Progressive Metal Guitar

An Advanced Guide to Modern Heavy Metal

Published by www.fundamental-changes.com

ISBN: 978-1-911267-28-7

Copyright © 2016 Rob Thorpe

The moral right of this author has been asserted.

All rights reserved. No part of this publication may be reproduced, stored in a retrieval system, or transmitted in any form or by any means, without the prior permission in writing from the publisher.

The publisher is not responsible for websites (or their content) that are not owned by the publisher.

www.fundamental-changes.com

Cover Image Copyright: ShutterStock *Melis*

Engineered and mixed by Declan Pearson of Colossus Audioworks

Other Books from Fundamental Changes

The Complete Guide to Playing Blues Guitar Book One: Rhythm Guitar

The Complete Guide to Playing Blues Guitar Book Two: Melodic Phrasing

The Complete Guide to Playing Blues Guitar Book Three: Beyond Pentatonics

The Complete Guide to Playing Blues Guitar Compilation

The CAGED System and 100 Licks for Blues Guitar

Fundamental Changes in Jazz Guitar: The Major ii V I

Minor ii V Mastery for Jazz Guitar

Jazz Blues Soloing for Guitar

Guitar Scales in Context

Guitar Chords in Context

Jazz Guitar Chord Mastery (Guitar Chords in Context Part Two)

Complete Technique for Modern Guitar

Funk Guitar Mastery

The Complete Technique, Theory and Scales Compilation for Guitar

Sight Reading Mastery for Guitar

Rock Guitar Un-CAGED: The CAGED System and 100 Licks for Rock Guitar

The Practical Guide to Modern Music Theory for Guitarists

Beginner's Guitar Lessons: The Essential Guide

Chord Tone Soloing for Jazz Guitar

Heavy Metal Lead Guitar

Exotic Pentatonic Soloing for Guitar

Heavy Metal Rhythm Guitar

Voice Leading Jazz Guitar

The Complete Jazz Soloing Compilation

The Jazz Guitar Chords Compilation

Fingerstyle Blues Guitar

The Complete DADGAD Guitar Method

Contents

Get the Audio 3

Introduction 5

Chapter 1: Neoclassical Phrasing 6
    Pedal Point 10
    Arpeggios 13

Chapter 2: Legato 19

Chapter 3: Tapping 24
    Rhythm Tapping 30

Chapter 4: Alternate Picking 35
    Odd Rhythmic Groupings 40

Chapter 5: Economy/Sweep Picking 43

Chapter 6: Recasting Pentatonic & Blues scales 47

Chapter 7: Exotic Scales, Substitutions & Beyond 53
    Harmonic Substitution 53
    Exotic Scales 57
    Symmetrical Scales 58

Chapter 8: Harmony Guitar 64
    Rhythm Guitar Harmony Riffs 73

Chapter 9: Meter and Cross-Rhythm 78
    Cross Rhythmic Riffs 82

Chapter 10: Demo Solos 88

Chapter 11: Forging Your Own Style - You Can Do It! 110

Get the Audio

The audio files for this book are available to download for *free* from **www.fundamental-changes.com** and the link is in the top right corner. Simply select this book title from the drop-down menu and follow the instructions to get the audio.

We recommend that you download the files directly to your computer, not to your tablet and extract them there before adding them to your media library. You can then put them on your tablet, iPod or burn them to CD. On the download page there is a help PDF and *we also provide technical support through the form on the download page*.

We spend a long time getting the audio just right and you will benefit greatly from listening to these examples as you work through the book. They're free, so what are you waiting for?!

We would like to thanks Declan Pearson of Colossus Audioworks for engineering and mixing the audio for this book.

Kindle / eReaders

To get the most out of this book, remember that you can **double tap any image to enlarge it**. Turn off 'column viewing' and hold your kindle in landscape mode.

For over 250 Free Guitar Lessons with Videos Check out:
www.fundamental-changes.com

Twitter: **@guitar_joseph**
Over 7000 fans on Facebook: **FundamentalChangesInGuitar**
Instagram: **FundamentalChanges**

Introduction

Welcome to Progressive Metal Guitar, the third volume of my series on playing Metal guitar!

This book gives advanced guitarists a greater stylistic understanding of the genre as a whole, and offers fresh ideas to help you break out of a creative rut to reinvigorate your playing.

If you've been following the series, we've seen how metal emerged from electric blues and hard rock in the '60s and '70s, and became increasingly diverse and technically challenging. We've explored the style from both a rhythm and lead standpoint by analysing how each idea is constructed on a musical level, while at the same time honing your technique.

In this third volume we're going to expand on what we've already learnt, looking at specific stylistic choices as well as how these techniques can be employed in more unusual and creative ways.

After discussing the advanced use of specific guitar techniques, I'll address compositional tools like harmony and arranging for multiple guitars, beginning with classic harmony guitar from Iron Maiden and Judas Priest. I'll then get in-depth with rhythmic riff writing by focussing on the modern cross-rhythmic style used by bands such as Meshuggah, Periphery, Tesseract and others.

From the '90s onwards, the metal and progressive rock genres increasingly overlapped. The more 'art-music' and complex approach to writing music (a defining feature of prog rock), has affected a greater proportion of metal music. After being hinted at in the songs of Iron Maiden and Fates Warning, the progressive metal sub-genre exploded with bands like Queensrÿche, Dream Theater and Symphony X. These musicians mixed the longer song structures and concept album approach of progressive rock with the increased technical level of the shred-metal movement. This created a style that was at once heavy and technical while including depth and creativity in songwriting.

In the '90s Thrash metal developed into death metal, taking the traits of aggression, dissonance and speed to their logical conclusion, with vocals becoming more guttural. The lyrics also took a more cerebral turn, exploring gruesomely vivid imagery with clinical objectivity, as well as dystopian futures, science fiction and robotics. This subject-matter related well to the direction of the music which started to feel increasingly mechanised and inhuman.

Certain bands within the genre introduced the unlikely influence of jazz fusion in the early '90s. Death's later records, as well as the work of Atheist, Watchtower and especially Cynic showcased an intricate and dynamic way in which these two styles could be melded successfully.

Use of advanced harmony and rhythm not found in other forms of popular music but instead recalling classical music of the 20th century has become more common. Comparing the music of composers such as Stravinsky, Béla Bartok, Prokofiev and Schoenberg to the more experimental metal of Spastic Ink, Buckethead, Fantomas and Meshuggah suggests some influence.

I hope you enjoy working through this book and find much of interest to use in your own music. As always, most benefit will come from taking these ideas as a starting point and applying them creatively to form your own unique voice.

Thank you and good luck!

Rob Thorpe

Chapter 1: Neoclassical Phrasing

We will begin by exploring the characteristic ideas from neoclassical metal, popularised in the '80s by guitarists like Yngwie Malmsteen, Jason Becker, Vinnie Moore, Tony MacAlpine and others. As rock guitar became a more formally studied craft at schools like G.I.T, Berklee and the Musician's Institute, the technical bar was continually raised. In these environments, it made sense that guitarists would look to classical music, the archetype of formally taught music, for inspiration.

Neoclassical 'shred' metal is closely associated with the Shrapnel record label, the owner of which, Mike Varney, discovered and promoted guitarists who were on the cutting edge of rock technique.

As you might expect, emulating these players is a daunting task. Very precise technique is needed to achieve such speed and clean execution. To play these licks we'll be using the techniques we learnt in *Heavy Metal Lead Guitar*. However, it's not all about shredding; you can draw inspiration from the style and apply it at whatever speed you like, without having to retreat to a hermitage to spend years with a metronome!

The 'classical' element mainly draws on the Baroque period of music, as exemplified by the instrumental works by J.S. Bach, Vivaldi and Handel. This involved lots of scale runs, patterns and sequencing, pedal point and arpeggios which we'll apply to the guitar.

At the end of the book is a transcription of Paganini's Caprice No. 16, originally written for solo violin but arranged for electric guitar. This piece is a goldmine of interesting arpeggio-based licks and will be a great workout for your technique.

I'd like to quickly address the theory we'll be working with so that you can digest the musical information and get writing your own neoclassical licks right off the bat.

Harmonic Minor

Harmonic Minor is a scale very similar to Natural Minor (or Aeolian mode) with which you should already be familiar. The difference is that the 7th note of Harmonic Minor is sharpened by a semitone. This sharp note has several knock-on effects to the way the scale can be used.

Firstly, chord V of Harmonic Minor, is a dominant 7 chord rather than the minor chord found in Natural Minor. This allows for the very dramatic-sounding V7- i progression, common in classical music but not often heard in hard rock before the Neoclassical movement.

Secondly, Harmonic Minor's raised 7th creates three pairs of semitones (2-b3, 5-b6 and #7-R). These can be exploited melodically to add tension and excitement, as each pair contains a note in the tonic chord and an approach note.

Finally, the Harmonic Minor scale contains both a Diminished 7th chord, and an Augmented triad. Major modes don't contain these dark and dramatic sounds. The Diminished 7th chord and Augmented triad are symmetrical, meaning that they are formed by stacking intervals of the same distance. This means that once you know one Diminished or Augmented shape you can move anything you play with them up or down by the intervals used to build them.

We'll focus more on that in Chapter Eight.

Arpeggios

An arpeggio is simply a chord played one note at a time. In Metal lead guitar playing, this translates as using the notes of a chord melodically, and not letting the notes ring into each other. Much of western classical music has concerned itself with harmony, chord progressions, and cadences. Arpeggios are commonly used because they enable us to spell out chord progressions while playing a melody.

We will look at some different arpeggio ideas in the Chapter Seven, but the best place to start is to use one arpeggio per chord to give your solo a strong connection to the rest of the music (rather than just wailing regardless of the harmony). Arpeggios are frequently played with sweep picking or tapping, which help us to perform wide intervals easily.

Sequencing

In the first book of this series, *Heavy Metal Rhythm Guitar*, I looked at how sequences can develop to be quite complex and mathematical; but for the neoclassical lead style we will be sticking to moving a scale fragment up and down within a key, just like baroque composers such as Bach. Our ears are adept at identifying patterns in music and quickly latch on to sequences. The use of sequences helps to make fast playing more comprehensible to the listener.

Pedal Point

A pedal is where one note or motif alternates with a changing note or motif. The static part is often the lowest part and is known as the pedal, from its origins on the church organ. Bach was principally a church organist who wrote many works for the organ including the famous Toccata & Fugue in D minor. Pedal point helps maintain energy in faster playing as the ear will naturally pick out the moving part as separate from the pedal.

To kick things off here's a simple sextuplet scale pattern. In this chapter we're more concerned about the note choice and phrasing than specific techniques so feel free to use either legato or picking. Either way be sure to make the timing even.

Example 1a

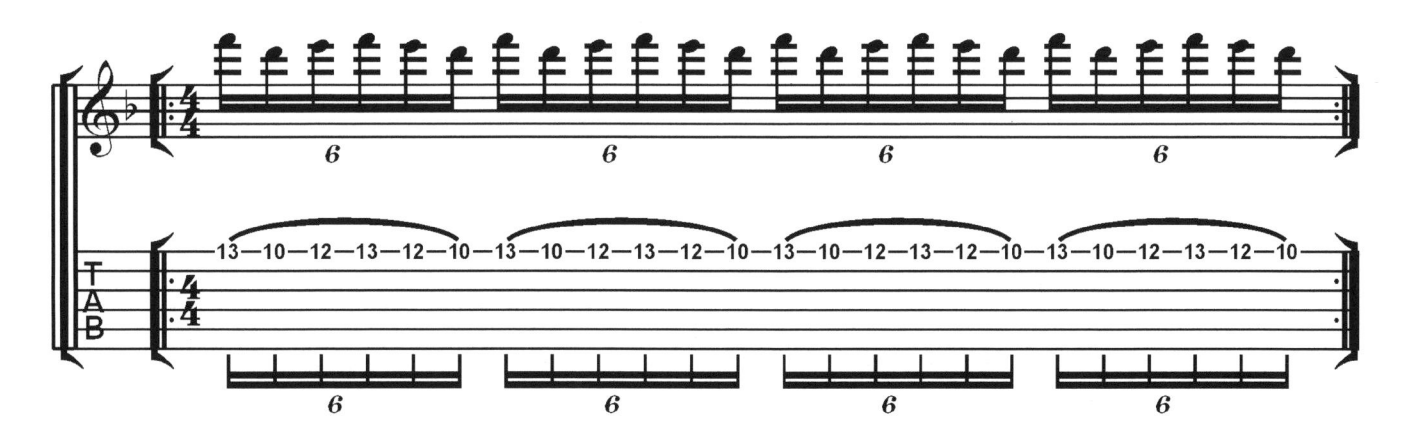

Next we apply the basic motif to the A Natural Minor scale. If the wider spacing of the lower strings proves difficult, practice each string's pattern in isolation before trying to move from string to string.

Example 1b

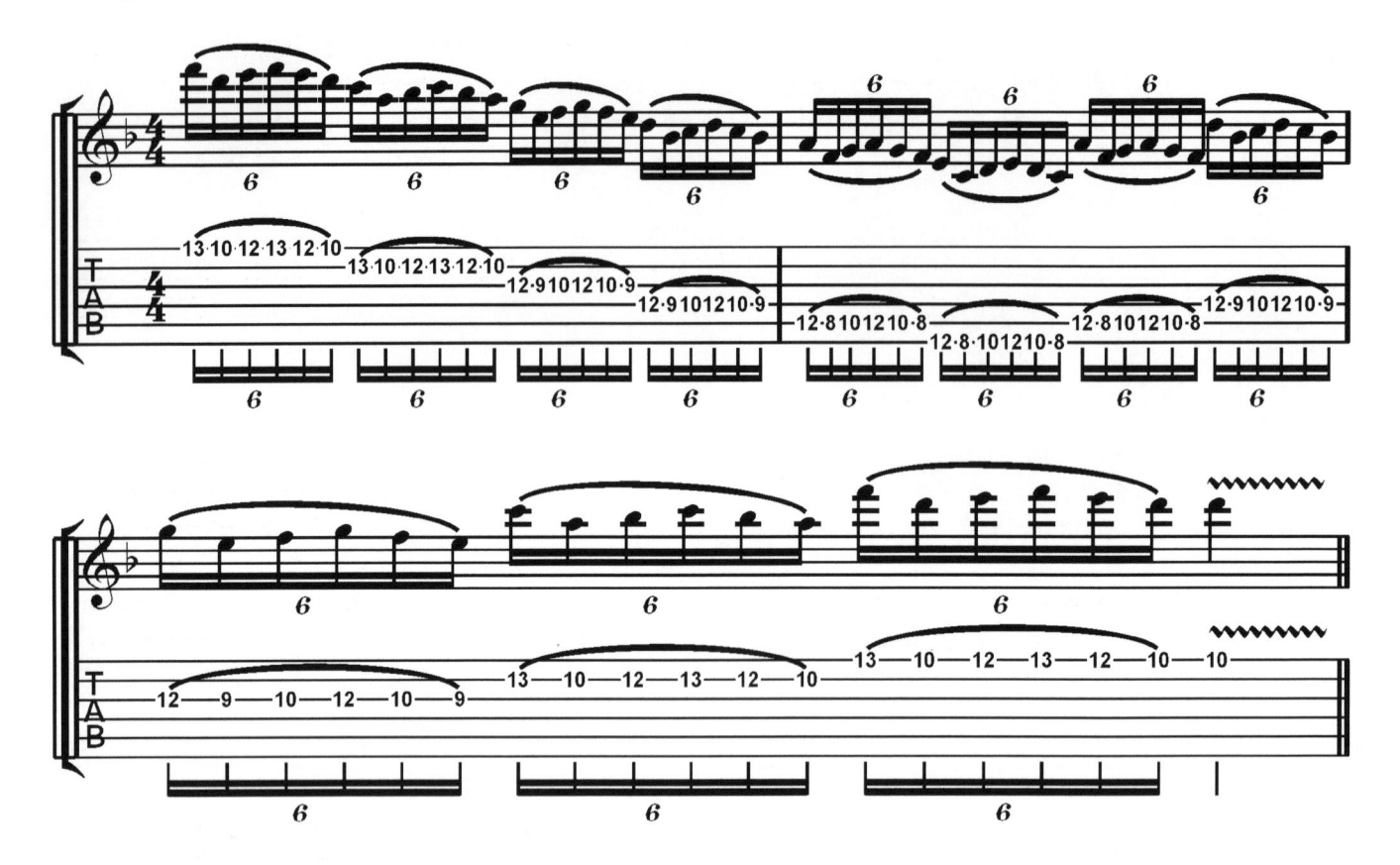

The following baroque-inspired Yngwie lick involves groups of four notes sequenced through the A Harmonic Minor scale. We're taking this at a fairly pedestrian pace, but listen to any of Yngwie's recordings to hear the potential of these single string lick.

The main challenge is the position shifts with the index finger. Practice each position slowly and accent the first note of every four with a harder pick stroke to help keep the hands in sync. Also watch out for the wider Harmonic Minor stretches at the start.

Example 1c

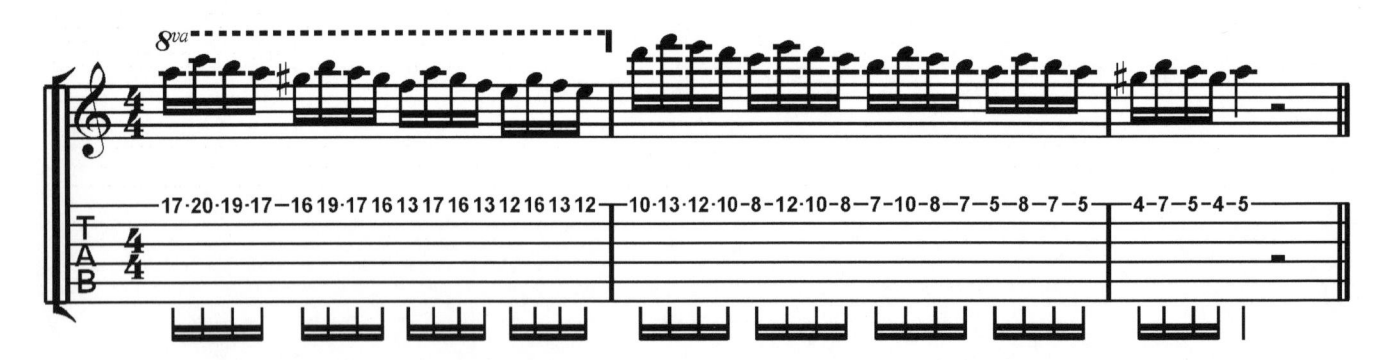

Next we have the ascending version of the same lick. This one is a little more difficult because the position shifts are made with the pinkie, but the same approach should be taken as before and with regular practice they will like second nature.

Example 1d

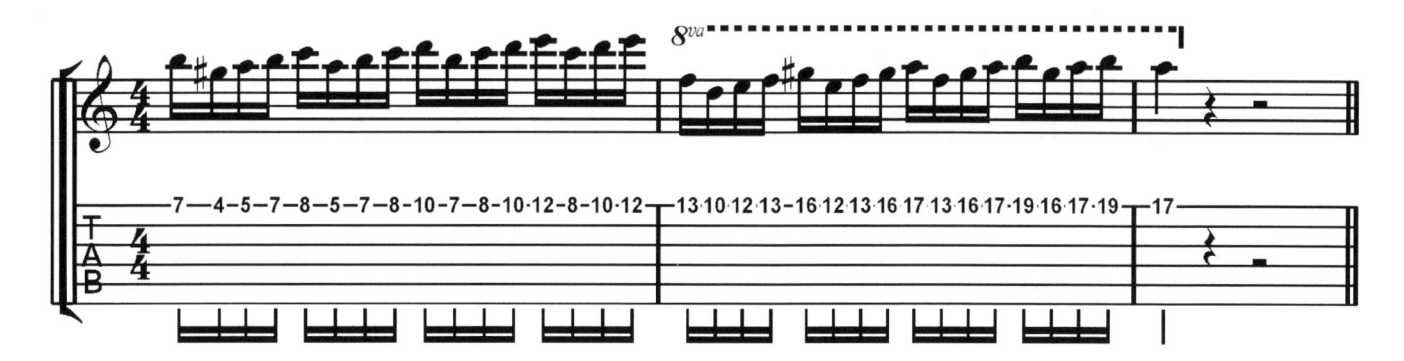

This time our four-note sequence traverses the strings. Groups of ascending four notes are moved up through the E Harmonic Minor scale, however to mix things up, I've displaced the rhythm so that the groups of four start on the final 1/16th note of each beat to make the lick sound little less predictable.

I've opted for legato here to keep things varied but you can try picking too. Always practice a lick with a range of techniques so you can choose how to articulate it, and not become limited to 'painting in just one colour'.

Example 1e

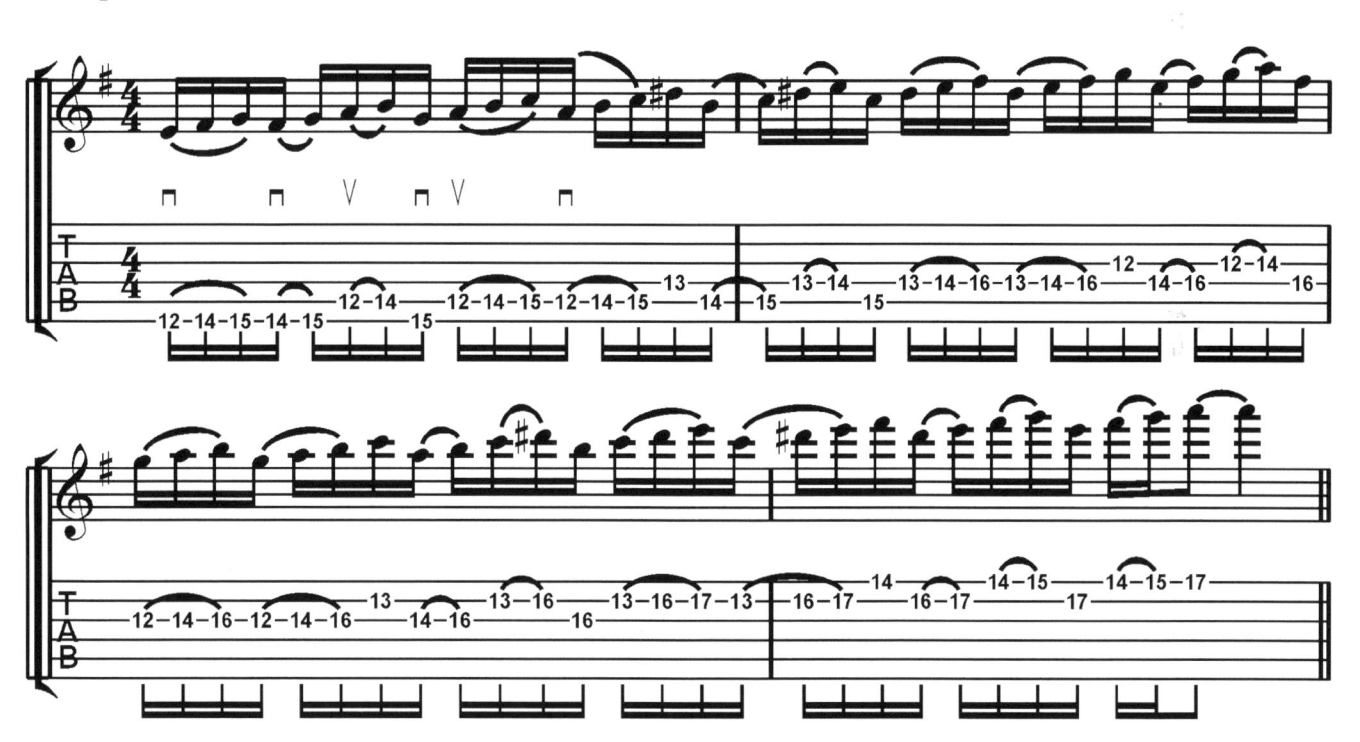

In our final sequential lick, we play ascending steps while the line gradually descends

Example 1f

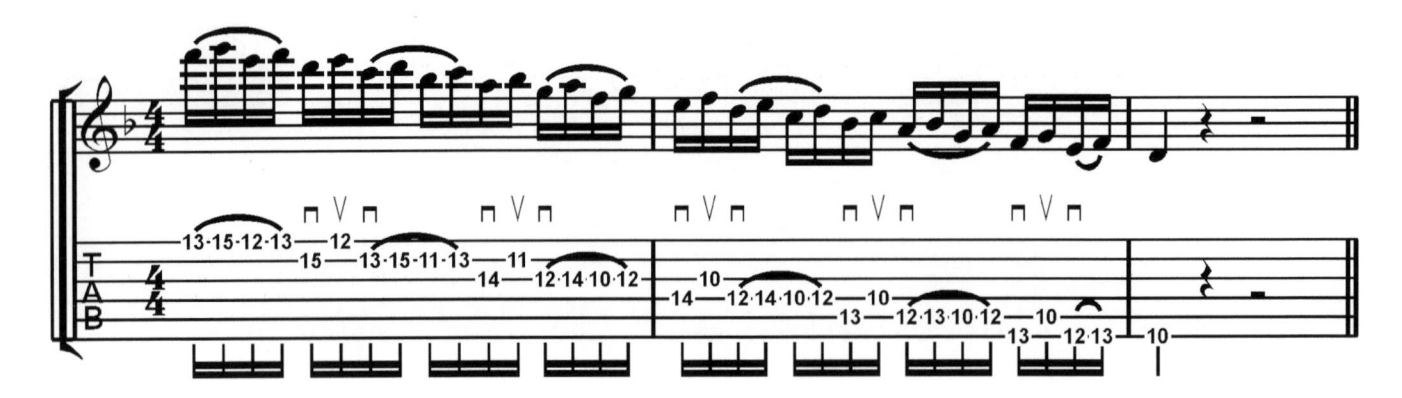

Try experimenting with sequencing ideas of your own by taking different motifs or lengths of scale fragment; then vary the direction of the sequence, making note of ones that you particularly like. It can be helpful to use notation or sequencing software to help with this so you can be objective about listening to new licks, before attempting to get them under your fingers.

Pedal Point

Our first pedal point lick illustrates the 'pedal' concept very clearly. The fretting hand plays the E Harmonic Minor scale along the length of the string. 'Pulling off' to the open E provides the pedal. Follow the suggested fingering for the fastest and most fluid results.

This type of lick is easier than it sounds, as the open string is doing half the work for you. Learning scales along the fretboard is an often-neglected skill but one that really opens up the fretboard for you.

Example 1g

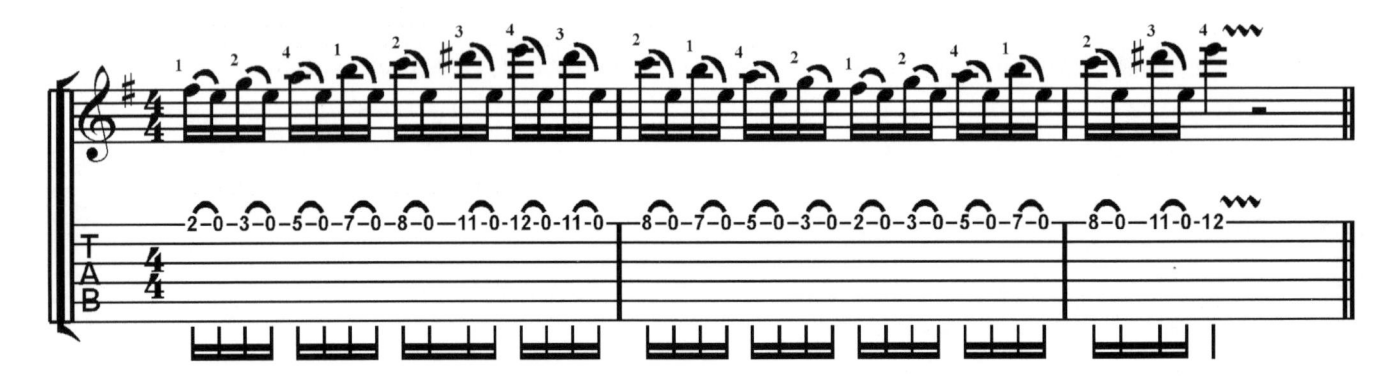

Here's another common neoclassical lick that uses the same idea, but this time the pedal is the highest note rather than the lowest. Getting the correct fingering can be tough at first due to the weaker 3rd and 4th fingers, so be patient and try to keep them relaxed.

Example 1h

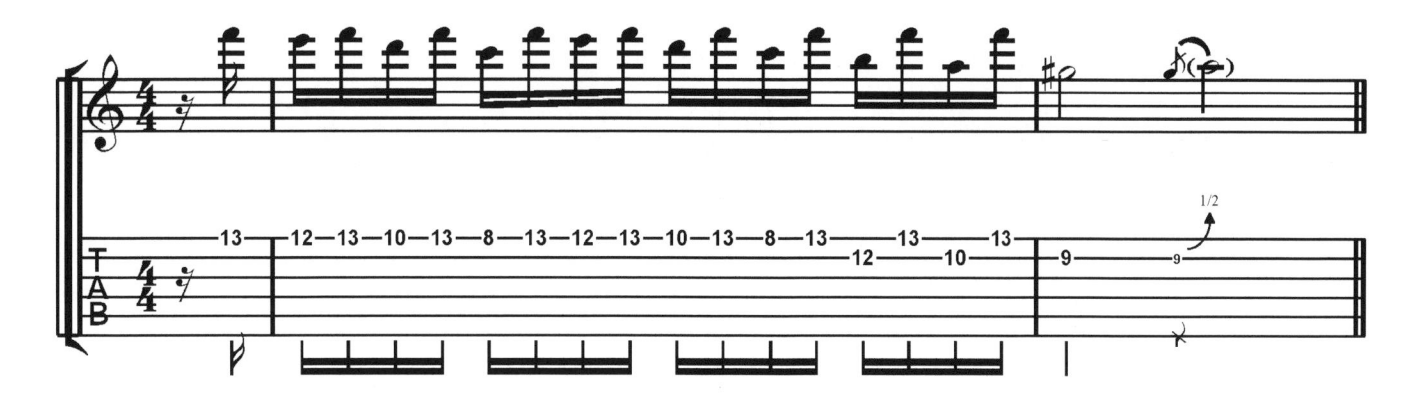

An alternative way to play example 1h would be to use the picking hand to tap the high pedal note, while the fretting hand takes care of the melody part. This can open up more interesting lines rather than just descending the scale.

In the following example, the fretting hand plays a descending sequence of three notes against the pedal. Tapping ensures a completely legato articulation, which may, or may not, be the sound you're looking for...

Example 1i

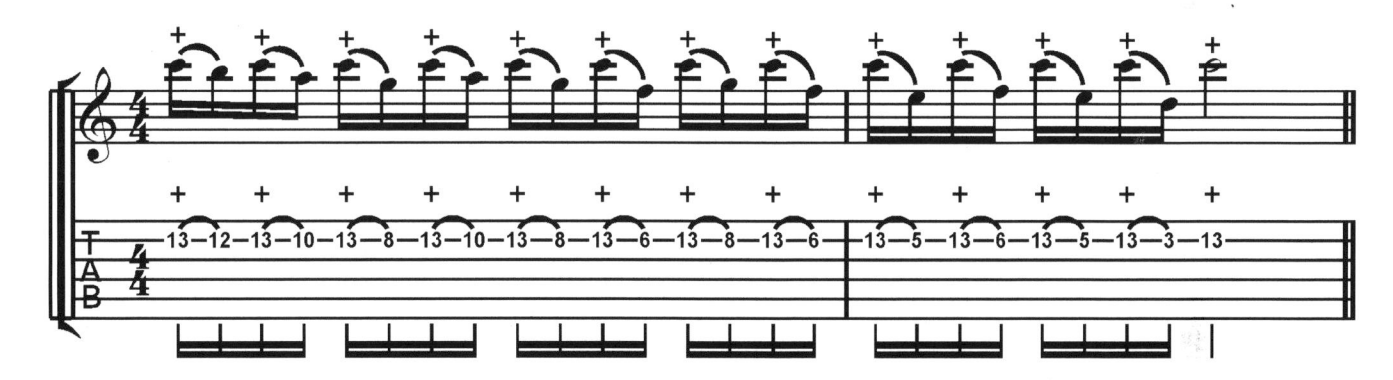

If example 1i proved unsatisfyingly slippery, the following pedal point idea reaches for a less common guitar technique in metal: hybrid picking, to deliver a bit more bite!

To play the following example, hold the pick normally and use down-strokes to play the lower notes. Use the middle finger of the picking hand to pluck the high B notes (12th fret).

In the notation I've indicated upstrokes when all the notes are on one string as this is how I played it. Many players however, would pluck with the middle finger throughout, try both and see which you prefer.

For an added classical influence, I've used the Melodic Minor when ascending scale with the major 6th and 7th (G#, A#) intervals and reverting to the Natural Minor intervals b6 and b7 (G and A) when descending.

Example 1j

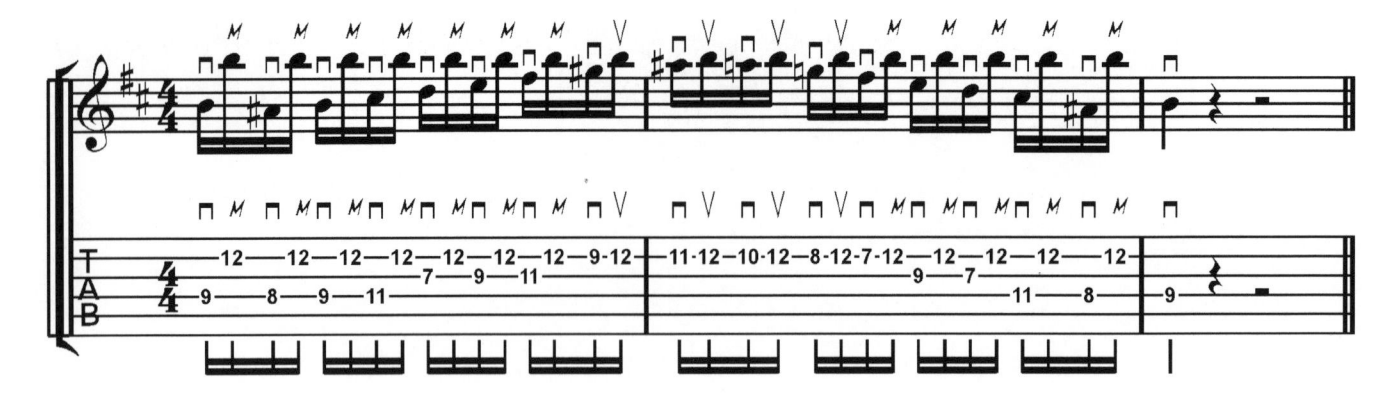

The final two pedal point ideas substitute the pedal tone for a three-note motif. The first is inspired by Vinnie Moore and uses alternate picking. Be careful of the wider stretches on the highest notes, if they prove difficult it will help to keep the thumb lower on the back of the fretboard and angle the guitar neck a little higher.

Example 1k

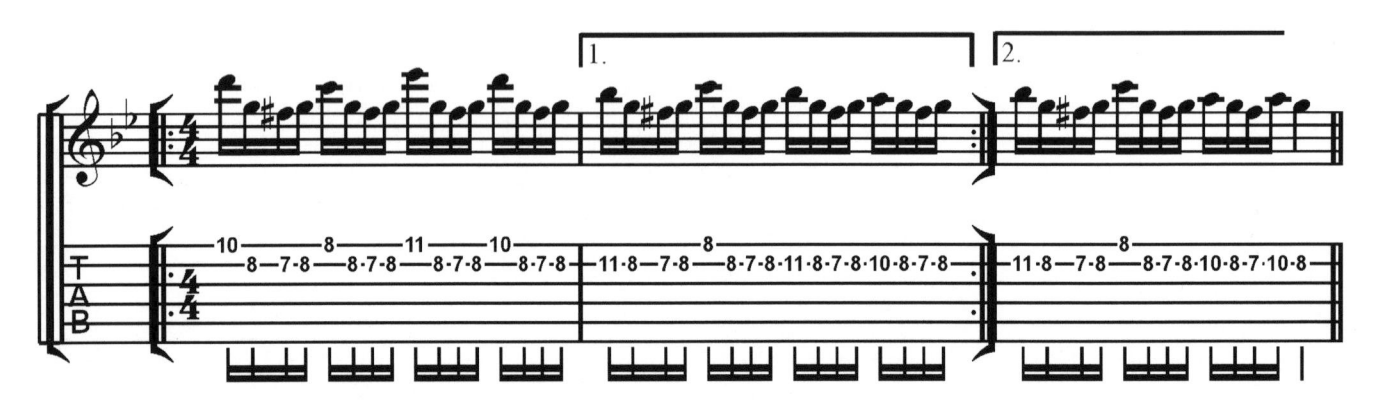

To conclude our collection of pedal point licks, we'll revisit the tapping of example 1i. This time, however, the tapping hand provides the moving part while the fretting hand repeats the pedal motif. To really nail the tapped bend on the last note, hold the D# (16th fret) with your tapping finger and apply the bend/vibrato from behind with the fretting hand as if you were fretting the note as normal.

Once you're comfortable with this lick, try moving the scale fragment *and* the tapping hand along the string to create some very interesting intervallic phrases.

Example 1l

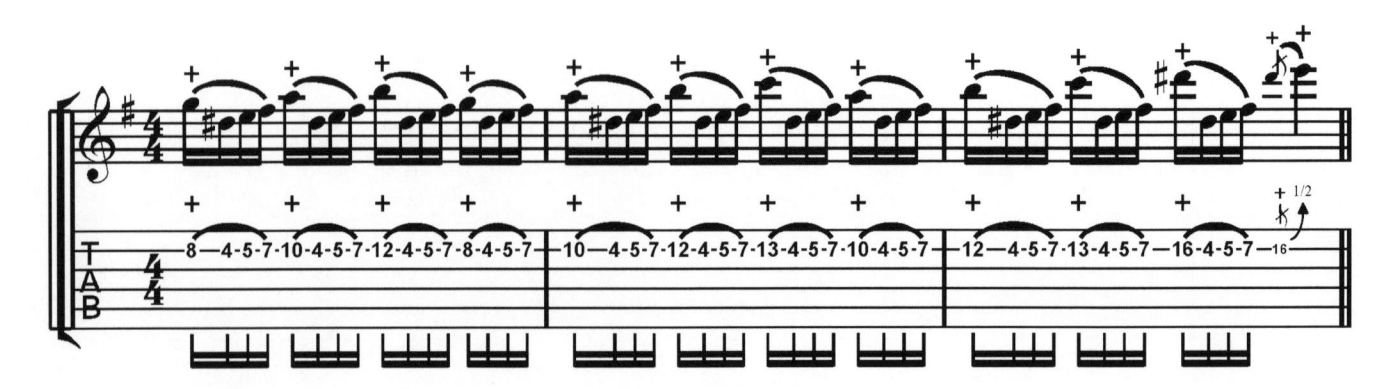

Arpeggios

To break up these long streams of notes, here's a more melodic phrase demonstrating the use of arpeggios to outline a chord progression. Try to identify the familiar open position chord shapes behind these fragments.

To create a cohesive structure, the same melodic contour is used over each chord while the notes themselves change to fit the harmony.

Example 1m

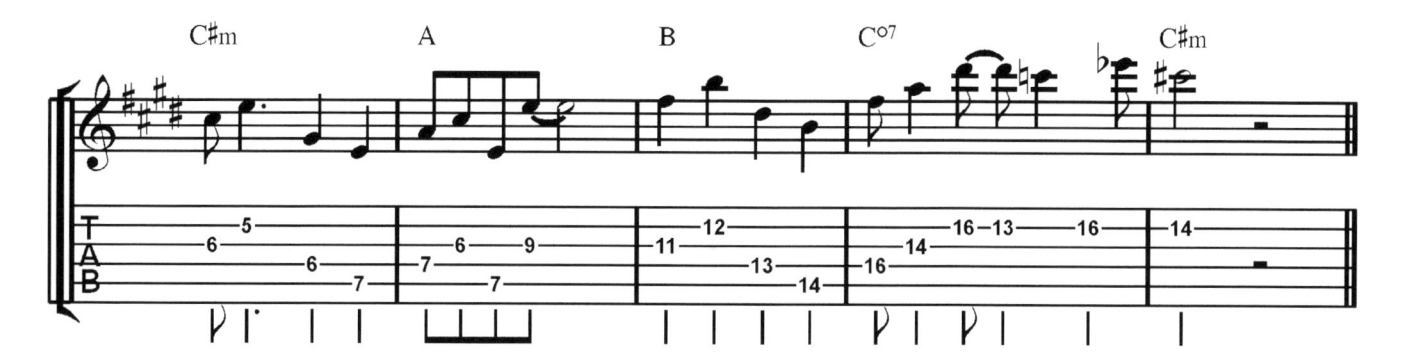

An important chord progression in western music is the circle of 5ths. This sequence of chords gives us our system of key centres and forms the foundation of classical music's functional harmony. The basic principle is to move chords in intervals of a 5th, each chord being the dominant of the next one. After twelve movements the cycle will return to the starting chord.

For example:

C G D A E B F# C# G# D# A# E# C (note: E# = F)

When ascending a 5th, the musical result is an increase in tension as you move through the keys in a constant cycle of I-V progressions or *imperfect cadences*. Descending in 5ths (or ascending in 4ths) gives a sense of continual resolution, as we're going V-I, V-I repeatedly in a long chain of *perfect cadences*.

The following example outlines descending circle of 5ths progression with arpeggios. The arpeggio shape used is built on the common open D chord shape with the root on the B string.

Example 1n

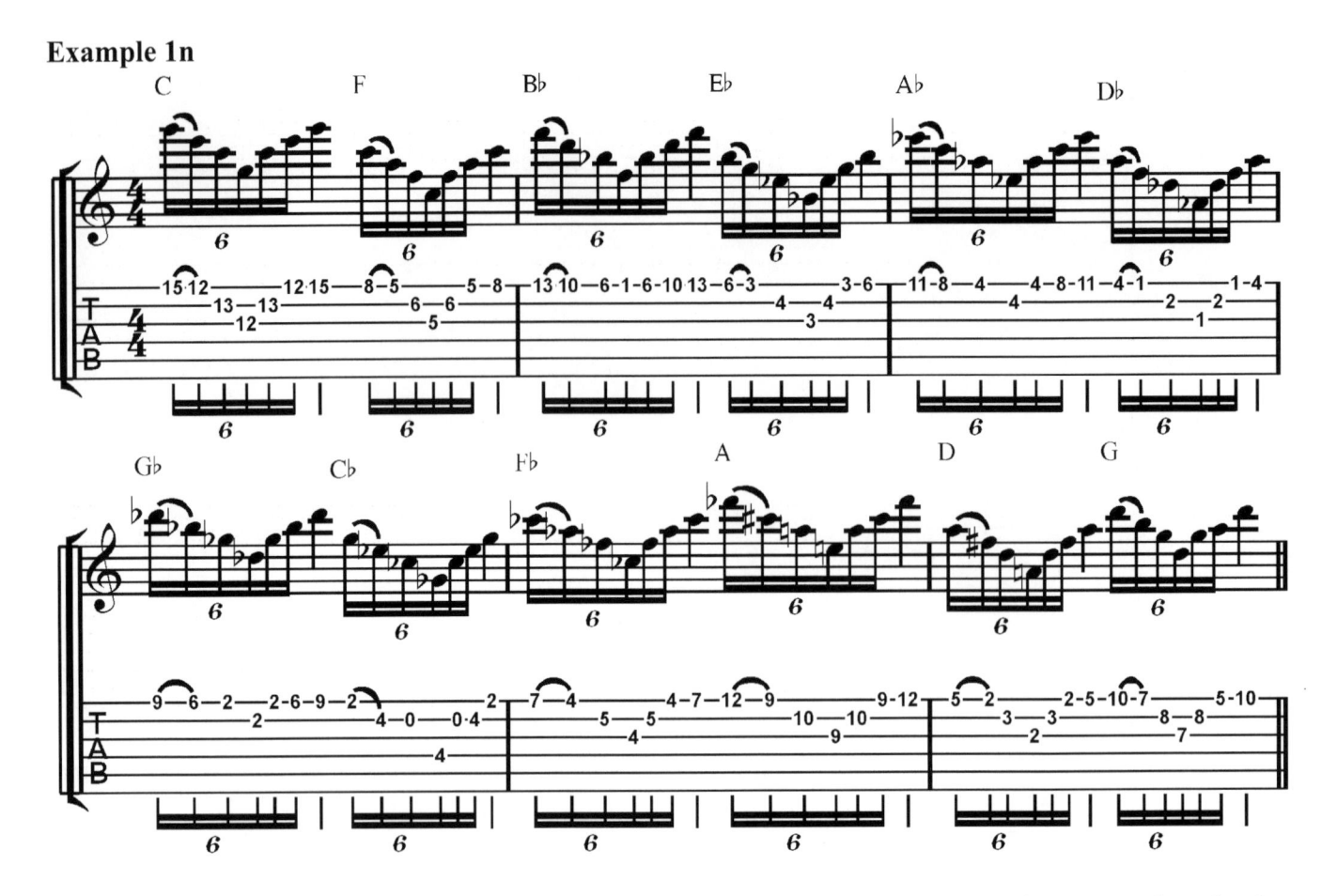

In the previous example I moved one arpeggio shape all over the neck to illustrate the progression clearly, but to get the most flowing melodic line we should start each arpeggio to on the closest note in the next chord. Rearranging the notes of a chord in different orders is known as the different *inversions* of a chord, which I covered in Heavy Metal Lead Guitar.

The next example plays the same circle of 4ths but uses all three inversions to keep the line as smooth as possible with no sudden wide leaps between chord changes. The progression is referred to as a circle because after twelve changes you should arrive back at the chord you started on, in this case C major.

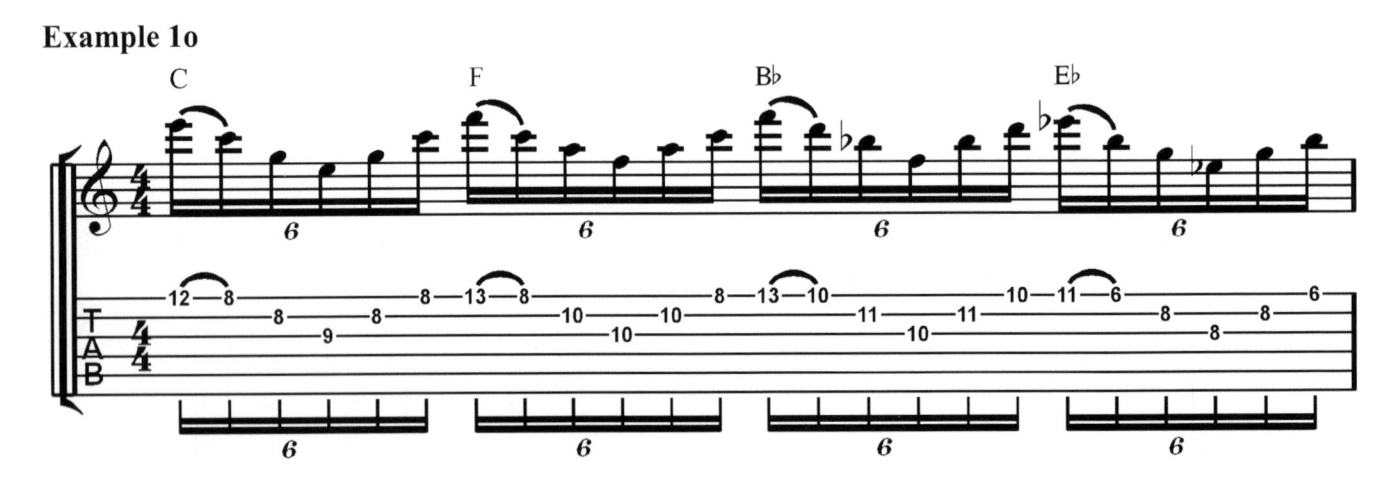

Example 1o

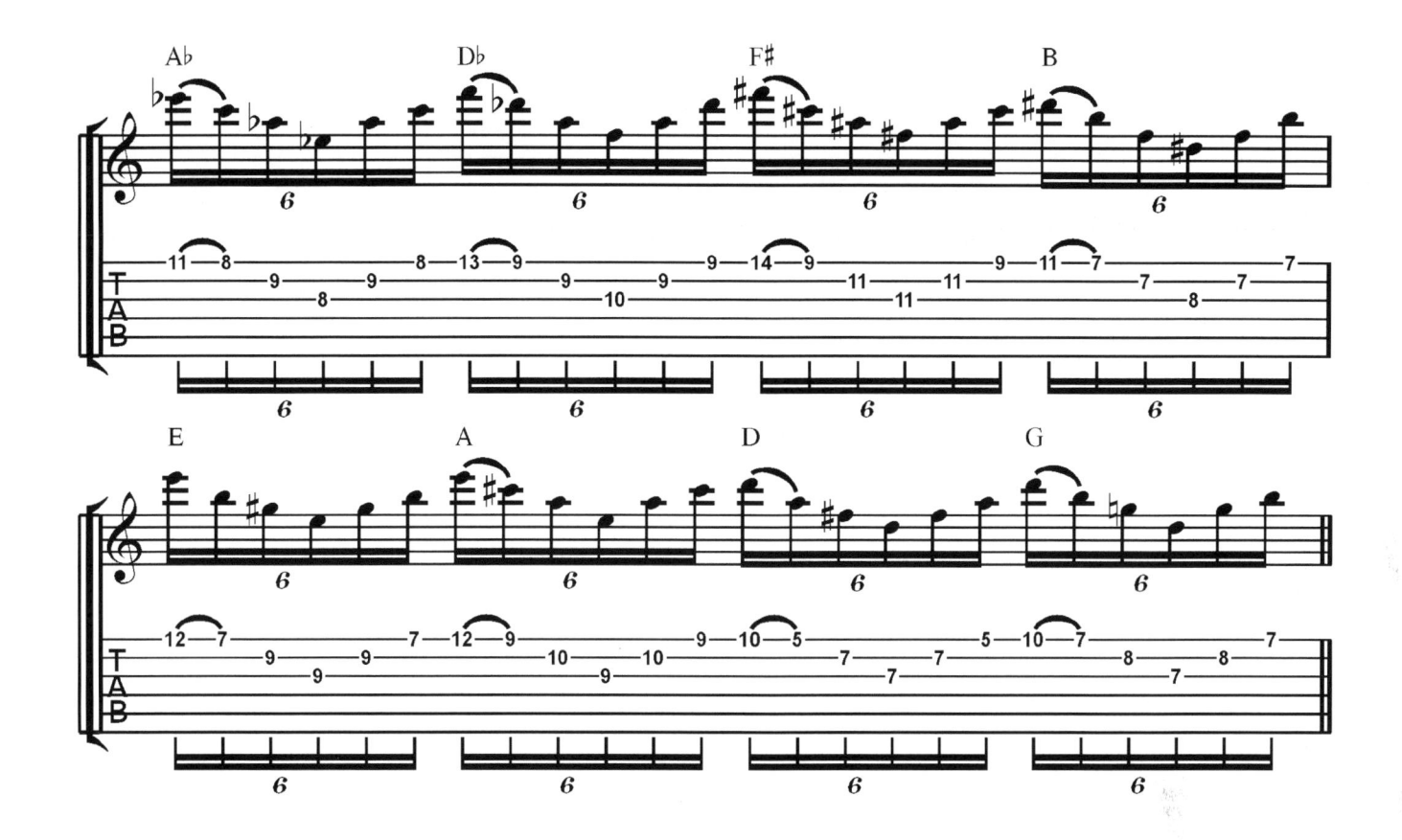

To get really familiar with this chord sequence and the different arpeggio shapes, try playing this example starting on different chords and with each of the three inversions. Remember to always look for the closest inversion of the next chord.

Using Diminished Chords

The strongest harmonic resolution is the perfect cadence (moving from chord V to chord I). The effect of which can be heightened by the tweaking of notes in the V chord to make it even more dissonant, and make the tonic more consonant by comparison. Without wading too far into the murky waters of chord theory, one of the notes we could add is the b9, or second degree of the scale, measured from the V's root.

In the key of D minor, the V chord is A7, which can be 'extended' to include a 9th (stacking another 3rd above the 7th). In minor keys this is a flattened ninth (Bb).

The V chord (now A7b9) contains A C# E G Bb. The final four notes (C# E G Bb) create a Diminished 7th chord. Because of this, Dim7 chords can act much in the same way as a V7 because they share most of the same notes. For example, you will often see the chord Bb dim7 used as a substitute for an A7 chord. By playing a Bb dim7 chord over an A bass note we create an A7b9 chord.

Compare the following pair of chord diagrams and you'll see that the only difference is the Bb in the Diminished arpeggio has replaced the A in the A7 diagram.

15

A7   Bb dim7

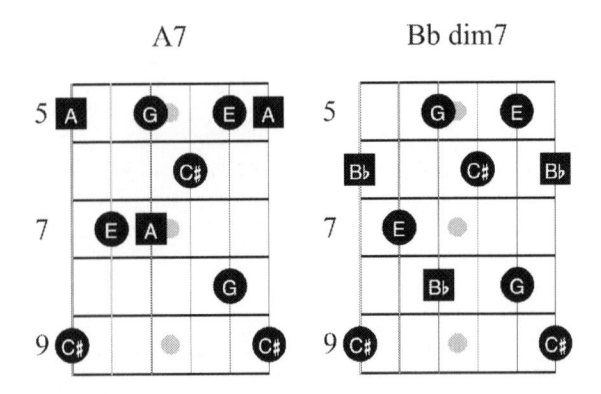

Diminished chords contain a flattened 5th and double flattened 7th which gives them a dark and dissonant sound compared to minor chords. They are often used as a source of tension before resolving to the minor scale or arpeggio. The lick signs off at the end of the bar by returning to the safety of a D minor phrase.

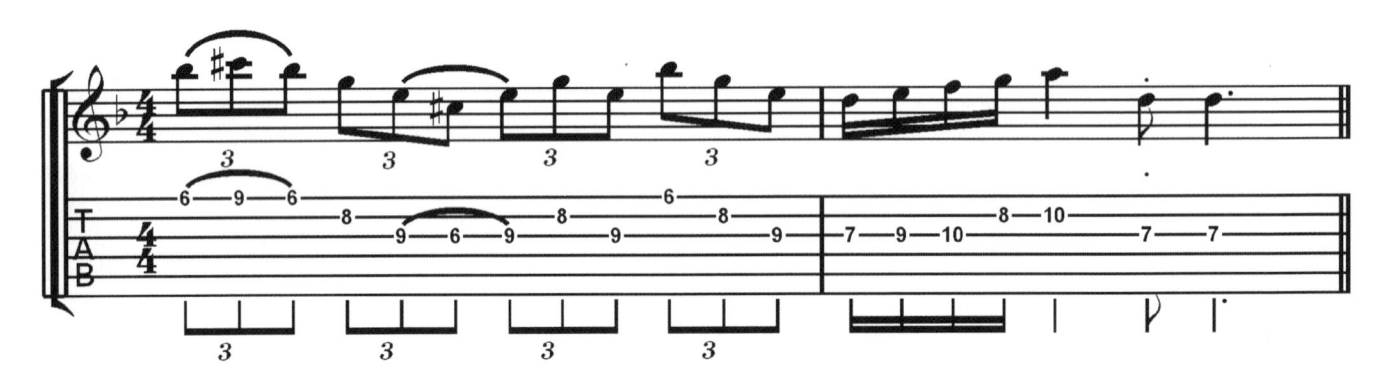

Example 1o

In the next example, we use the symmetry of Diminished chords to move a lick up the neck. Each note in a Diminished chord is a minor 3rd (three frets) apart, so it is common to move the same idea around the neck in three-fret intervals. After three *inversions* of the pattern the line finishes with an E Harmonic Minor run.

Example 1p

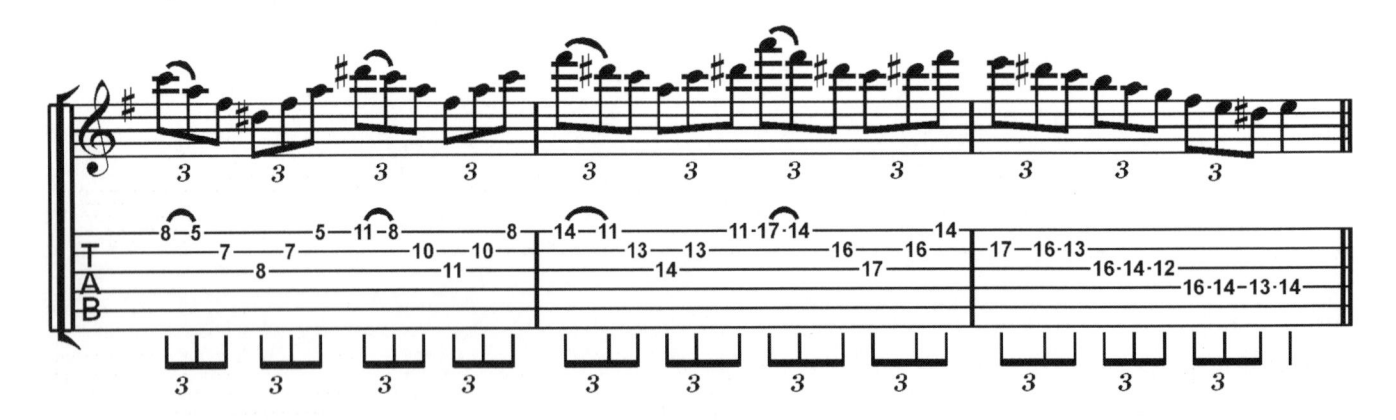

Next, the Diminished arpeggios are used in conjunction with the major and minor triad shapes we studied in book two. Pay special attention to the position shifts and try to 'hear' the chord changes go by as you play through the example.

Example 1q

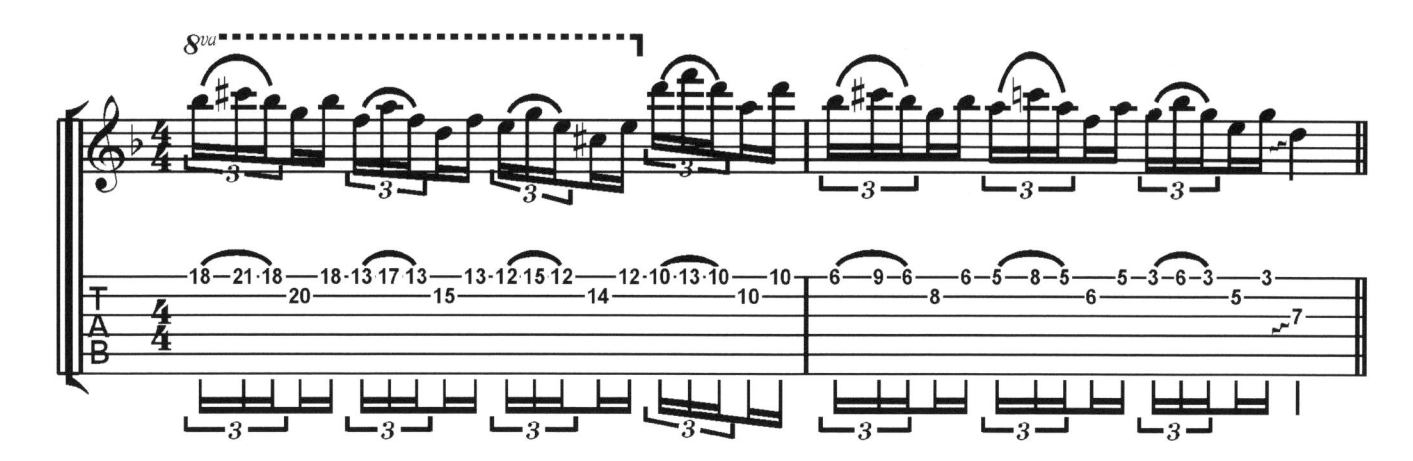

We couldn't visit neoclassical metal playing without looking at a frenzy of crazy arpeggios in the style of Paul Gilbert's work with Racer X. This lick is demanding, but playing two notes on each string feels more like a stretched out Pentatonic line, so the general approach should be familiar.

This line follows the written chord changes and uses Diminished arpeggios to resolve into the different chords. Warm up with smaller stretches and take this very slowly at first - don't strain yourself!

Example 1r

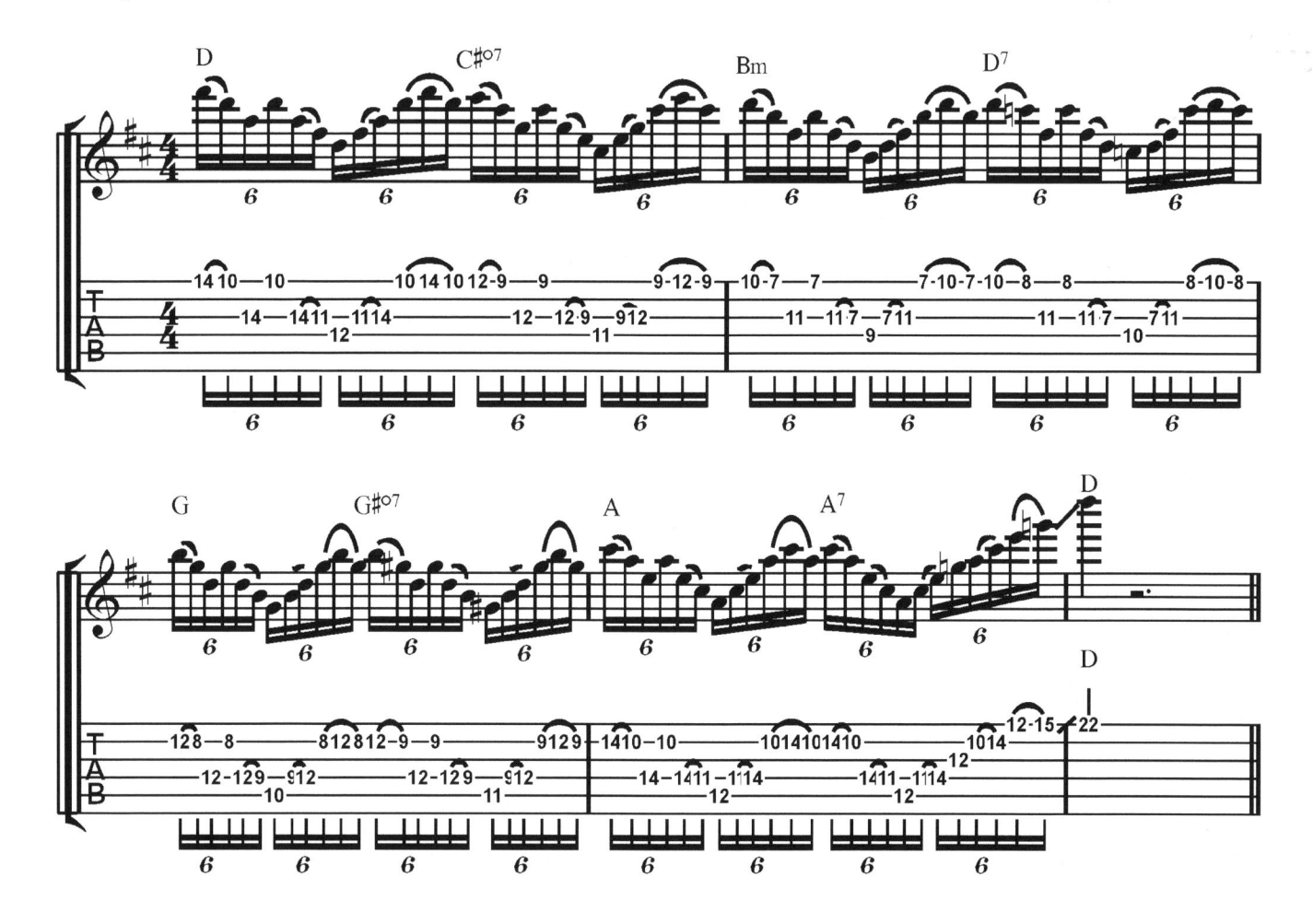

At the end of this book we'll go back to the classical source with a transcription of a piece of music originally written for violin. Among violin virtuoso Nicolo Paganini's (1782-1840) best known compositions are a set of twenty-four caprices. We'll be looking at the 16th caprice, in G minor. I've arranged the original violin part onto the guitar fretboard in the most playable way possible.

The piece makes use of all the techniques we'll develop over the next four chapters. The smaller size and 5ths tuning of the violin also means several of the phrases force us to deal with unnatural position shifts.

Recommended listening for neoclassical metal and baroque influences:

J.S. Bach – 15 Two Part Inventions
Handel – Flute Sonatas
Vivaldi – The Four Seasons
Scarlatti – *Sonata K. 1 in D minor*
Paganini -5th Caprice (from the 24 Caprices)
Deep Purple – Highway Star
Ozzy Osbourne (w/Randy Rhoads) – Over the Mountain
Yngwie Malmsteen – Black Star
Racer X - Scarified
Cacophony – Speed Metal Symphony
Jason Becker – Altitudes
Symphony X – Eve of Seduction
Adagio – Fire Forever
Sonata Arctica – What Did You Do in the War, Dad?
Time Requiem – Optical Illusion

Chapter 2: Legato

This chapter teaches you to use legato playing to navigate the fretboard with great fluency. We look at linking up the positions in different ways before exploring ideas using wider stretches in four note-per-string and string skipping ideas.

One of the biggest challenges with any legato technique is keeping unwanted string noise to a minimum. Be strict with yourself when practicing: Pay attention to reducing unwanted noise, and also play with only a mildly overdriven sound. It's very tempting to use more gain and distortion to help the intended notes sustain but this also increases the volume of unwanted noise too.

It's become popular to dampen the strings at the nut with a hair band or other soft material, which makes your playing sound cleaner, but I would recommend always practicing without one to be as critical as possible, as you probably won't have the mute onstage mid-song. This means you're not using a crutch to mask weaknesses in your technique.

Our first lick features lots of 4th intervals which gives it a modern fusion flavour. The fingering pattern should feel consistent with Pentatonic rock licks but the wide stretches along each string add an extra level of difficulty. Playing 4ths in one position means we get a repeated note when changing between strings. The different tone of each string makes it musical, resulting in a stuttering melodic contour.

The second half of the lick changes position to avoid the repeated notes and the position shifts can become unwieldy as the speed increases. Train the index finger to change position while the pinkie is fretting, so that the hand moves up the fretboard in a more dynamic way.

Example 2a

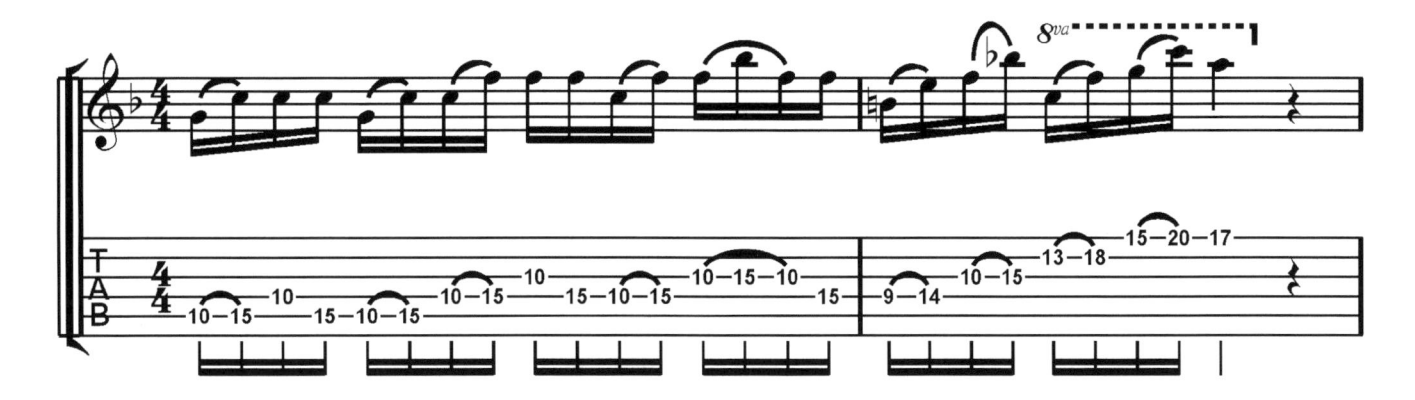

This next single-string idea features slides to jump between positions. The jumps are quite wide here as we're skipping up and down the neck. The quintuplets should arrange themselves quite easily so long as you concentrate on performing the shifts on the beats.

Example 2b

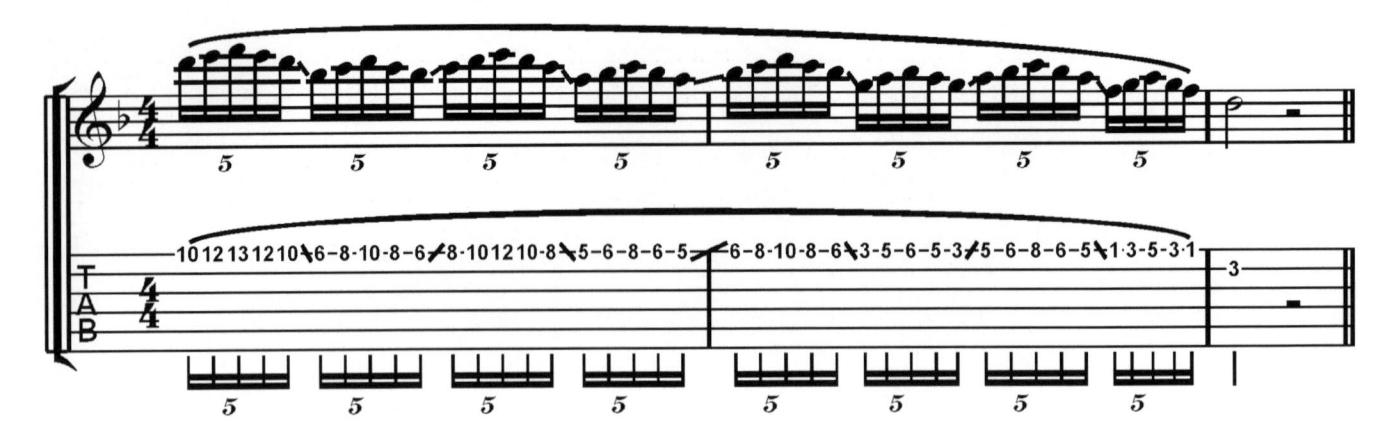

The next four examples demonstrate that small legato fragments can be put together to create long legato passages that span the fretboard.

Using a twelve-note fragment, we descend through the different positions of F# minor along the neck. Practice the position shifts slowly at first. Concentrate on moving your pinkie towards the new position while the first fragment is being completed. This may sound like a lot of multitasking but it will stop you having to jump abruptly between shapes.

Take it slowly at first and note where the position shifts occur, and the fingering used to achieve them.

Example 2c

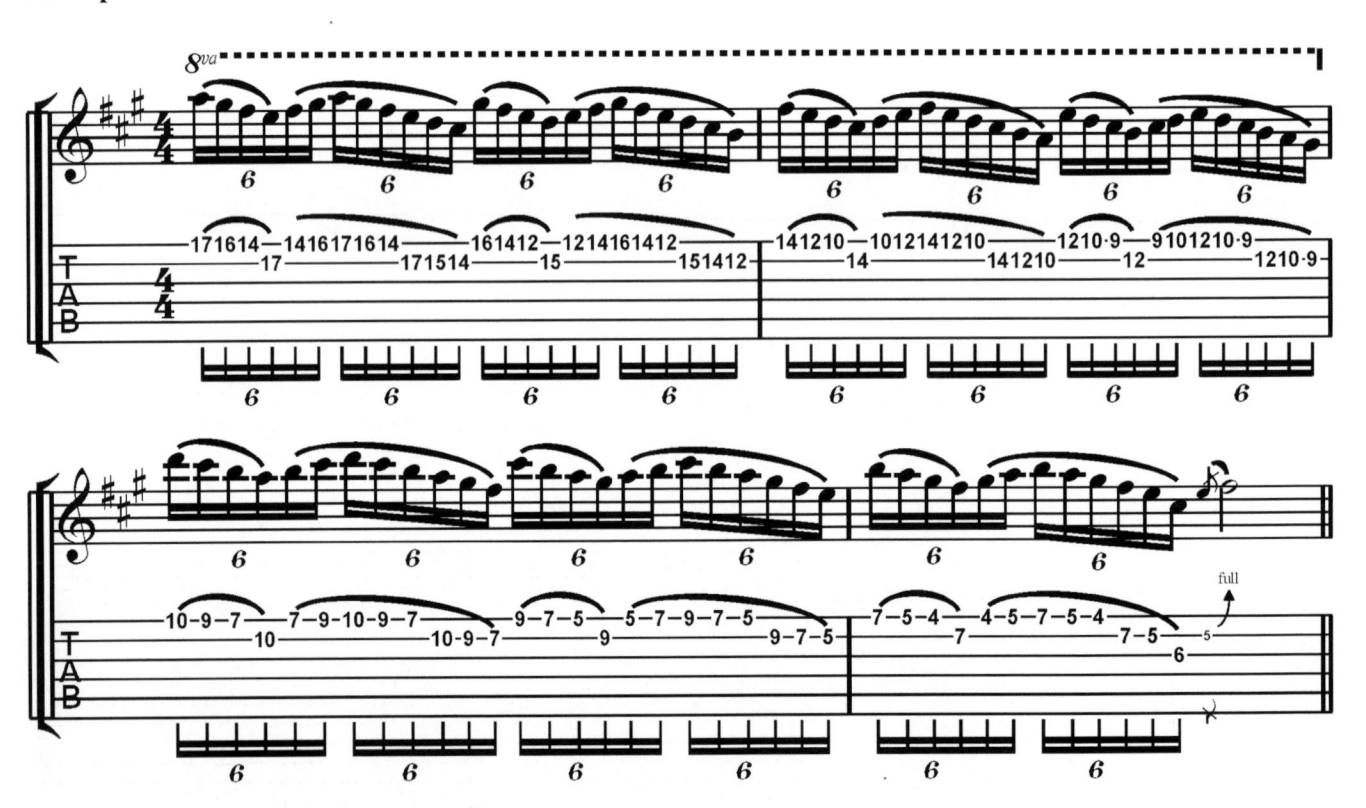

The next fragment-based legato lick uses a consistent eight-note pattern with a slight variation at the end. Once the basic building block is practiced, focussing on the starting note of each group will help to stop all that movement getting out of control.

Example 2d

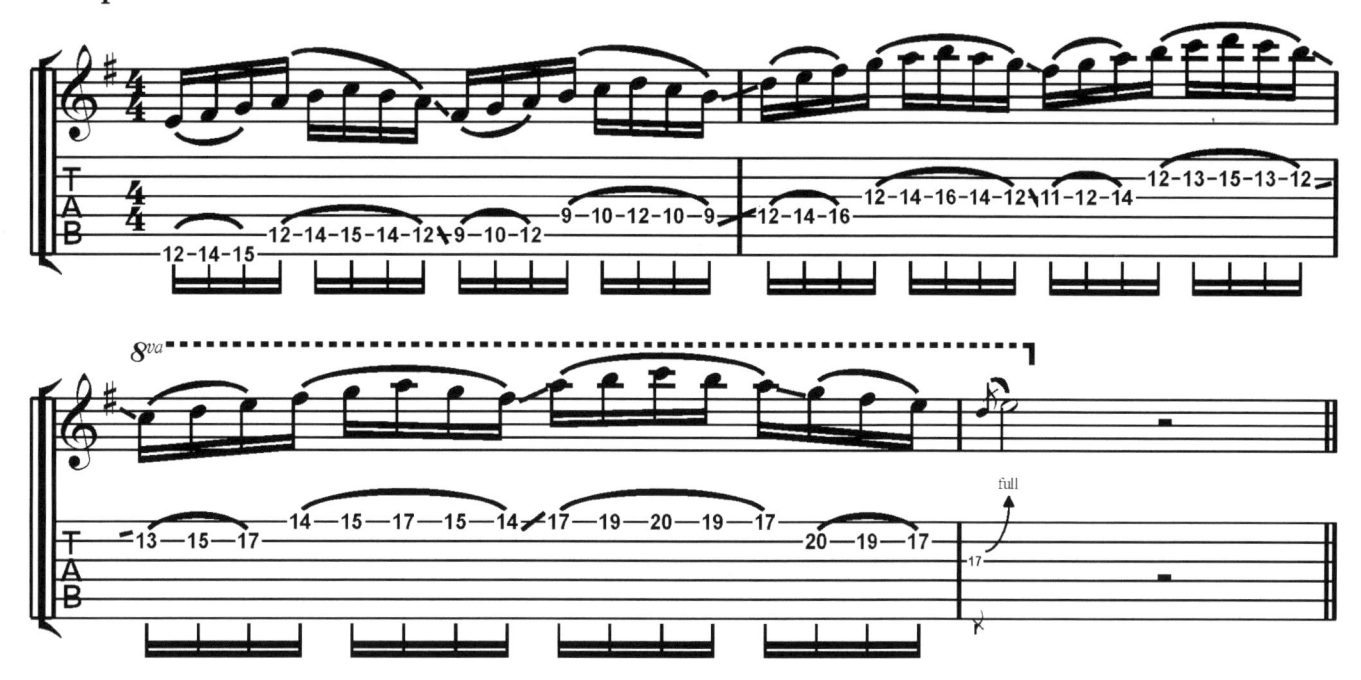

The melodic line in example 2e is deceptively varied, so work through it in small chunks to memorise the whole passage accurately.

Instrumental rock/metal legend Joe Satriani stands out as having a strong command of this type of super smooth legato playing so check out any of his music to hear it in action!

Example 2e

Our second, longer legato run involves string skipping as an added hurdle. Continuous stepwise motion can be a little monotonous and skipping strings can help to break this up by adding ear-catching wide intervallic leaps into the scalic phrases. Brett Garsed's, and the great Shawn Lane's playing both exhibit this approach.

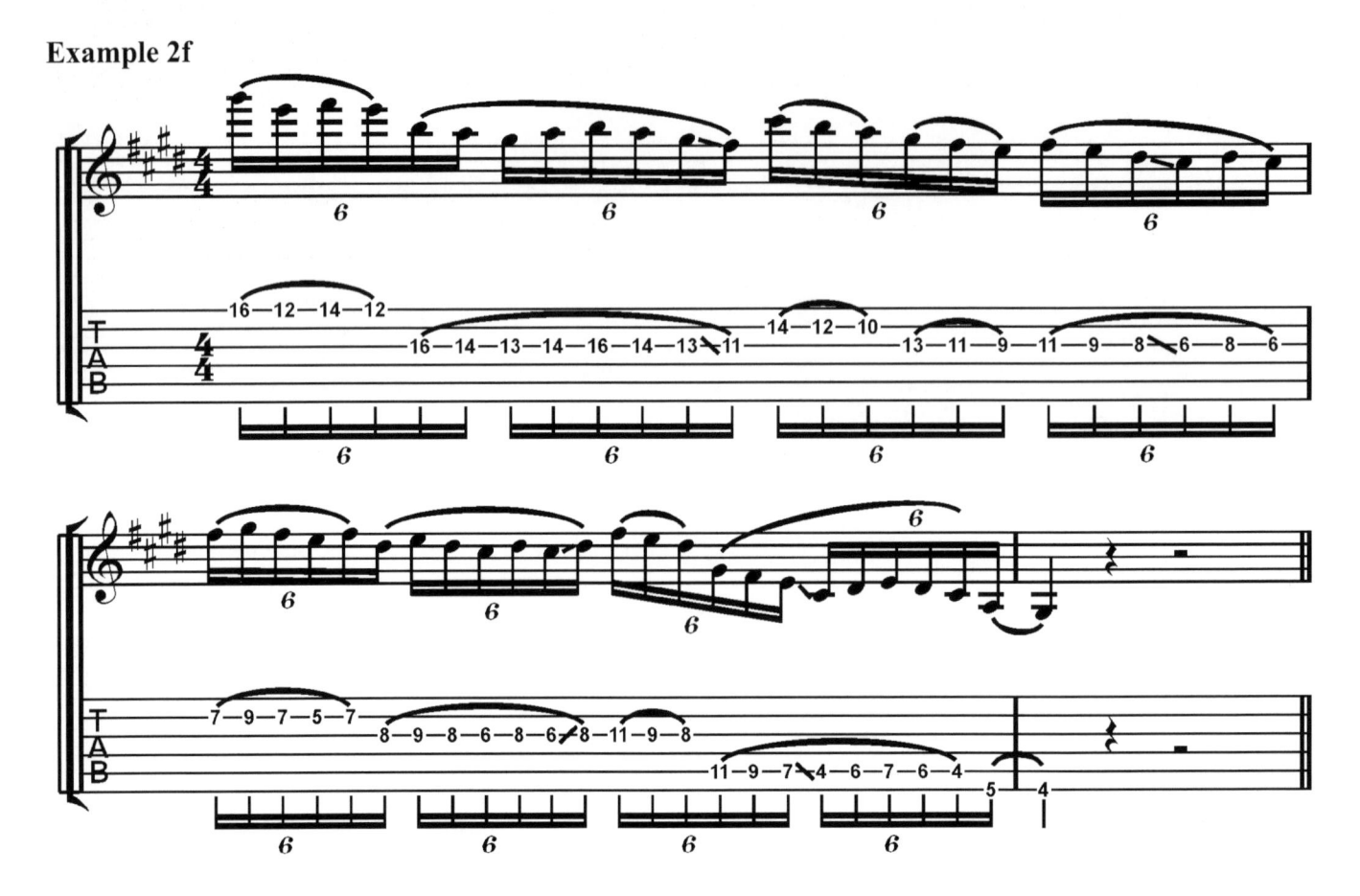

Example 2f

The following Diminished lick comes with a health warning! The wide stretches will take a good level of dexterity and stamina to maintain, so make sure you're warmed up before playing and stop if you feel any stress in the wrist or fingers. Keeping the thumb low on the back of the neck and angling the neck more vertically will both help with the wide stretches.

Notice how we resolve the dissonance of the Diminished arpeggio onto a Dm arpeggio spread out along the D string and end on notes from D Harmonic Minor.

Be careful when sliding to the final note (A) at the 22nd fret. It can be helpful to bunch the other fingers up behind it and slide the whole hand as one rather than just the pinkie. Don't forget to add some suitably ostentatious vibrato!

Example 2g

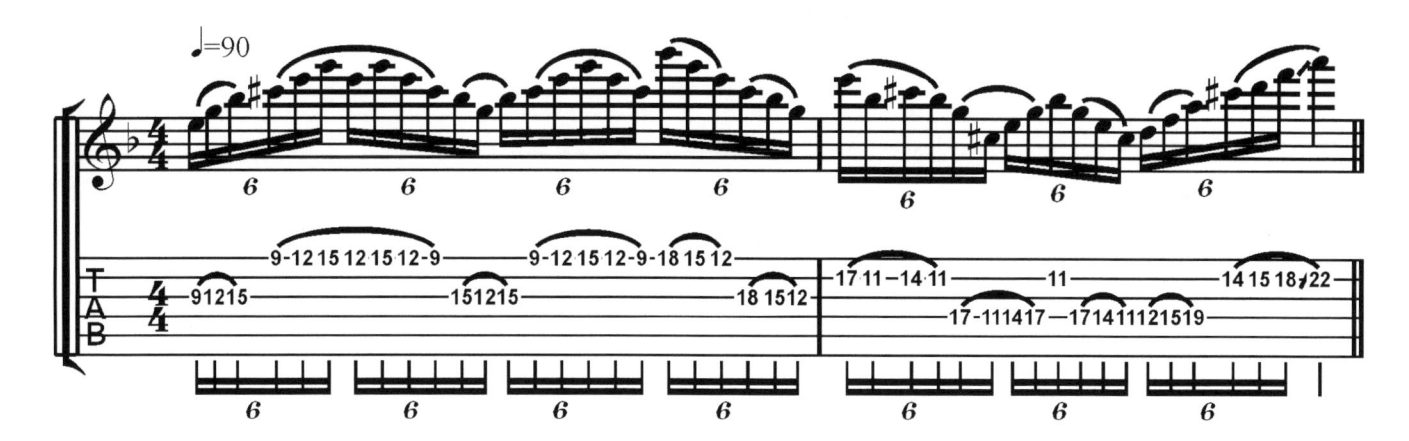

Recommended listening for examples of great legato:

Joe Satriani – *Crystal Planet*
Symphony X – *Savage Curtain*
Sikth – *Scent of the Obscene*
John Petrucci – *Curve*
James Murphy – *Epoch*
Opeth – *Heir Apparent*

Chapter 3: Tapping

In Heavy Metal Lead Guitar, many of the tapping licks we explored were based around arpeggios in the style of Van Halen and Randy Rhoads. In this chapter we're going to look at more scalic lines. Tapping as an extension of legato technique allows for the smoothest possible sound by fitting more notes on each string.

We'll return to arpeggio tapping towards the end of the chapter but with a more contemporary slant, focussing on the string skipping tapped arpeggios of players as diverse as Greg Howe, Guthrie Govan and Michael Romeo of Symphony X.

It's usual to phrase tapping licks with the tapped note on the beat. However, it's important to break away from these limiting muscle memory associations. To be most liberated, we want to be able to place any note on the beat so that the technique enhances the music instead of dictating it. At first this may be confusing for the hands so take each lick slowly to get the interaction between the hands as even as possible.

Both Van Halen and Paul Gilbert use their index finger for tapping, however, it's now common practice for modern players to use their middle finger. This is the better option for two reasons: Firstly, you are able to keep hold of the pick as normal so making the transition back to regular playing is easier. Secondly, if you wished to use multiple fingers to tap (such as example 4h), then the middle and ring fingers provide the strongest combination.

After exploring some advanced lead applications of tapping, I have included several riffs that incorporate the technique. In modern metal and instrumental rock, textural and pattern-driven compositions have blurred the division between 'rhythm' and 'lead' vocabulary. Death, Limp Bizkit and Funeral for a Friend often use tapping to create riffs in this way.

Progressive bands like Sikth and more recently Scale the Summit have used tapping to create intervallic riffs that would be impossible without the two handed approach.

Our first line is played as straight 1/16th notes, and the taps do not fall on beat one of each group. This can feel uncomfortable, but breaking the dependence on a physical reference point for rhythm will improve your ear and sense of pulse.

Start slowly, and make sure you know which notes fall on the beats so you can keep in time. A great way to practice this rhythmic freedom is to break the lick up into small chunks and, with a metronome, practice stopping on different beats. This will show you if you're really staying in time throughout the lick, or just cramming notes together between two beats.

Use the fretting hand add the vibrato from behind the tapping finger on the final note.

Example 3a

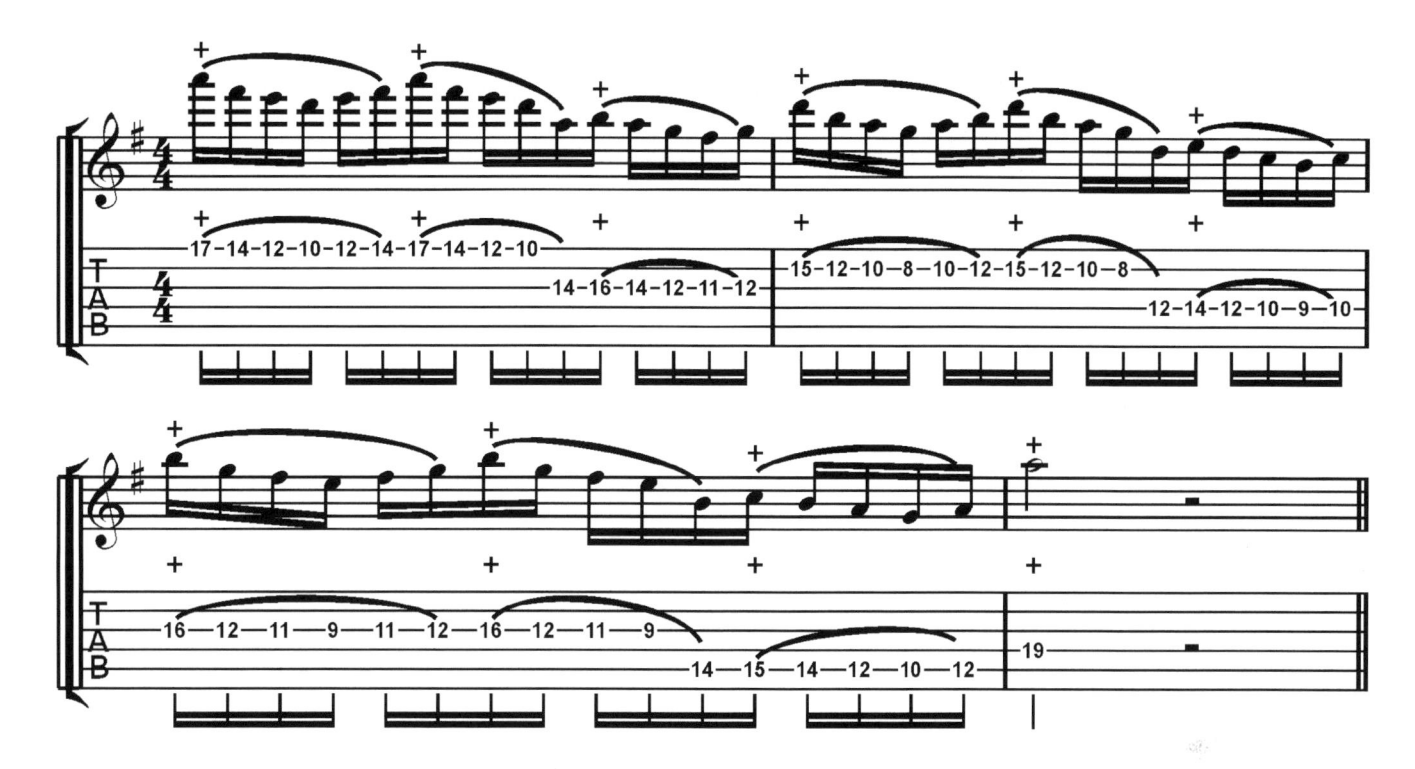

```
17-14-12-10-12-14-17-14-12-10
                              14-16-14-12-11-12      15-12-10-8-10-12-15-12-10-8
                                                                                 12-14-12-10-9-10

16-12-11-9-11-12-16-12-11-9
                            14-15-14-12-10-12    -19-
```

The main challenge is hammering-on to a new string with the first finger of the fretting hand. This poses two problems: Firstly the first finger is actually surprisingly weak for most people because normally it never needs to hammer-on, and secondly, the force of the hammer-on often causes unwanted string noise.

Unfortunately, the index finger is rather overworked as it must simultaneously play the desired note *and* mute the other five strings. To tackle this, experiment with how you hammer-on so the first finger not only lands on the desired pitch, but also mutes the adjacent lower string with its tip and the higher strings with the side of the finger. To consistently get all three things right may take some time, but once you've mastered it, the knock-on effect will pay dividends for your playing in general.

Our next lick spans three octaves of a B7 arpeggio and focuses on hammering-on from nowhere with the fretting hand. The basic triad is in the fretting hand with the tapping hand adding the b7 (A).

Example 3b

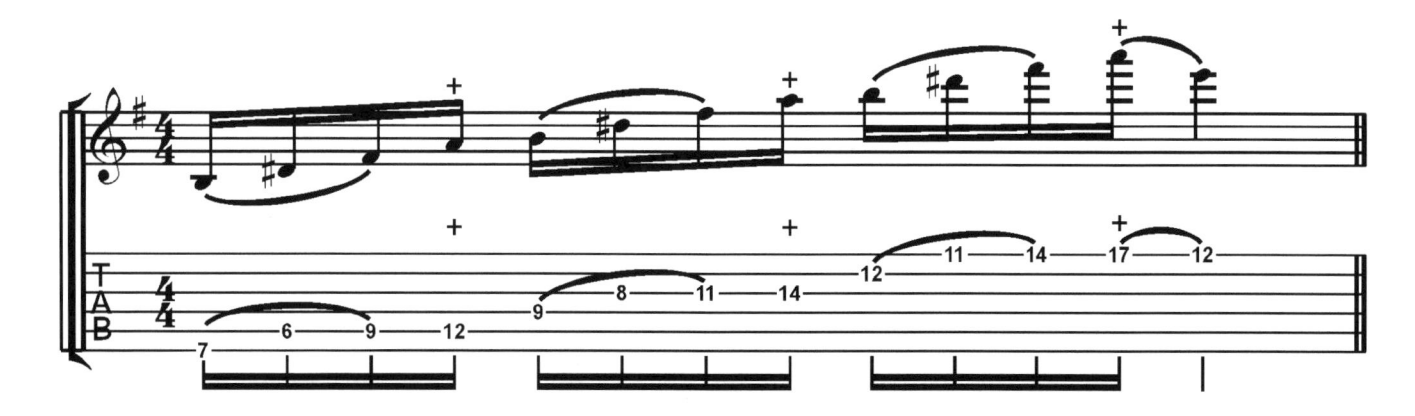

```
                                                              11-14-17-12
                                              8-11-14    12
                                      9
              6-9-12
    7
```

Building on the previous idea, the following lick combines the B7 with a Cmaj7 arpeggio found right next door. Focus on the first note of each four-note grouping to keep track of where you are and initially practice the fretted part before adding the tapping.

The combination of the two arpeggios gives a strong B Phrygian Dominant flavour, just as you would get by strumming the two chords one after another.

Example 3c

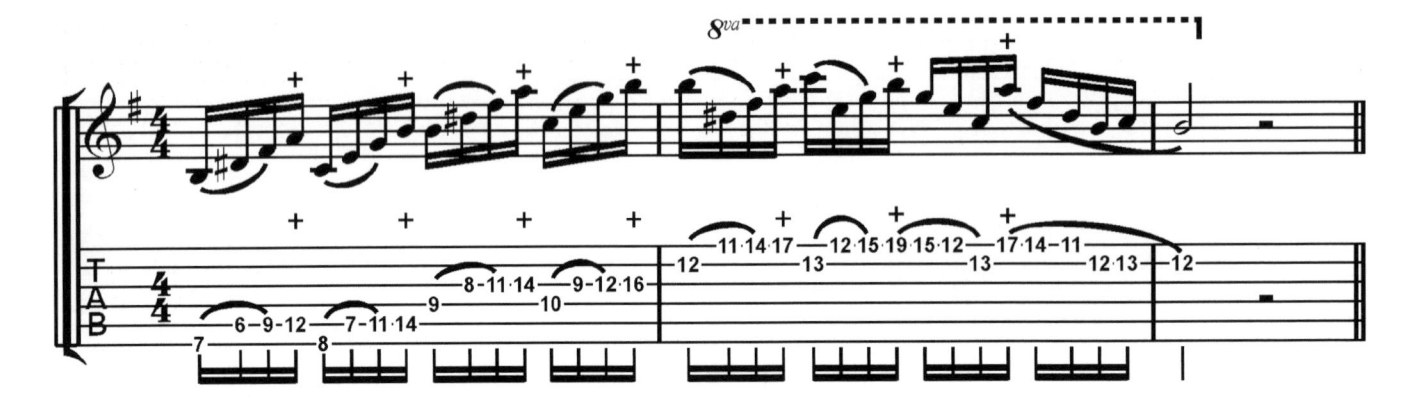

In the following example we lay out the notes of an Em7 arpeggio in one position, based around the 'A shape' Em barre chord.

Michael Romeo of Symphony X has a masterful command of this type of lick; incorporating them musically into his highly technical neoclassical soloing style.

Example 3d

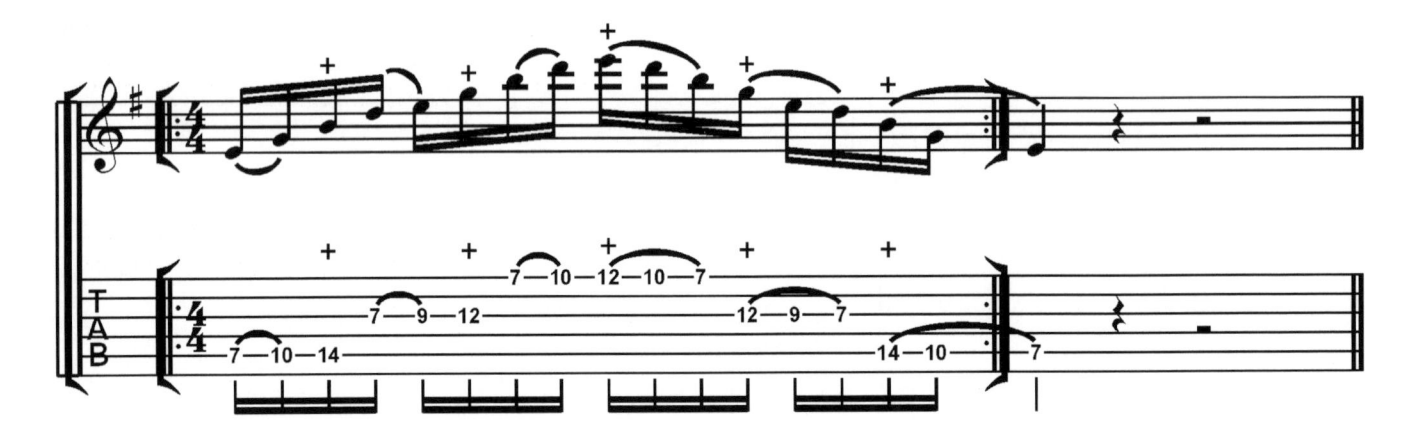

Here's the same shape, but this time using sequences of four notes. To get this idea clean will require serious muting and strong hammer-ons, otherwise the notes will disappear in a muddy mess of distortion and open strings. Remember to keep fretting hand fingers flat against the strings to mute them, playing with the pad of the finger rather than the tip.

Example 3e

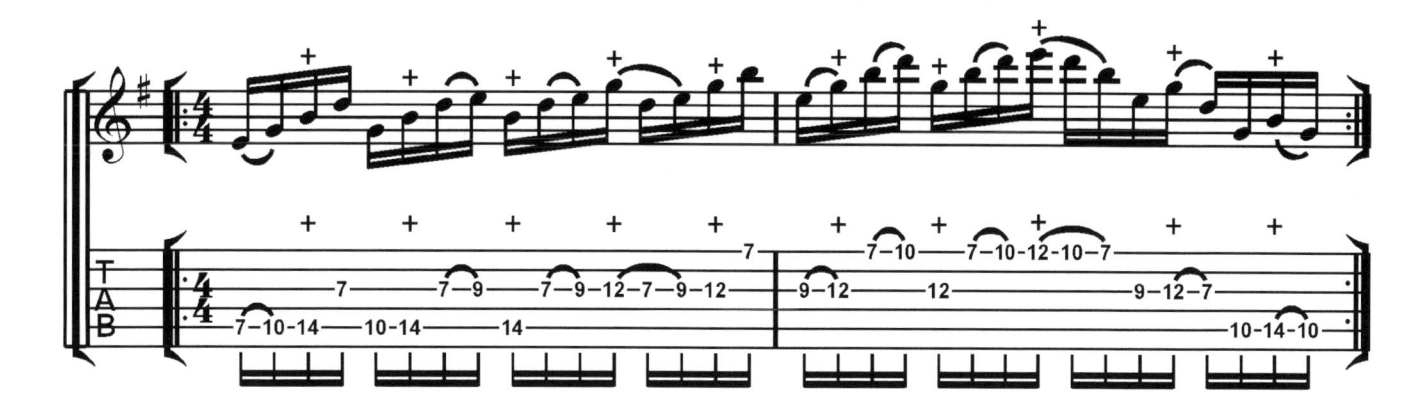

The same Em7 arpeggio can be played with all four chord tones on one string and repeated in octaves. This is easier to visualise when improvising, particularly in less familiar keys. Keep the thumb low on the back of the neck to make the five fret stretch more manageable and, as always, be vigilant against unwanted noise.

Example 3f

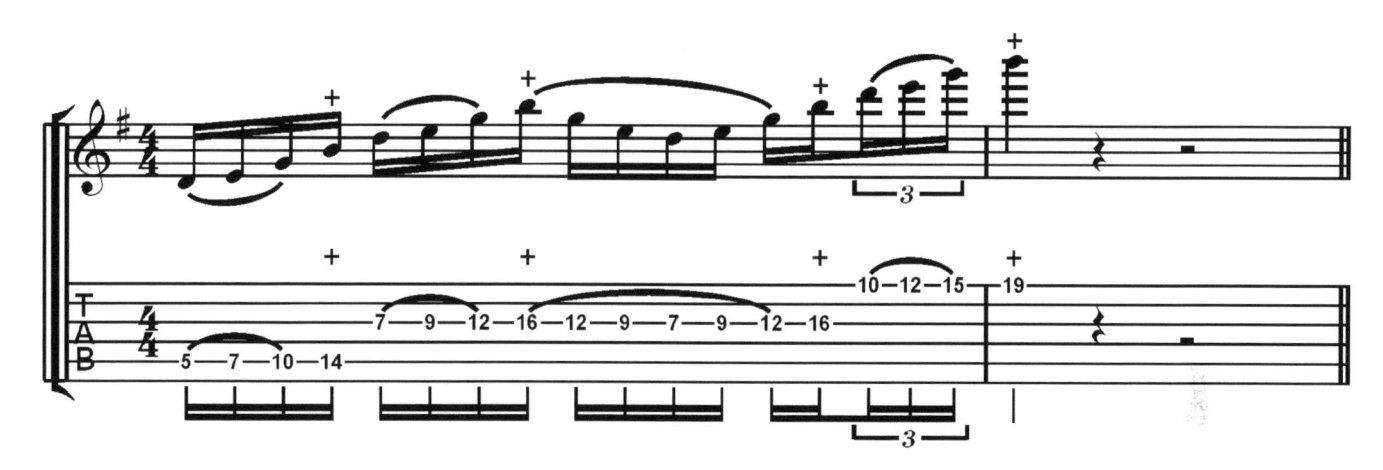

Here's a descending pattern in the same fashion as example 3f but this time in D minor. The stretch for the fretting hand may be a little awkward because of the bunching up of the index and middle fingers. Guitar wizard Guthrie Govan quite often employs phrases like this to achieve a wonderfully fluid saxophone-inspired articulation. Listen out for a preposterous example at the start of the solo on his track Fives that combines several different arpeggios into one phrase.

Notice how we've relocated three octaves of the same arpeggio onto the E, D and high E strings. Although a wider string skip is needed, the fretting hand avoids the lateral movement found in the previous lick. This should make moving backwards and forwards between each string more fluid.

Example 3g

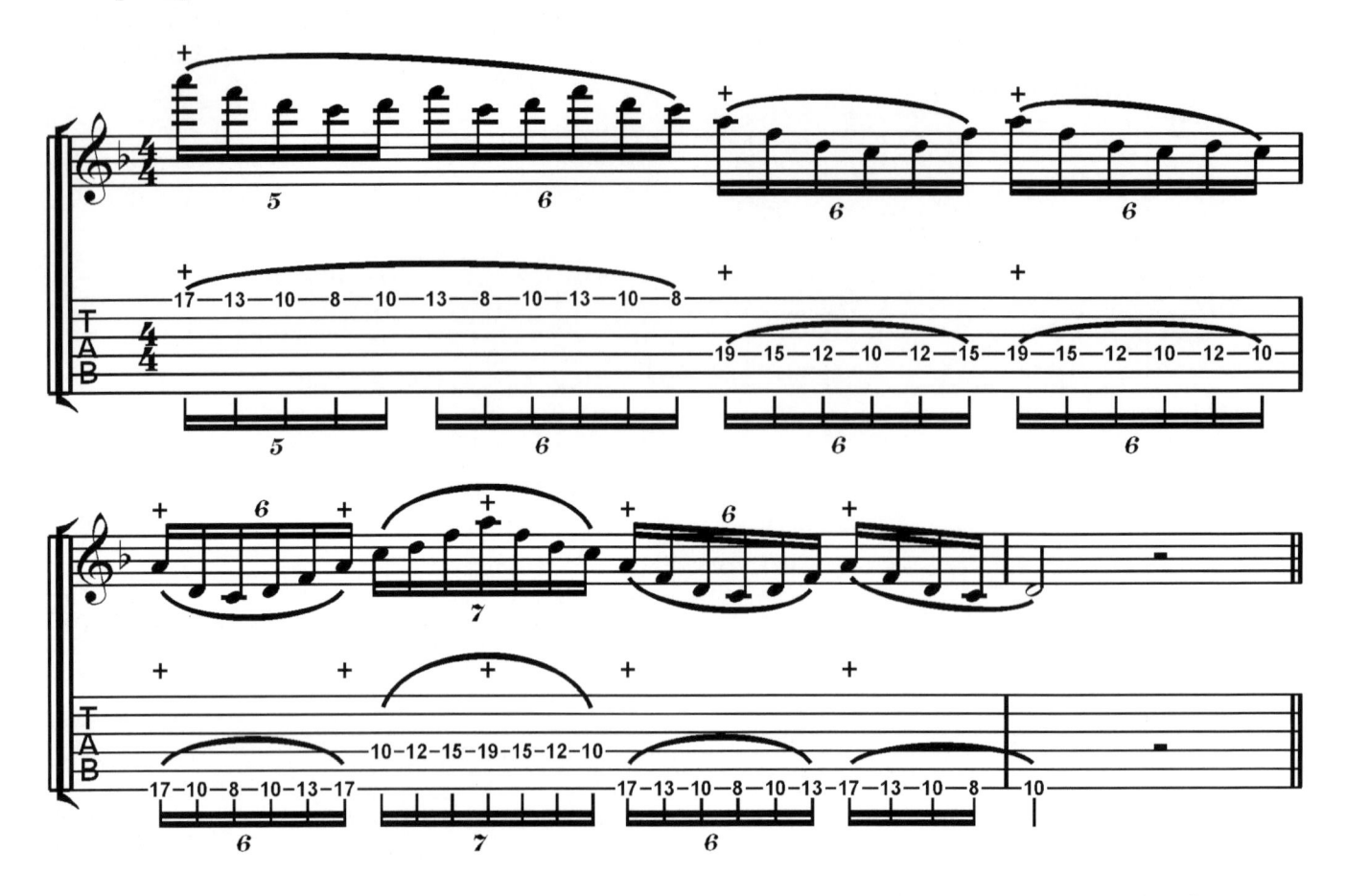

Let's explore this concept even further by tapping using two fingers on the picking hand to give five notes on one string. If you've not used more than one finger on the picking hand to tap with before, then don't panic, the ring finger operates in exactly the same way as the middle finger, although a subtle pull off is needed from the ring finger after tapping to give the third tapped note sufficient volume.

Practice the first four notes in isolation to get a feel for hammering-on and pulling-off between the tapping fingers.

The fact that there are three consecutive tapped notes allows a sufficient time for the fretting hand to change string. I prefer to pull off upwards into the palm but pulling off either upwards or downwards is equally valid if the results are comfortable and sound good.

Example 3h

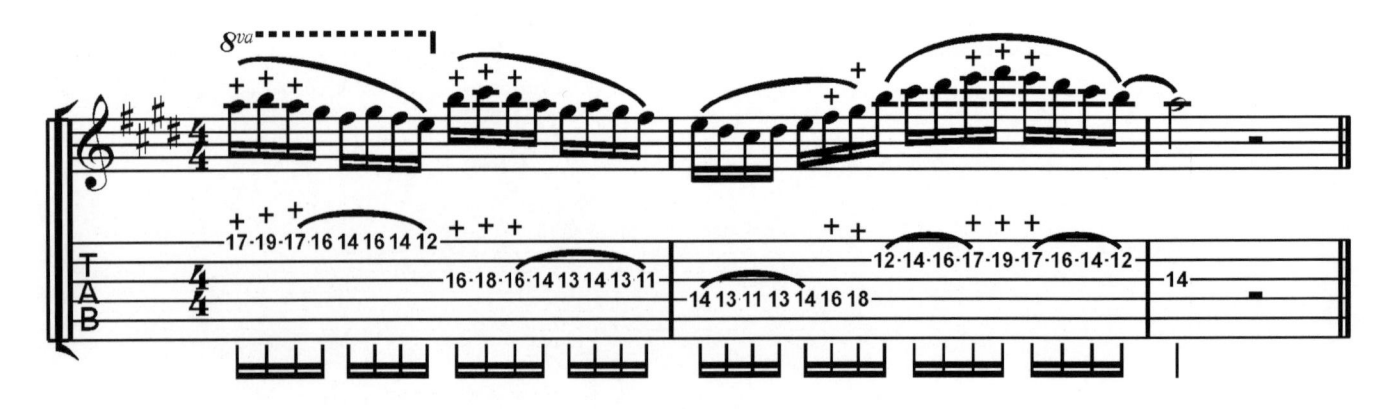

As with the previous lick, example 3i uses two tapping fingers to help the fretting hand. In the spirit of Van Halen (and later Greg Howe), we're using tapping to share the work of each hand in what is otherwise a quite conventional sounding blues lick.

You'll have to hammer-on with the fretting hand for the F#m arpeggio on beat one, so be on guard against unwanted noise. Lift each finger as the next one comes down, while once again using the tips of each finger to mute the adjacent lower string.

The lasting appeal of Van Halen is that despite using flashy technical ideas, at the core he is still in touch with The Bluesy vocabulary inherited from hard rock. Listening to, and learning some of his solos will help you to integrate these two aspects successfully.

Example 3i

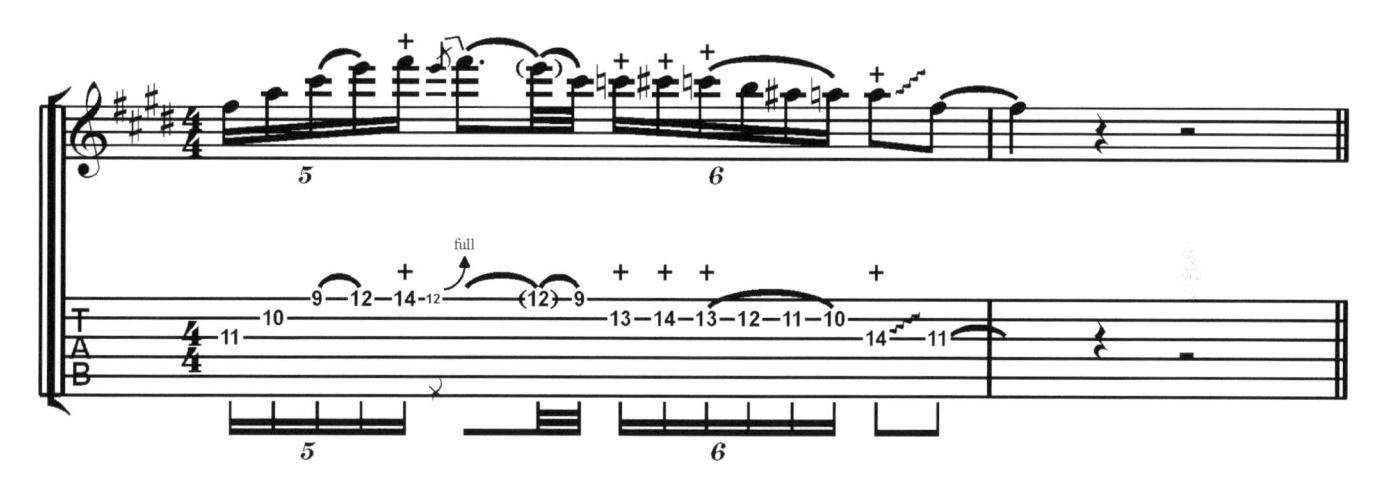

For the next example we're using the Whole Tone scale which lends the lick a tense 'Augmented' sound, ideal for dark and dramatic moments. Although the Wholetone 'fits' over Augmented triads and V7b5/#5 chords, try using it over other chords to create an 'outside' sound on an otherwise diatonic solo. If your ears like the results, go for it!

Notice how this lick momentarily moves outside of the E Whole Tone scale as we move chromatically up the top E string. Also, the final two tapped notes start with the ring finger (unlike our other examples). Be sure to get things dialled in slowly and accurately.

Example 3j

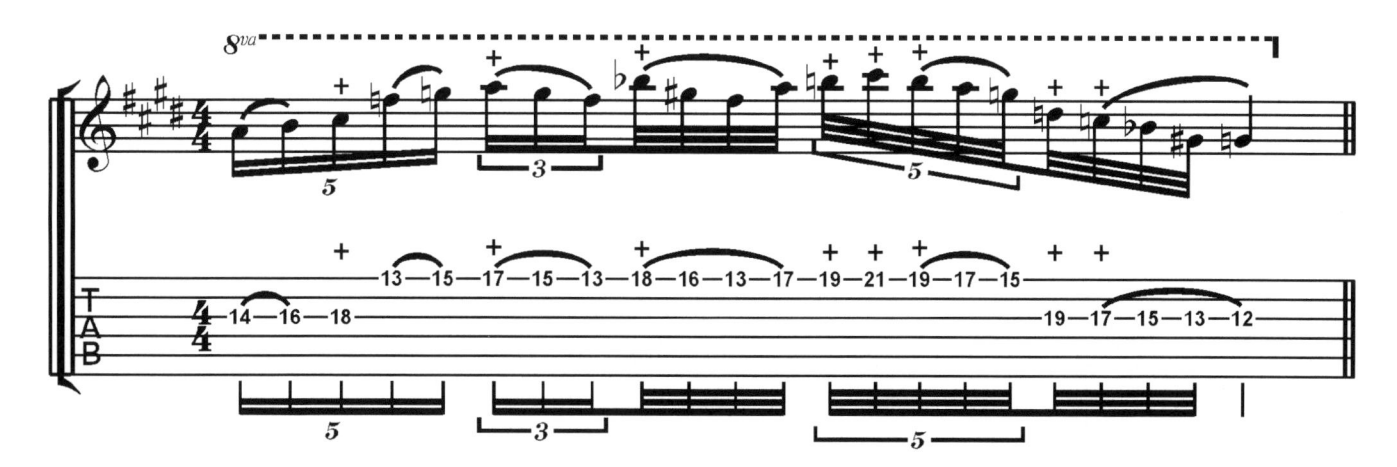

Sliding tapped notes is an interesting alternative to using two tapping fingers to extend a melody.

The following example demonstrates both of these characteristics by sliding a tone on the G string then sliding a major 3rd on the E string.

Example 3k

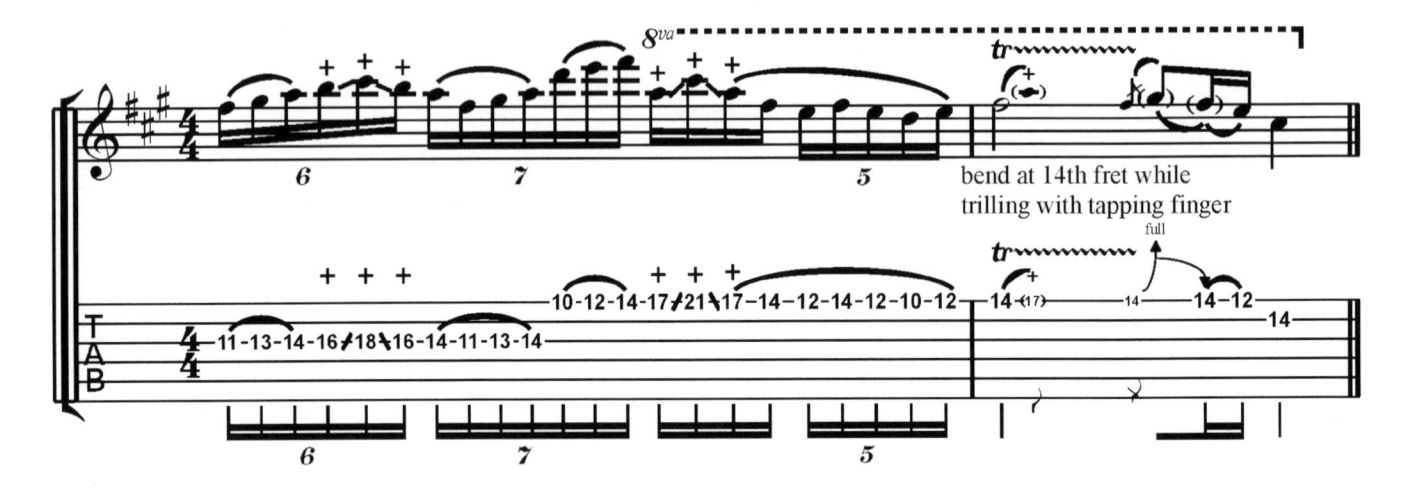

As with example 3j, try to ignore how complex the rhythmic groupings appear on paper, but observe which notes land on the beats.

Use the audio as a guide, and then just go for it! The way the notes float over the pulse enhance the legato feel, but it's important to keep a sense of time so that you can land on the beat whenever you choose… just as an acrobat controls their landing after somersaulting through the air!

Rhythm Tapping

The rest of this chapter explores riffs (rather than licks) that feature tapping. Tapping can provide high-pitched accents that would otherwise be impossible. It also allows wide interval patterns at higher tempos, and helps achieve a flowing, piano-like texture. Rhythm parts need to tightly lock in with the drums, so be prepared to practice your legato/tapping playing to the same rhythmic precision you would demand when picking.

Picking becomes problematic when several picking hand fingers get involved, so we become reliant on fretting hand hammer-ons. You'll find that with this amount of fretting hand hammer-ons, muting the unwanted strings becomes a serious challenge. Take each section slowly; making sure your technique is watertight by flattening the fretting-hand fingers and using the picking hand palm to mute unwanted noise.

We'll start off with a fairly straight forward riff that follows closely from our lead work. This has a distinctly classical sound to it, thanks to the use of pedal point. Be careful with the position shift of both hands at the start of bar four. Practice the fretting hand until it is fluent before adding the tapping.

Example 3l

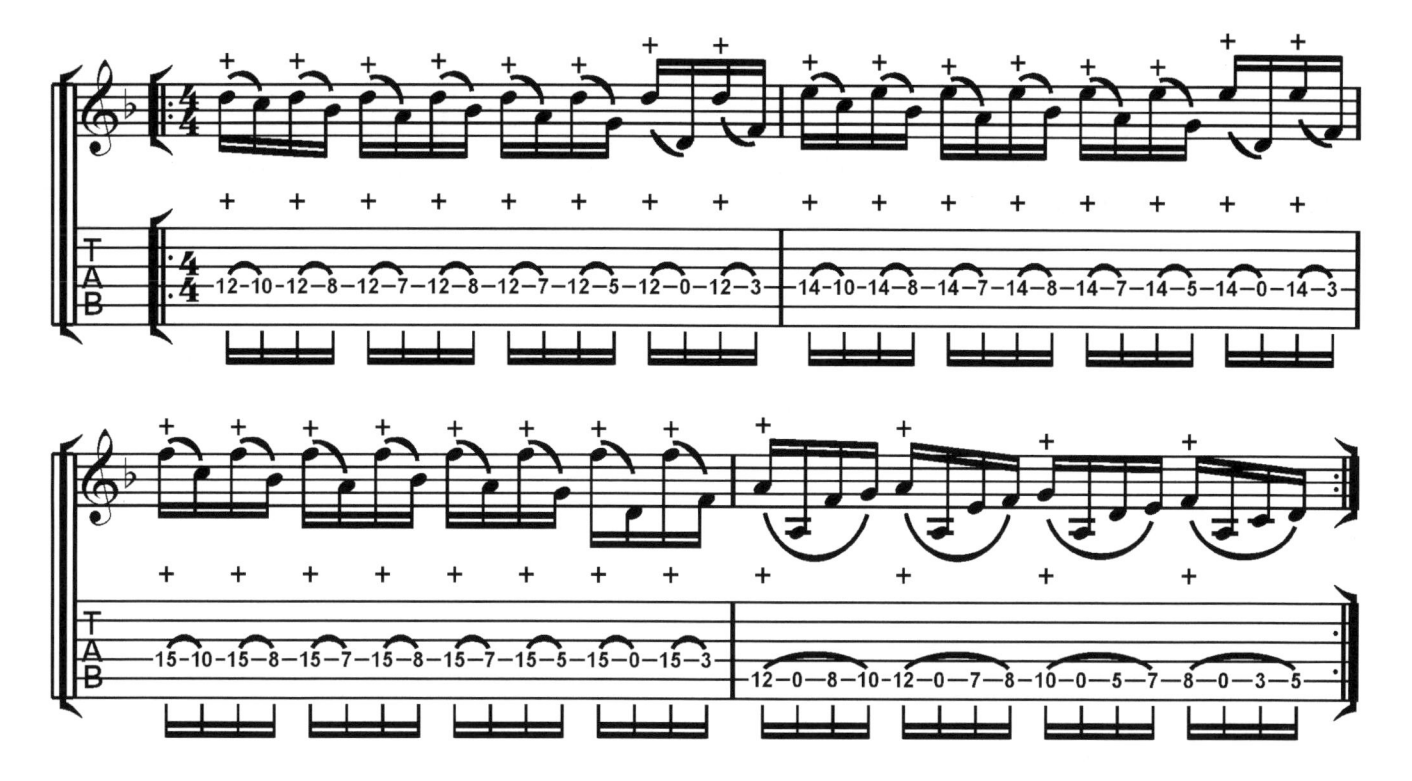

Tapping and picking don't have to be mutually exclusive! Here we augment a tight, thrashy triplet riff from Annihilator or Lamb of God with a descending tapping run. Work through the final bar in isolation before combining it with the riff. It has three, four-note groupings which fall across the main pulse, so count it out slowly before raising the tempo.

The movement of the picking hand between palm muting at the bridge and tapping at the fourteenth fret needs to be carefully rehearsed so that the rhythm and pick attack aren't compromised. It's a bit of a juggling act so use the legato at the end of bar three to cover the picking hand's leap. **Example 3m**

The next riff uses tapping to add extensions to a G power chord. Here we alternate between the Bb (b3) and A (9th), but you should go on to experiment with adding other notes with tapped notes.

After a strong Gm(add9) tonality in bar 1, the second half answers with a tenser G Dorian #11 phrase, a mode of D Harmonic Minor, (also known as the Romanian Minor scale)

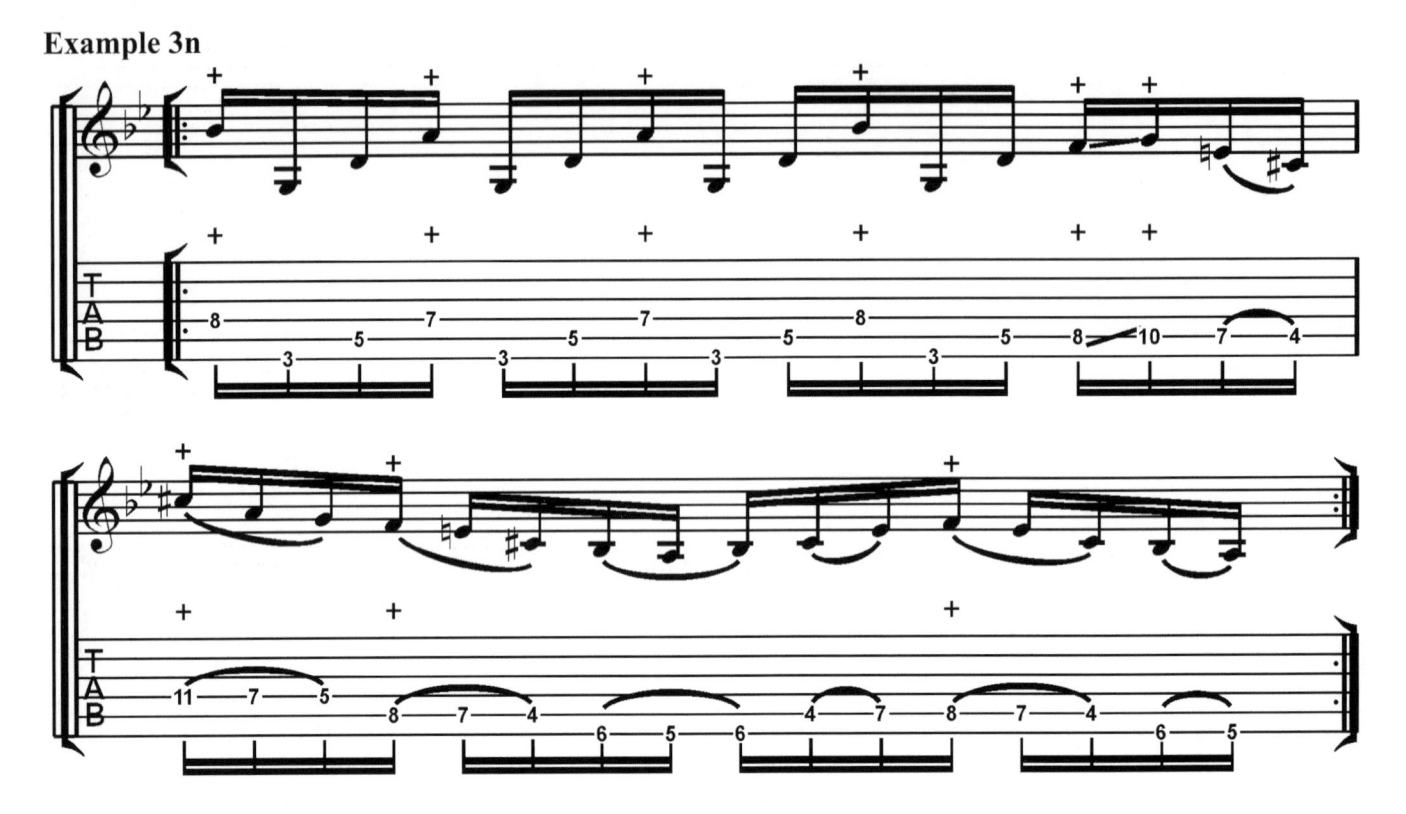

Example 3n

Keeping a power chord in the fretting hand remains a common theme, but now the fretting hand is leading rhythmically.

Listen to the audio to absorb the odd rhythm until you hands can tap the rhythm in each part. Many of these ideas feel like drumming between the hands, so learning to coordinate the two hands in different ways is the best starting point.

In this example, I've actually brought the thumb into play to gently pluck the open E string in bars two and four. This is marked with the symbol 'p' in the notation.

The softer attack of the thumb blends closely with the tone of the tapped notes. Also the first tapped chord in bar four is most easily played with a combination of index and ring fingers.

Example 3o

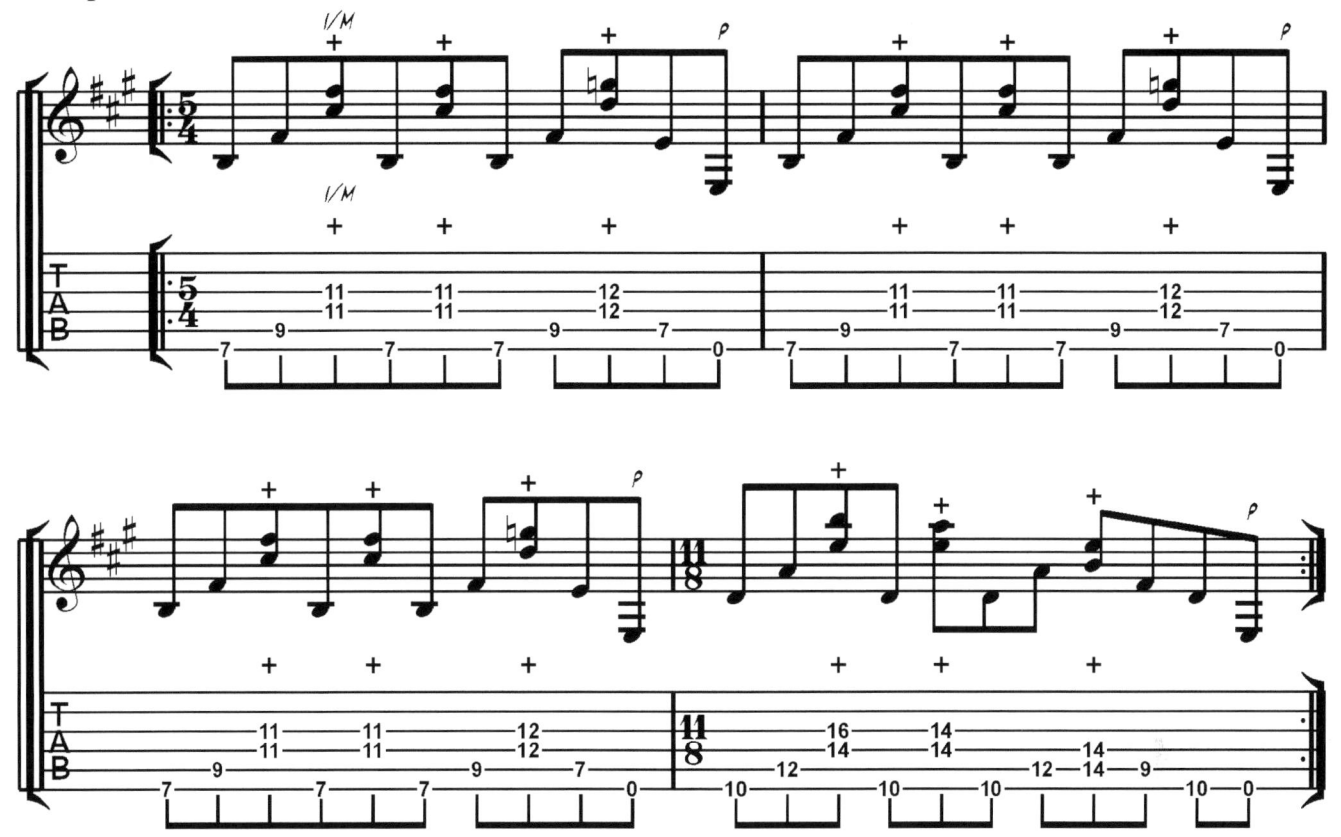

All of the previous examples used a constant stream of even notes, but the final tapping riff adds more rhythmic interest. This increases the difficulty as the notes can no longer be lined up evenly. Be sure that the hammer-ons are locking in tightly with the 1/16th note pulse.

We outline a chord progression of D, D/C, Bm and G, although several passing scale notes are included on each chord. Bars one and two employ sliding taps, while bars three and four use two tapping fingers to play notes on adjacent strings. Practice this movement in isolation to avoid letting the two notes ring into each other. I used the middle and index, as in example 3h, so the pick can be kept in its usual grip ready to return to a normal playing position.

Example 3p

Recommended listening for tapping techniques:

Meshuggah – *Future Breed Machine*
Sikth - *Skies of the Millennium Night*
Animals as Leaders – *Cafo*
Periphery – *Zyglrox*
Scale the Summit – *Dunes*
Chon - *Knot*
Protest the Hero - *Bloodmeat*

Chapter 4: Alternate Picking

A strong picking technique is essential to great metal playing, and most of your time will be spent 'locking in' with the drums and bass as a member of the rhythm section. Locking in with the rhythm section requires a very high degree of precision and this accuracy will carry over into your lead playing to give your licks polish and crispness.

As we all know, the best way to achieve accuracy is with a metronome or a drum loop. Practice one lick slowly until it feels like it can't go wrong, and then start gradually raising the tempo to build your speed while remaining relaxed. Keep your foot tapping on the beats and sync up your hands by accenting the notes that land on each beat.

Once you're feeling confident with the three-note-per-string runs we worked on in Heavy Metal Lead Guitar, it's time to step up a gear. In this chapter we're going to be looking at alternate picking licks that make more demands of your technique. The speed at which you play any of the licks is of course up to you, so we'll be raising the bar in terms of rhythm and string crossing, rather than just shredding harder!

Keep the heel of the picking hand in contact with the bridge, and move it across the strings as you change string with the pick. Having this consistency will give an even attack and help you to avoid losing control when skipping strings by having a constant point of contact.

To start with, we've got a couple of picking runs that demonstrate how we could develop some diatonic fragments. After practicing different patterns and clusters of notes we can stitch them together to form longer runs full of twists and turns.

Example 5a switches from a sequence of four notes to three notes, then into a straight scale with a quick legato turn at the end. Split the line into short two-beat sections and make sure they feel easy before you combine them into the full run.

Try playing this idea descending, then combine other sequences to build your own phrases.

Example 4a

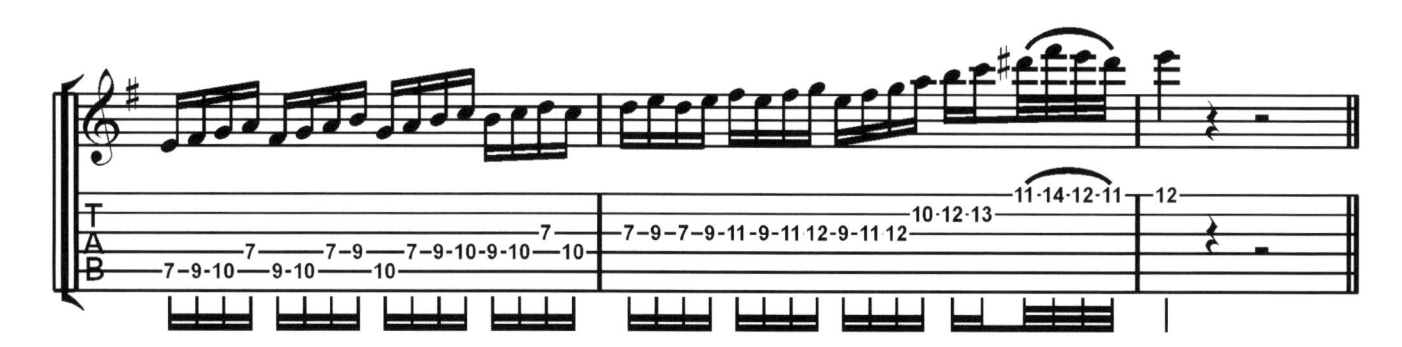

The second example maintains stepwise motion throughout the line, but changes direction at different times to keep the contour of the lick less predictable. Practicing the different permutations of each two string cell will enable you to improvise runs like this with ease, because you're assembling small building blocks, each of which have been carefully rehearsed.

Example 4b

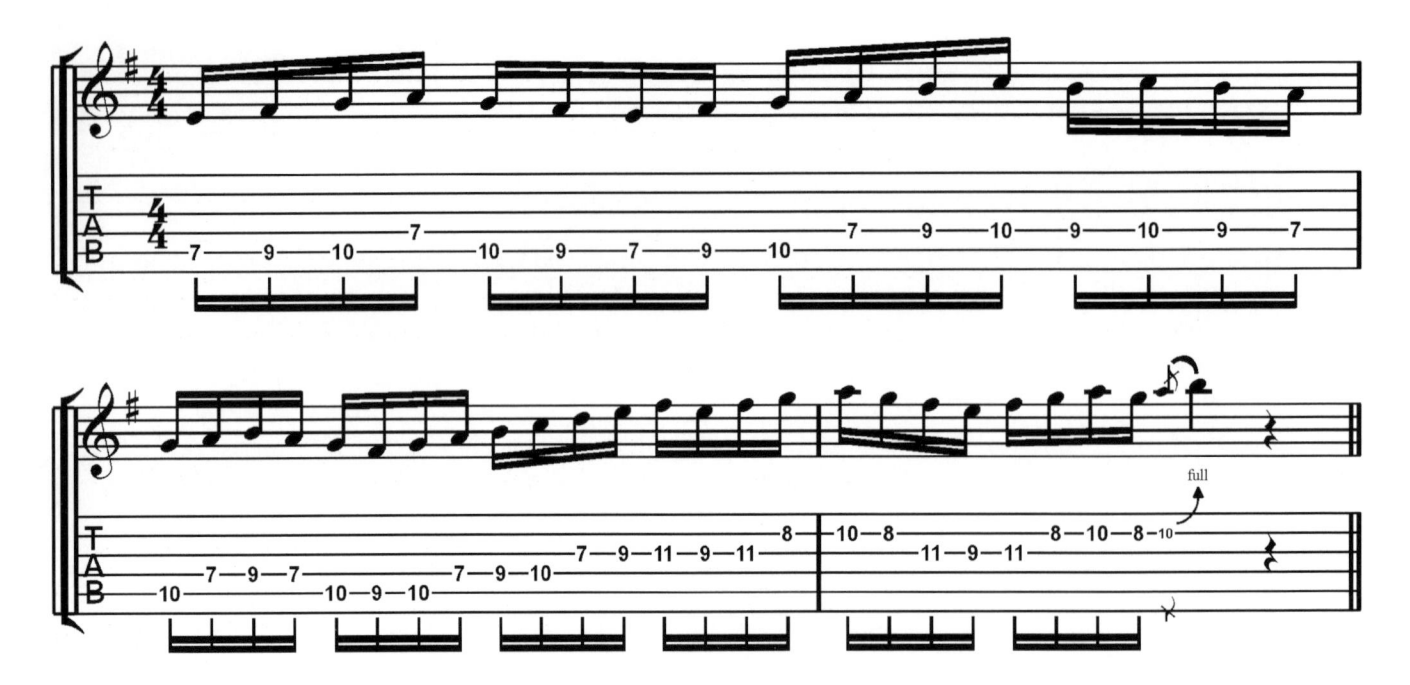

Michael Angelo Batio is one of the fastest shredders, and his picking prowess is in no doubt despite using an unconventional hand position. This demanding string-skipping lick is his style and will test your control, but the leaps in pitch make for an exciting pattern that covers a large range.

Moving the picking wrist as you change strings is even more important when you skip strings. Start slowly to check your pick crosses over the skipped string with minimal clearance. The pick should not be noticeably 'lifted' out from the strings but rather the skip is an extension of the last pick stroke.

Example 4c

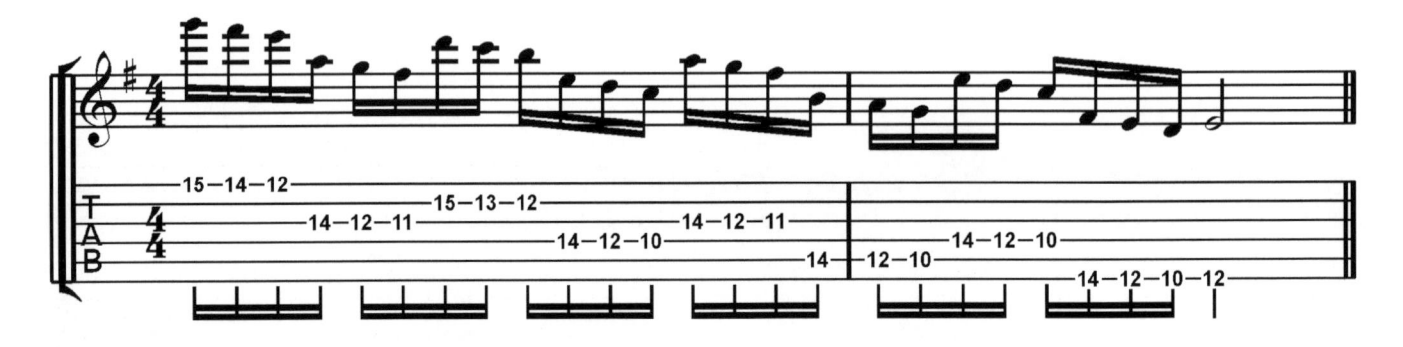

Now we've skipped one string at a time, let's skip two! Each melodic cell in the next example is repeated an octave below each time. The change of position and jump between strings may feel unwieldy to start with, but focussing on the destination fret rather than your hand should help build accuracy.

Practice the picking of this lick before worrying about the notes: Alternate pick eight strokes on each string using just one pitch so the picking hand learns its role.

Example 4d

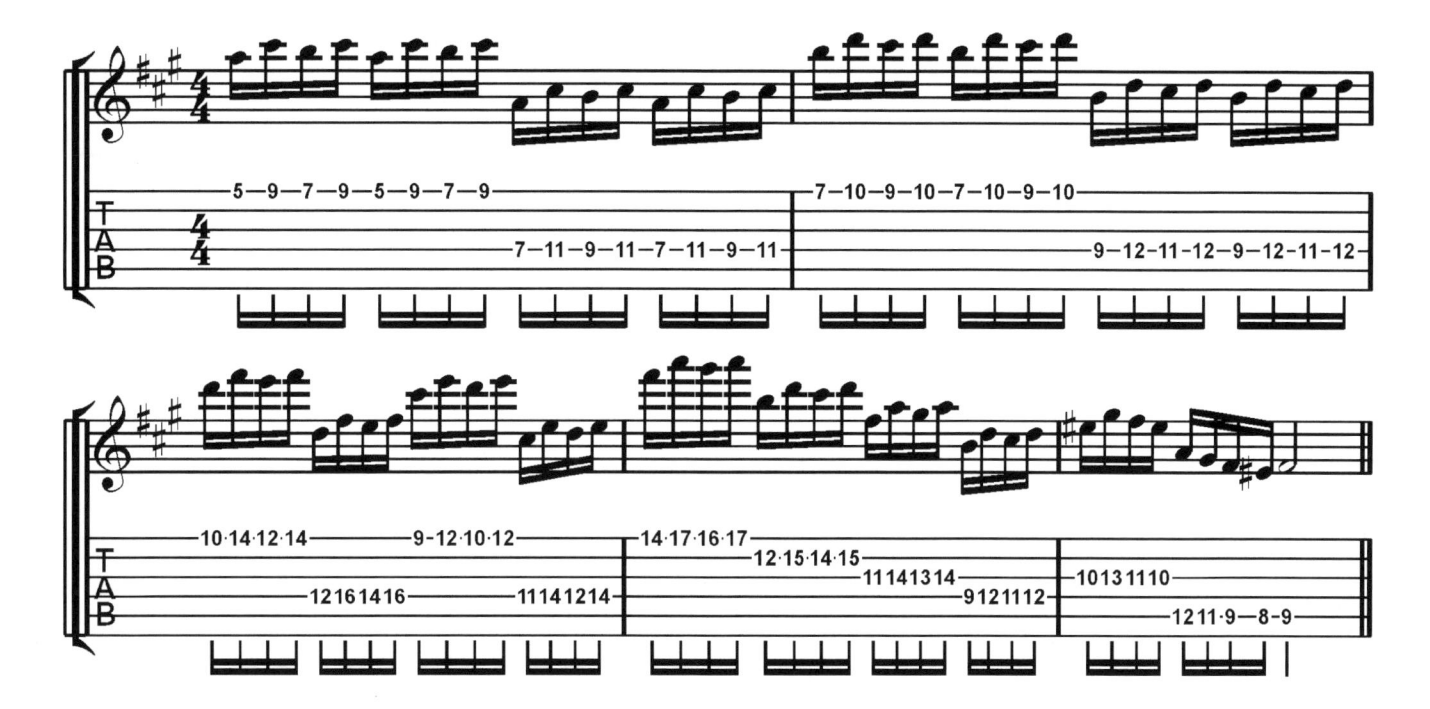

[Musical notation and guitar tablature for Example 4d]

Tremolo picking is playing a single note repeatedly at high speed, and is usually added as an effect to a slower melody without worrying about the actual subdivisions of the pick strokes. However, it's quite common for players to include sections of tremolo picking in particularly intense picking licks.

After ascending through a scalic phrase in the next example, the highest notes of each contour are tremolo picked. Repeating these notes helps to reinforce their melodic importance.

Keep in mind that while tremolo gives a sense of speed and frantic energy, the picking hand should remain loose and relaxed so that the rest of the scalic playing will be accurate.

Example 4e

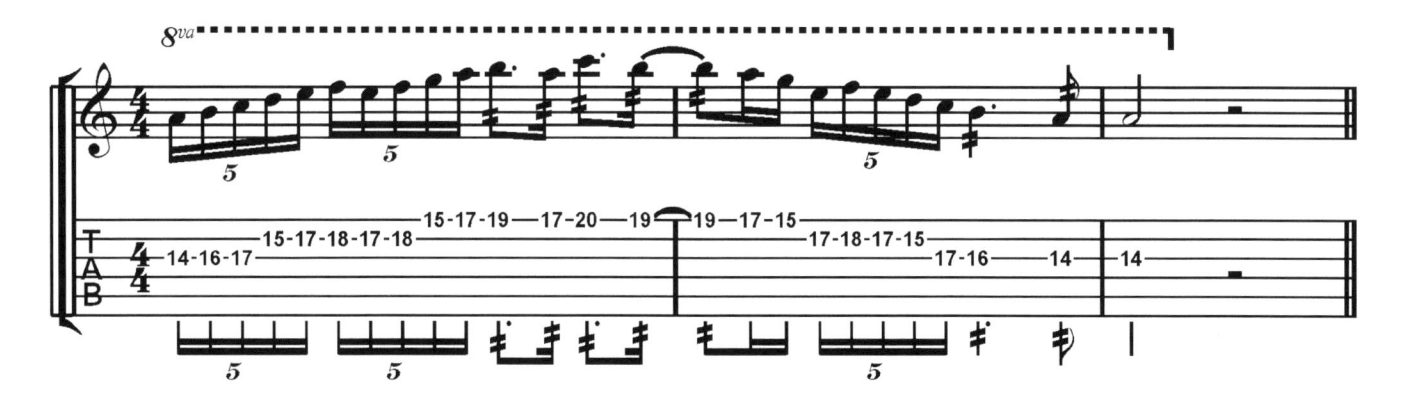

[Musical notation and guitar tablature for Example 4e]

In the legato chapter, learnt about either sticking religiously to the rhythmic pulse of the music, or floating over the time and cramming in notes so that the target note lands on the beat. It's worth developing the same freedom with picking, though the challenge is increased by having to keep both hands synchronised.

One way to work on this is to practice moving between different groupings of notes is shown in the next example.

Here we start in 1/16th notes before putting on a burst of speed to play two beats of sextuplets, ending with a mixture of 1/16th notes and 1/8th note triplets. Accenting the notes on the beat is again here your friend. Listen carefully to the audio to help gauge how much speeding up/slowing down is needed for each grouping.

Keep your foot tapping throughout, and with a good sense of time, you'll know when to drop back into rhythm at the end of runs of this type. Playing to a drum loop or metronome while you experiment with speeding up and slowing down will develop this illusive, but very expressive skill.

Example 4f

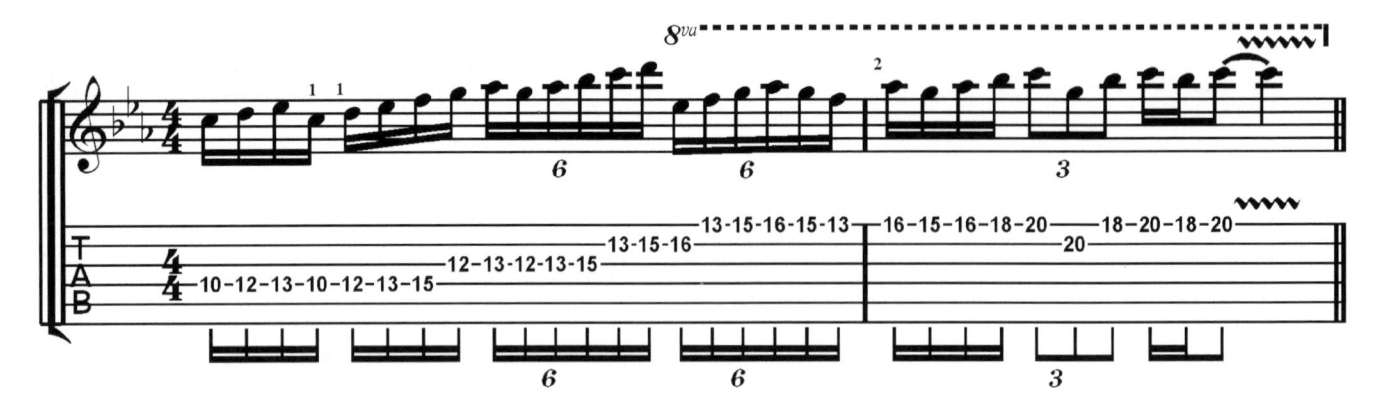

```
8va------------------------------
        1  1                              2
-------------------------------------13-15-16-15-13--16-15-16-18-20--18-20-18-20--
                                13-15-16-----------------------20---------------
                      12-13-12-13-15-------------------------------------------
    10-12-13-10-12-13-15-------------------------------------------------------
                6              6                     3
```

Now to touch on some intervallic licks after all that scale-based vocabulary. Obviously with lots of wider intervals in quick succession, there's going to be more jumping between strings. This first example involves lots of 5ths which provide a very angular yet consonant sound. First the line ascends by double picking each note in a line of 5ths before shifting a fifth motif up and down within the scale.

Here Steve Vai's influence is clear. Furthermore, Vai's use of 5ths licks likely comes from his time with Frank Zappa, so go back to the source!

Follow the fingering I've recommended to avoid getting tripped-up during the position shifts.

Example 4g

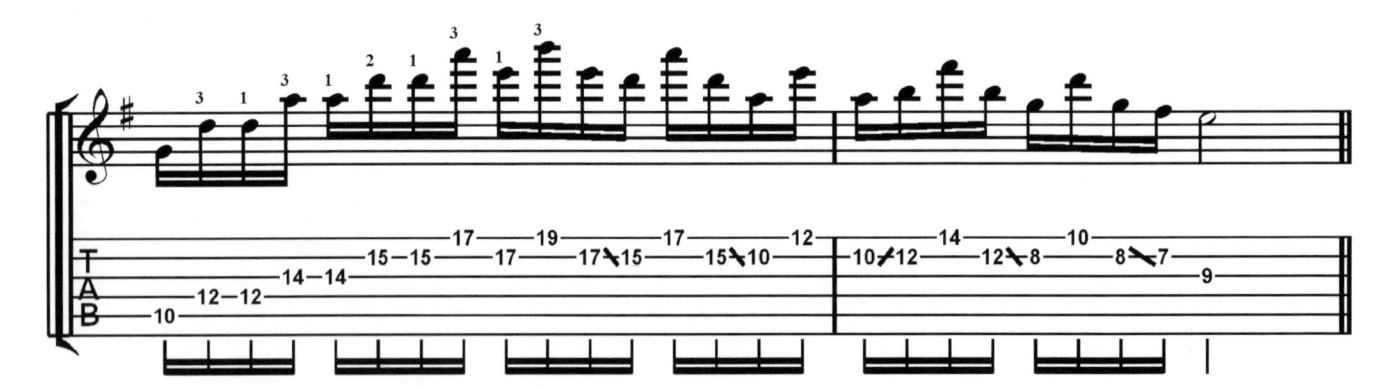

```
              3    3
        3   1    1
    3 1
-----------------17-----19-------17------12-------14--------10------
         15-15------17-------17\15------15\10---10/12---12\8------8\7---
     14-14----------------------------------------------------------9---
  12-12-----------------------------------------------------------------
10----------------------------------------------------------------------
```

You could also experiment by converting this lick to a version based on 4ths.

For some interesting intervallic licks check out John Petrucci's earlier work with Dream Theater.

In the following three examples we'll explore the possibilities of playing wider interval licks. Example 4h uses diatonic 6ths. Like 3rds, 6ths are sweet-sounding and harmonically strong, but the wider leaps make them more interesting.

There are lots of different patterns to explore with each of the different intervals. Finding a pattern you like, and then applying it to another interval is a great way of modifying licks to suit your taste. Explore the other intervals - 4ths, and 7ths – and note the flavour of each.

For more useful patterns, check out the Fundamental Changes book: **Guitar Fretboard Fluency**

Example 4h

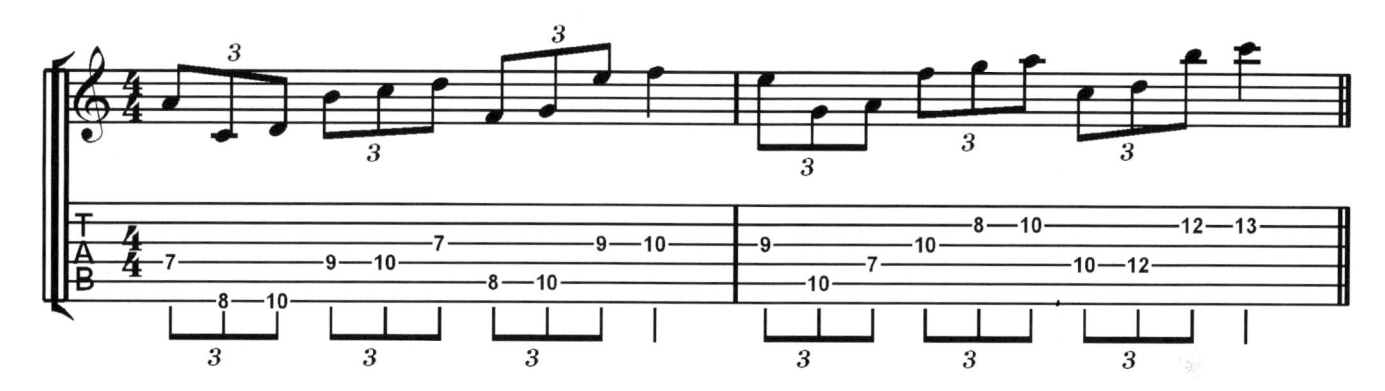

```
                                                                    8—10           12—13
                                      7              9—10      9            10          10—12
        7          9—10                        8—10          10          7
   8—10
```

The next intervallic lick uses octaves. Whereas other intervals have a distinctive musical flavour, the octave has a different effect. By moving the same note up an octave, we make it more prominent in the overall musical texture.

Simple lines can sound modern and individual if we move certain notes up by an octave. This technique is known as *octave displacement*. For example, this line of adjacent notes in the D minor scale, would be quite boring, but with octave displacement it takes on an entirely new sound.

Example 4i

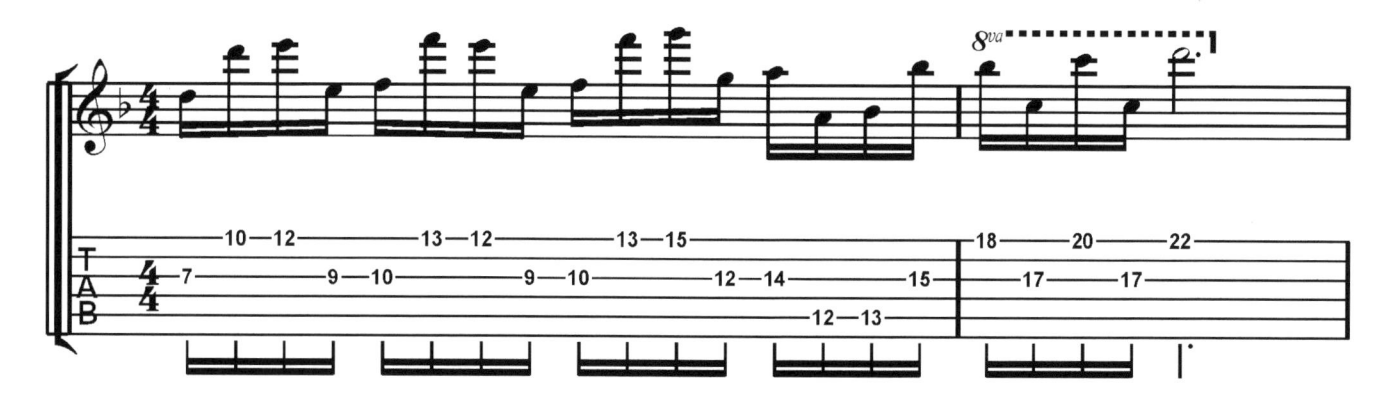

```
        10—12          13—12          13—15                      18          20          22
    7            9—10           9—10           12—14       15          17          17
                                         12—13
```

It might be tempting to use hybrid picking for this example, but alternate picking provides consistency of tone, plus it makes for a great exercise.

To me these erratic licks have a quality almost like a synthesizer's arpeggiator mode, where unconventional patterns are created that you wouldn't readily choose on guitar. I've deliberately avoided sticking to any one interval or sequential pattern for more than a few notes so as to make the most of the line's quirky and unpredictable appeal.

Example 4j

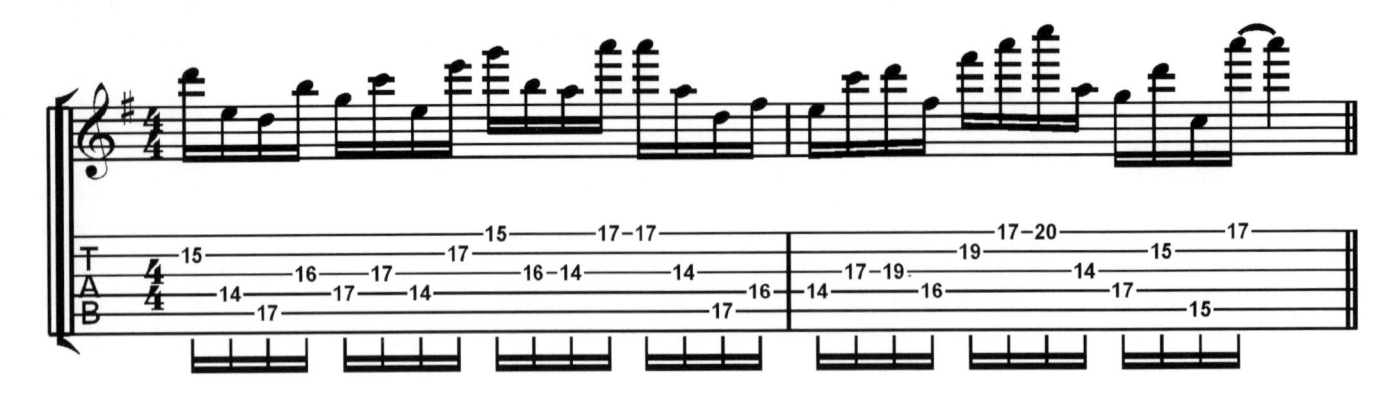

Odd Rhythmic Groupings

We have seen that longer runs are usually constructed from lots of connected cells that can be practiced individually. In the final portion of our chapter on alternate picking we're going to expand on that idea by using more creative groups of notes that break away from being rhythmically predictable.

The idea is to come up with cells that last an odd number of notes. When the pattern is cycled, a different note will be accented on the beat on each repetition. Rather than stringing several different fragments together, the constantly changing relationship between your lick and the underlying pulse is what maintains the interest, while retaining the consistency of each cell throughout.

When playing these ideas in a real musical situation, you must be aware of the main pulse of the music. As you become more adept at feeling different cross-rhythms, you'll more able to independently feel the underlying pulse, but begin by working out beforehand the beat of the bar your licks will end on. That way you'll immediately be able to fit back into normal time again reliably.

The first lick illustrates this idea by using a six-note pattern played in straight 1/16th notes. Here, focus on rhythm by accenting the start of each six with a louder pick to highlight the cross-rhythm. **Example 4k**

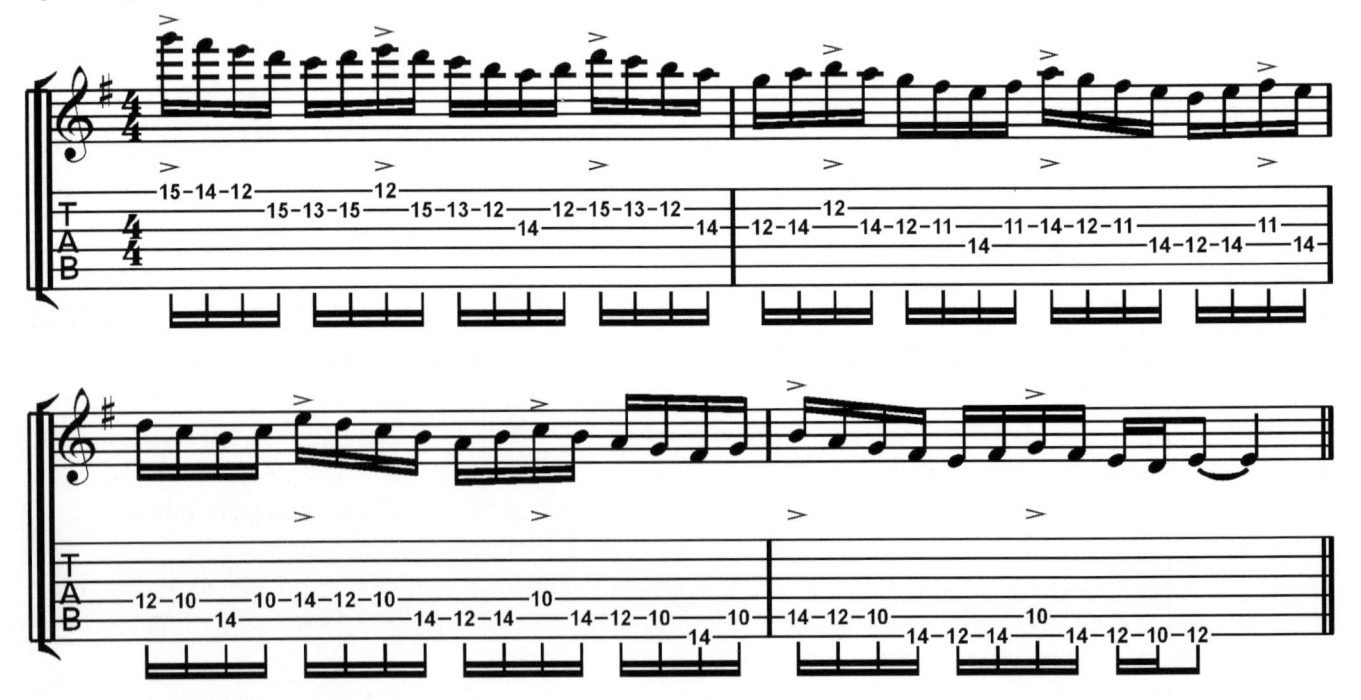

The following run uses less predictable groups of five. As you accent the start of each cell you'll notice that they fall on both down- and up-strokes. This is great practice for your picking control and teaches you that you don't need to play down-strokes on strong beat. This is beneficial when playing in odd time signatures.

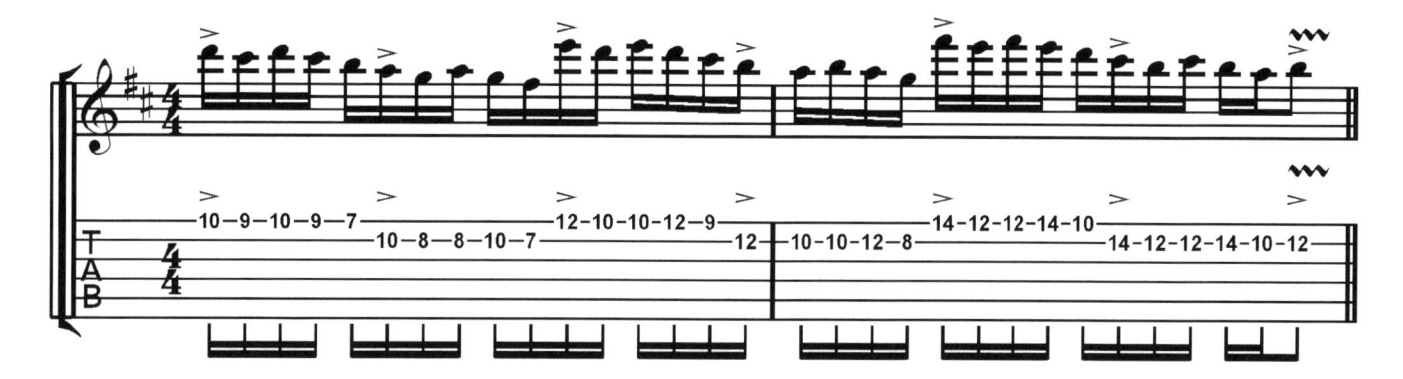

Example 4l

Example 4m uses a repeating fragment that lasts for eleven notes! This can be difficult to hear clearly, so work through the full line slowly. It can be helpful to play each fragment individually at first, and leave a short pause between them, before putting the whole line together using a metronome.

Example 4m

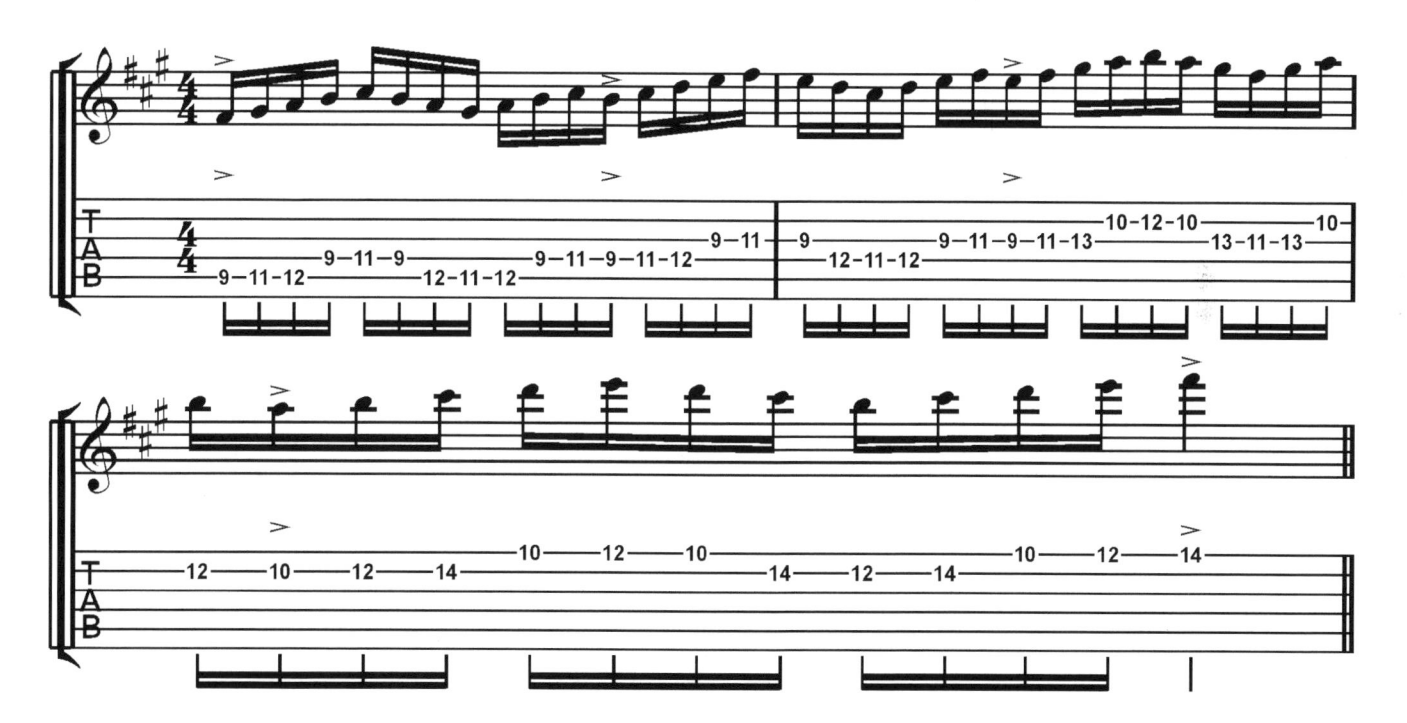

The last example in this chapter turns this concept on its head by superimposing a common phrase over an odd rhythmic grouping. This example has three layers of rhythm going on so hold onto your hats!

The main beat is subdivided into septuplets (seven notes per beat). Across these groups of seven, the melodic contour is divided into groups of four.

Physically this lick should hopefully be quite familiar as the sequence is a common one. To approach the rhythm, First, get comfortable with septuplets separately by ascending a scale or by picking seven notes on each string in turn.

Once the feel of the septuplets is confident, apply the four note sequence to them in small bursts. Start by playing just the first group of seven and landing on the following beat.

Seven notes per beat is quite fast so this type of lick is limited to songs with slower tempos. Later, in your own practice try applying similar ideas to other groupings such as triplets or quintuplets, which would work at faster tempos.

Example 4n

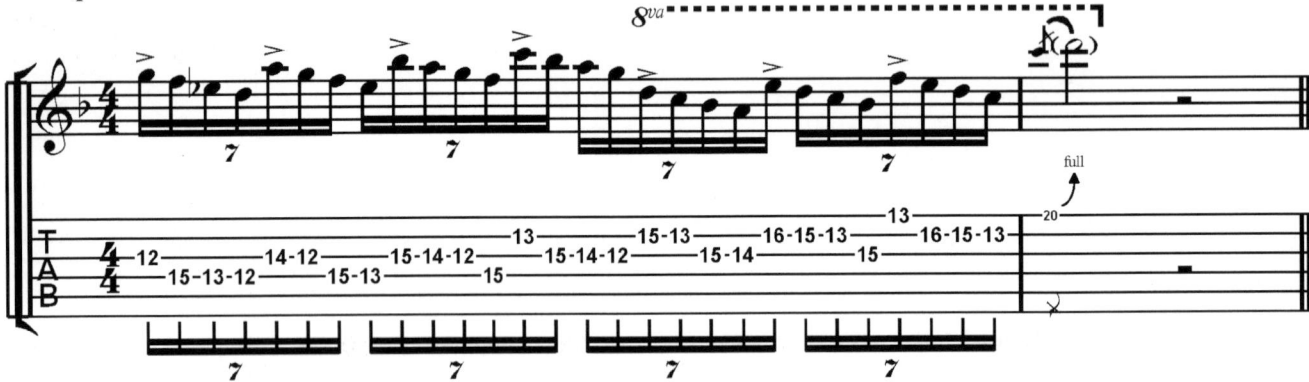

Recommended listening for examples of advanced alternate picking:

Dream Theater – *The Glass Prison*
Avenged Sevenfold – *Bat Country*
Cynic – *I'm But a Wave To…*
Disperse – *Profane the Ground*
The Contortionist - *Thrive*
Haken – *1985*

Chapter 5: Economy/Sweep Picking

I've left sweep picking until last because it requires a good sense of timing in the fretting hand, perfect synchronisation, and a grounding in alternate picking. Having discussed each of these elements in the previous chapters, you should now be well equipped to tackle some advanced licks.

Like tapping, sweep picking enables us to play much wider intervallic- and arpeggio-based lines at high speed. Whereas tapping achieves this by spacing intervals along the length of a string, sweep picking is used when we arrange notes roughly one-note-per-string, and then push the pick across the strings in a slow, controlled strum.

In Heavy Metal Lead Guitar, I presented major and minor triads and their different inversions across three strings. We then combined them in different ways to create sequences that outline chord progressions, before expanding to cover two octave arpeggios over five strings. Everything in this chapter will build on those fundamentals of shred vocabulary.

Sometimes the continual up-and-down contour of repeating five-string shapes can be a little too rhythmically predictable, so the following developments will provide variations to experiment with. Also, as shown here, they show how a more substantial lick can be created from a single arpeggio.

It's always important to pay attention to the quality of the final note or phrase, as a confident finish often provides musicality and credibility to some preceding shredding!

Example 5a

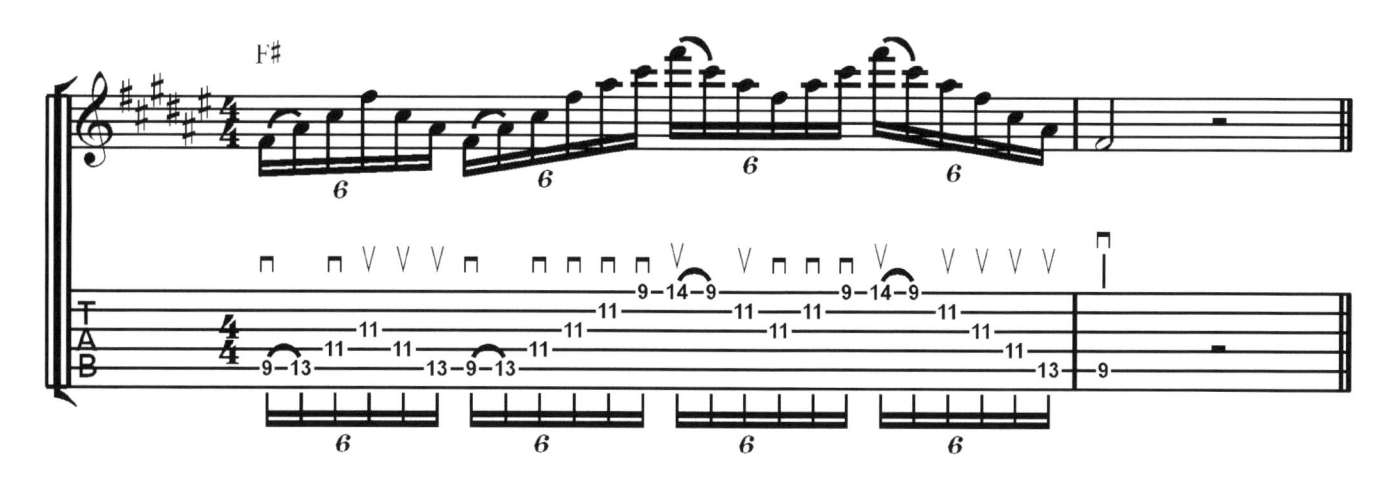

Taking example 5a further, we combine techniques by integrating a tapped note to extend the arpeggio. In the tapping chapter I suggested using the second finger to tap precisely because of licks like these. Keeping the pick ready makes the transition between the two techniques fluid and uncomplicated.

There are several different elements to contend with in this lick, so be sure to isolate each arpeggio shape, the position-shift, and tapped/legato section before trying to run through the whole idea. The rhythmic notation of beat three provides only a rough guide, but so long as the notes are even and you manage to land safely on beat two of the second bar, you'll achieve the desired effect.

As always, the creative benefit will come from inventing your own variations using the different shapes and ideas introduced here.

Example 5b

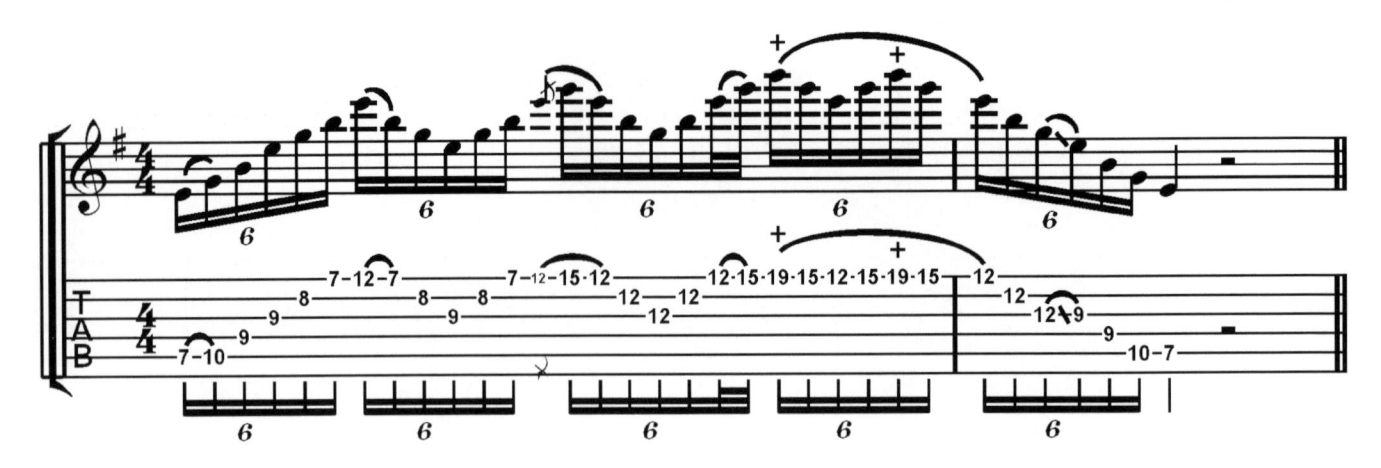

Six-string shapes are less common, but worth investigating if you wish to develop your arpeggio vocabulary.

The goal is to maximize the distance travelled in a single arpeggio. Starting in the fifth position, we move up through several positions using legato and slides. It takes control to break up the sweep pick with legato (rather than just ploughing straight through all the strings), so take your time to really internalise where the hammer-ons occur so the hands remain synchronised.

Example 5c

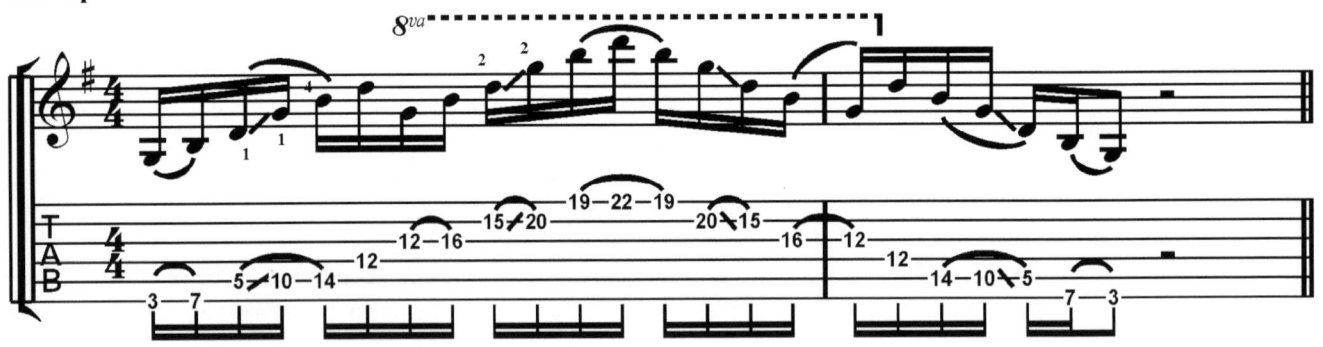

Here's a neat little way to play Diminished arpeggios across all strings. The notes are laid out in such a way that they can be picked while still sweeping from string to string. The quintuplets may feel a little unnatural to start with, but aim to begin each shape on the beat and the notes in between will, with practice, even themselves out.

To help fit this idea into your playing, try starting from different strings, and use just one or two shapes rather than the whole ascending or descending run.

Example 5d

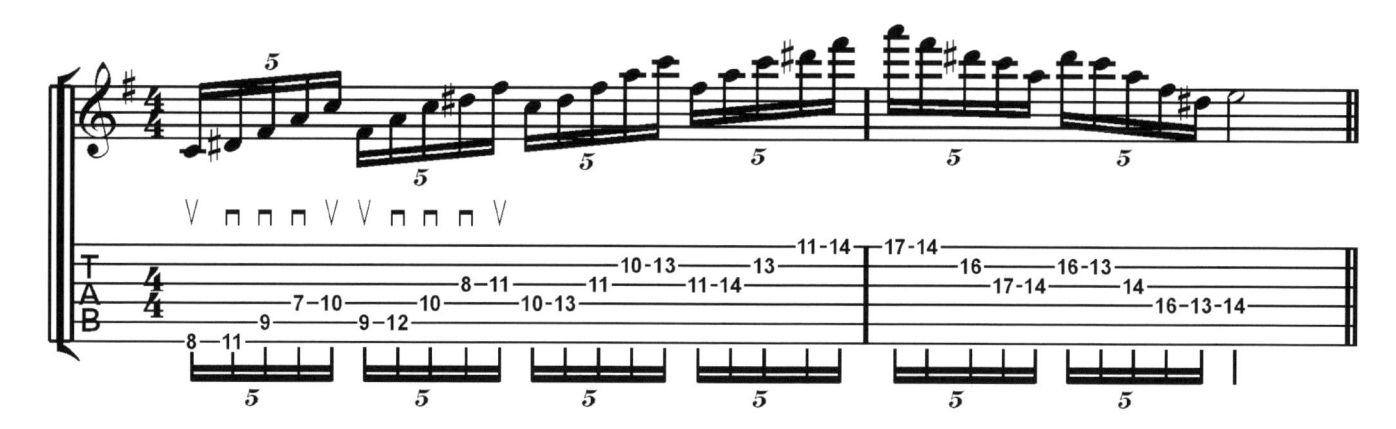

The same picking pattern gets recycled here, and is applied to the notes of the B Minor Pentatonic scale. Experiment with different triad or diatonic 7th shapes across the strings for more licks, and to get more mileage from your sweeping skills.

Example 5e

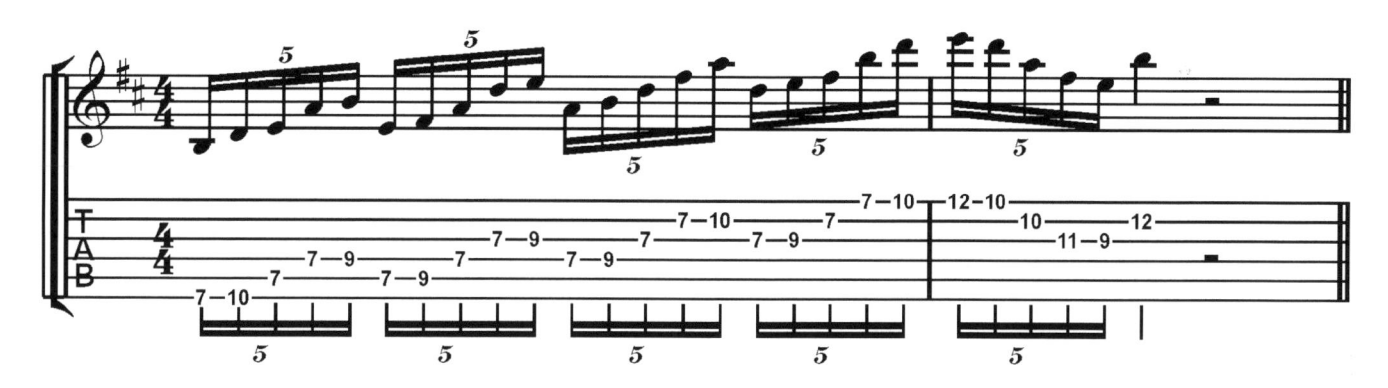

Frank Gambale, although a jazz-rock fusion guitarist, has had a discernible impact on metal lead guitar playing thanks to his frighteningly clean, fast economy picking technique. Economy picking takes sweep picking further by combining it with alternate picking to create a fluid combination of scalic and intervallic movement. The basic rule is to sweep from string to string wherever possible and then continue normal alternate picking while playing on the same string.

Example 5f

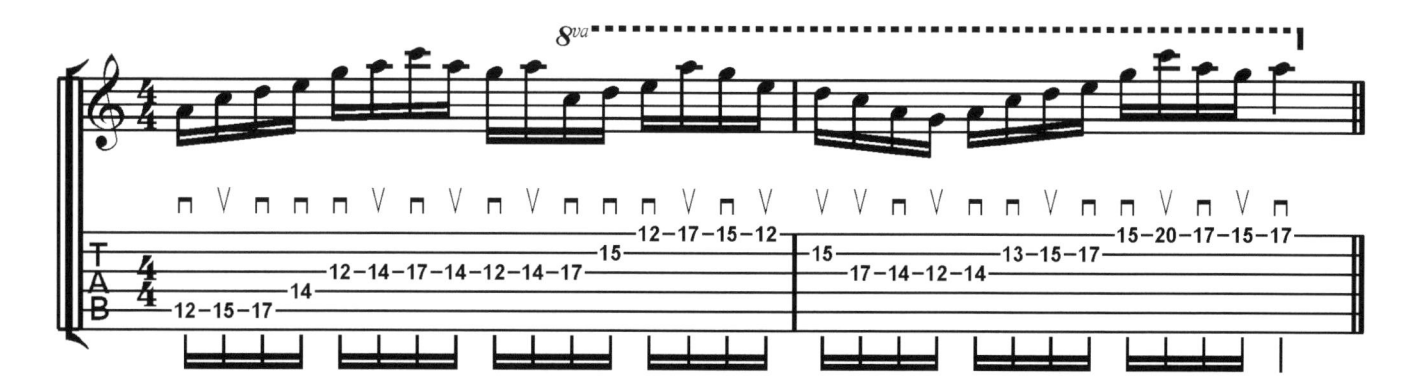

This example shreds its way up through the G Minor Pentatonic scale with a smoothness and rapidity that the standard two note-per-string approach could never match. Follow the picking directions carefully to start with and sweeping to each string should soon become second nature.

Another economy-picked idea here, though this time we use more angular sounding 4ths and 5ths instead of triads. Melodic use of perfect intervals (4ths, 5ths and octave) is still relatively rare, so they are a great source of fresh sounding ideas that will stand out in a solo. Keep the thumb low to help the stretch at the start of the lick and be careful of the barre roll on the 4ths at the end.

Example 5g

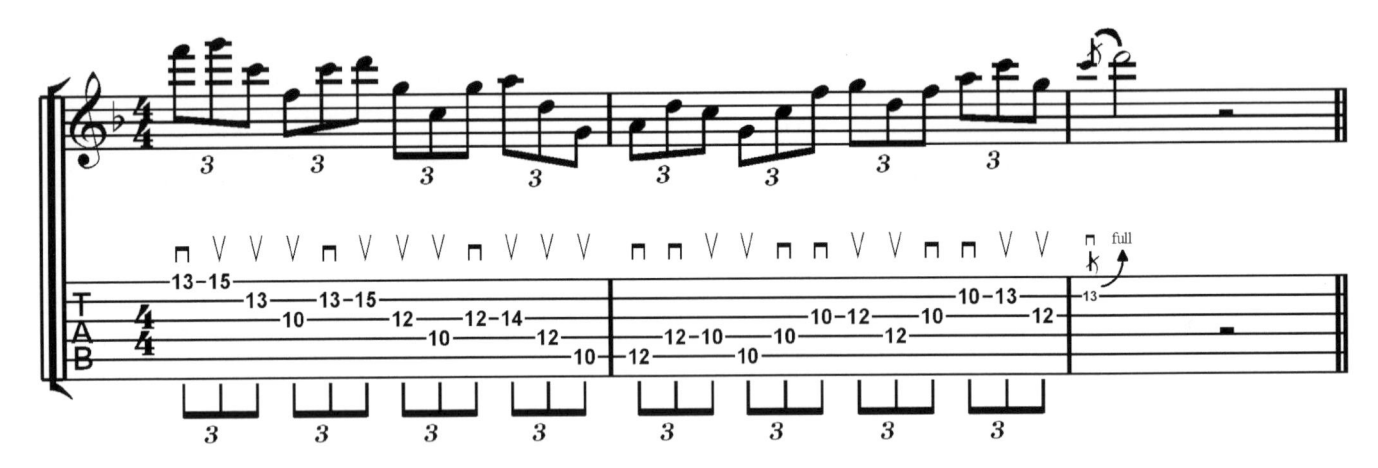

Our final lick is inspired by Cacophony/Megadeth guitarist Marty Friedman and his influence on modern players.

Marty's advanced arpeggio ideas stood out from the crowd in the late '80s and early '90s as being melodic and creative. Here I combine different diatonic triads to create a flowing and harmonically rich line. Try to identify the individual triads I've used and come up with your own licks by applying variations in contour and arpeggios.

Example 5h

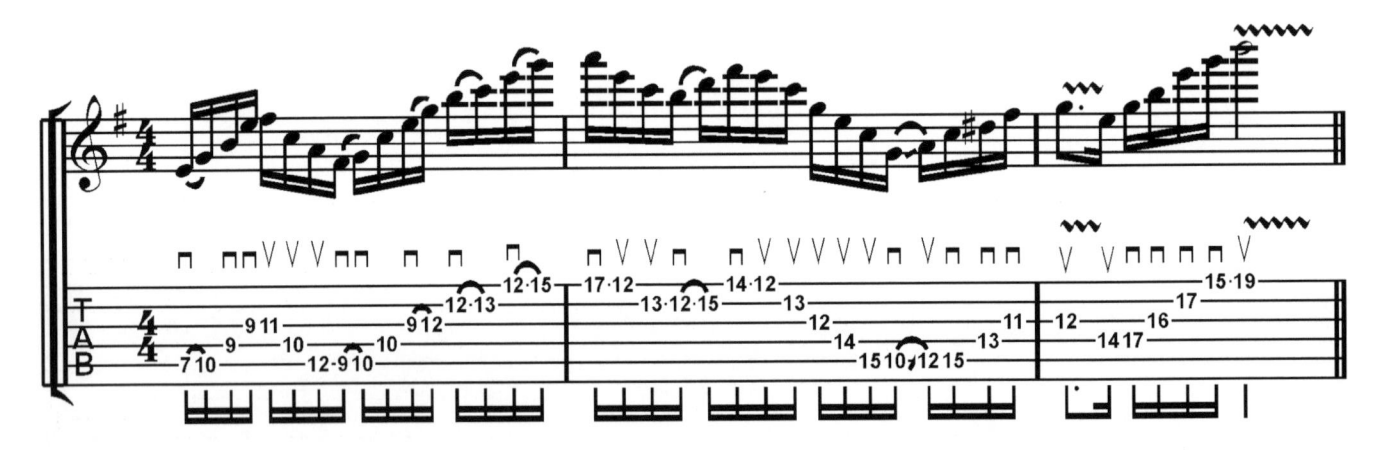

Recommended listening for sweep picking:

Yngwie Malmsteen – *Rising Force*
Megadeth - *Lucretia*
Steve Vai – *For the Love of God*
Slipknot – *Pulse of the Maggots*

Chapter 6: Recasting Pentatonic & Blues scales

I have already emphasised the importance of melody and understanding The Blues influence to the expressiveness of your playing, but in this chapter we'll look at less traditional ways to incorporate the Pentatonic and Blues scales into your music using various modern rock techniques.

Over the previous four chapters we focussed on developing each of the main techniques involved in playing Heavy Metal lead guitar. Now you got a feel for the vocabulary of each technique, we'll use them to create some interesting new licks.

The Pentatonic/blues sound is often heard in conjunction with rather predictable rock phrasing, but when that note choice is heard in a new context (such as a legato or sweep picked run) the results are fresh and exciting. It can be hard to avoid the neoclassical sound when playing with shred-influenced techniques, and this can sometimes create negative associations. Using The Blues scale is a great way to create excitement while using a familiar musical sound.

Much of this chapter deals with rearranging the Pentatonic scale on the fretboard using three or more notes per string, and sliding along strings rather than sticking to the standard 'box' shape of traditional playing. Spreading out Pentatonic scales in this way involves some serious stretches for the fretting hand, so be sure to warm up with some diatonic three-note-per-string playing beforehand, and take a break if any tension develops.

Dream Theater's John Petrucci uses chromatic passing tones in scale-based lines and acknowledges the influence of Steve Morse (Dixie Dregs, Deep Purple) on his playing. The trick to making this technique work is to start and end on strong chord tones. This is best done by approaching them chromatically and trying to place them on the beat.

Our first blues-influenced shred lick uses economy/sweep picking to play a Pentatonic fragment. The high note moves between the 4, b5 and 5 of the E minor blues scale to provide the melodic movement. The lick is rhythmically grouped into sextuplets, although the pattern repeats every four notes, so take time to internalise the resultant cross rhythm before attempting to speed it up.

The picking motion should be relaxed and use very little movement to achieve the speed.

Example 6a

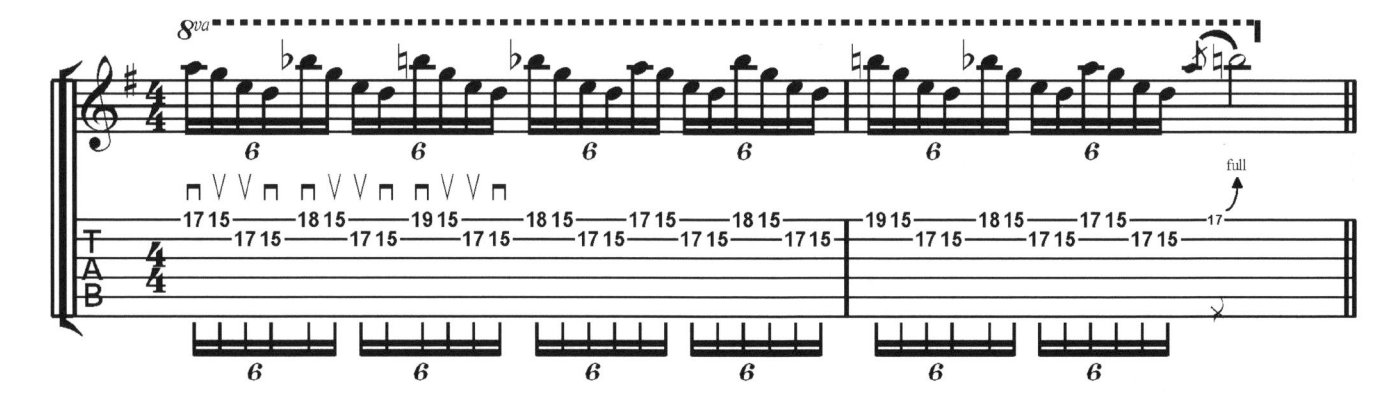

This Paul Gilbert-inspired idea uses a more conventional combination of picking and legato, but the chromatic notes added to the Pentatonic pattern allow for some frightening speed. Mixing the percussive accents of picking into the fluidity of a legato phrase creates a dynamic feel.

Example 6b

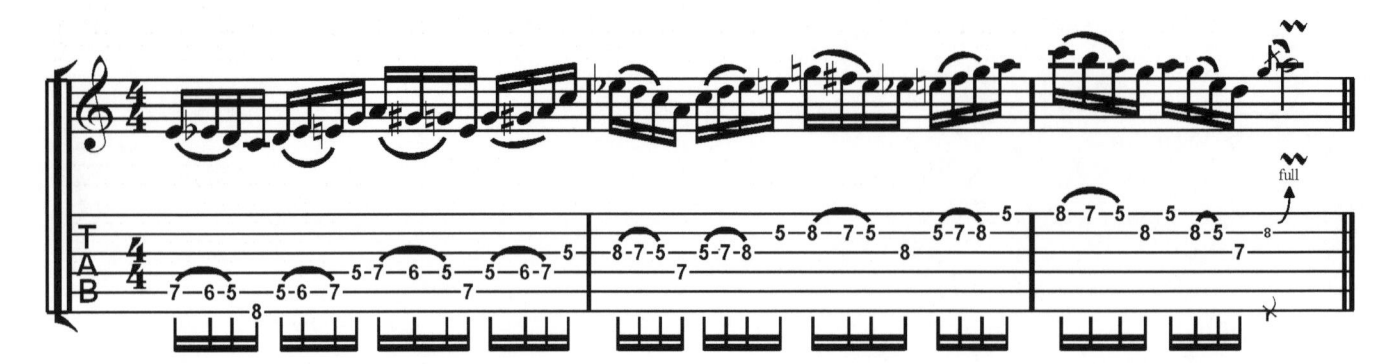

Now for a descending lick that uses the same hybrid scale shape as ex. 6b. The rhythmic combination of 1/16th-note and 1/16th-note triplets is the natural result of the picking pattern and the legato, so you should find that the rhythm sorts itself out.

The top three strings put demands on the ring and pinkie fingers together, so you may find that it takes time to build the strength to sustain these licks. However, once you can manage it, using fragments as repeating licks is an effective tool for building excitement and energy.

Example 6c

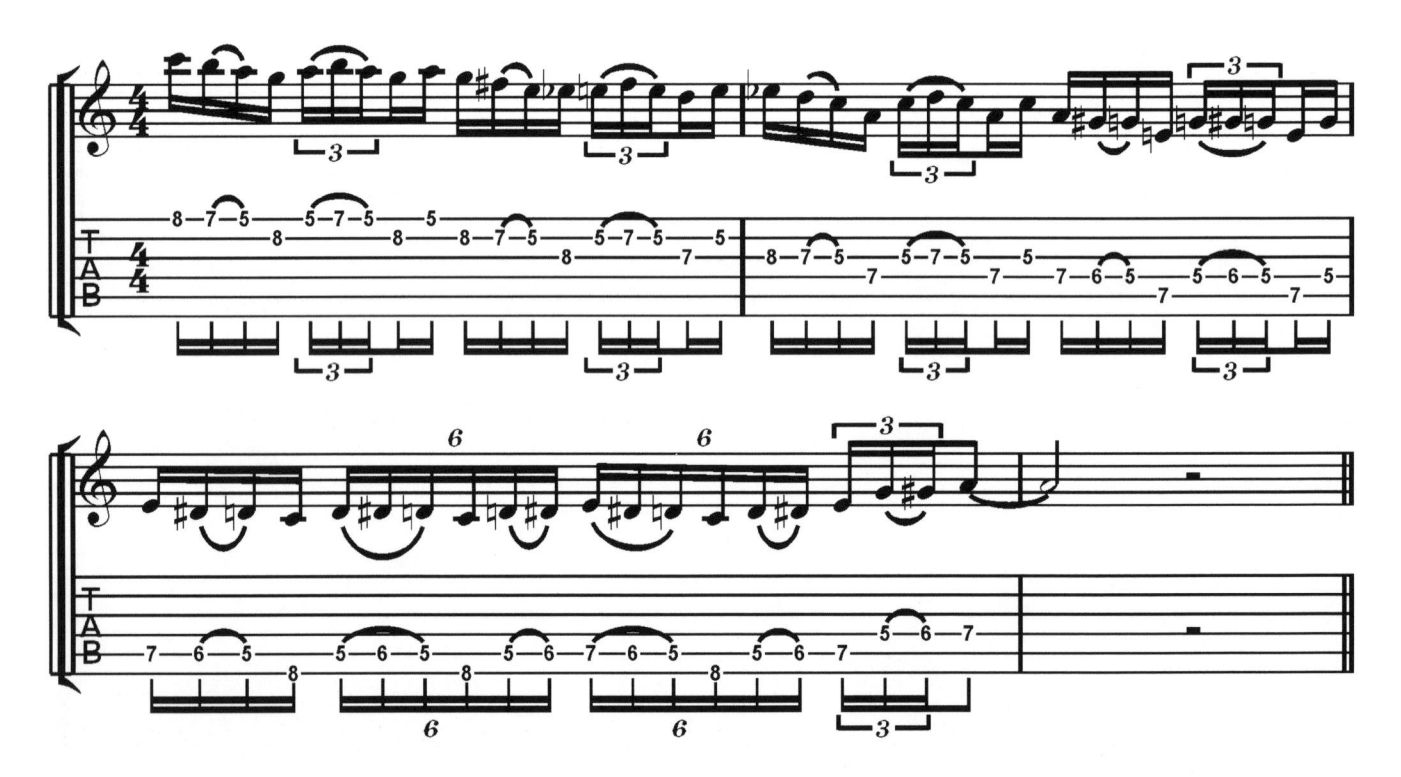

Applying bluesy note choices to shapes or patterns from the neoclassical or shred vocabulary is a great way to generate fresh licks, and that is exactly what I've done here. The sextuplet pattern we've used for several diatonic scale licks already has been stretched out to accommodate The Blues scale notes as well. Be aware of the wide stretches, and to make things easier, keep the thumb low on the back of the neck.

Example 6d

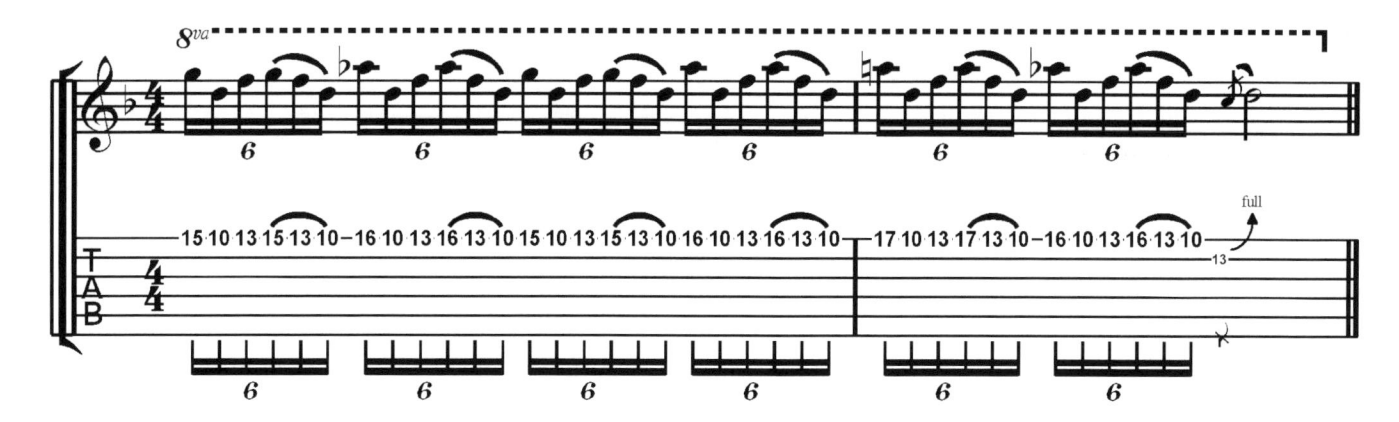

This three-note-per-string Pentatonic lick covers a lot of ground very quickly. Keeping the position shifts under control can be a challenge at first, but imagine trying to play the lick with the same speed and fluidity using two notes-per-string box shapes; the benefit of the alternative fingering is obvious.

Example 6e

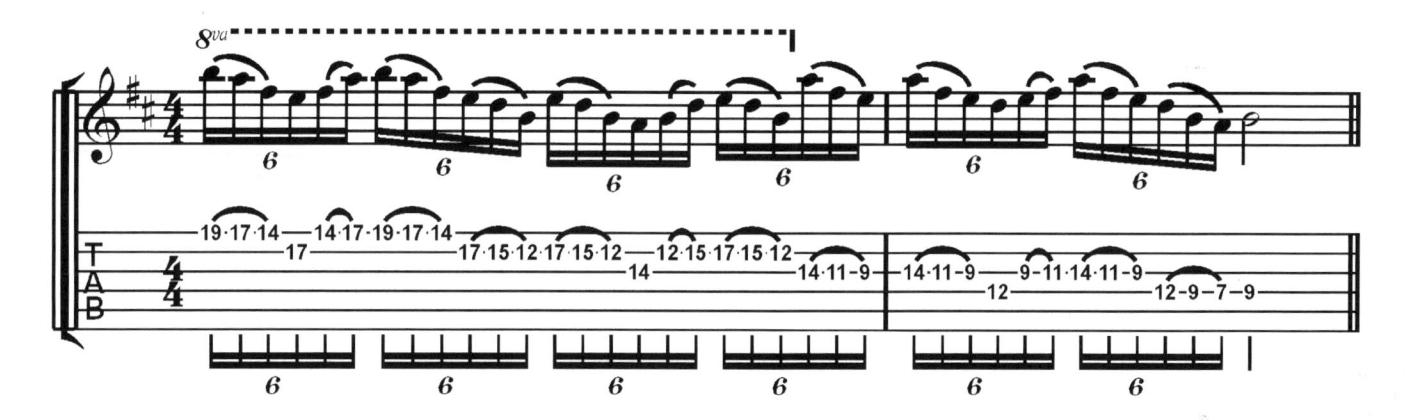

This is certainly not your typical E Minor Pentatonic lick, and isn't for the faint hearted! It comes with a health warning: The stretches involved can be very demanding, so remember to warm up well.

These 3 note-per-string Pentatonic fingerings cover two positions of Pentatonic shapes. Learning to visualise these new licks in terms of the shapes you're already familiar will help you integrate them in a natural and convincing way. To illustrate this, it finishes with a more typical blues phrase.

Example 6f

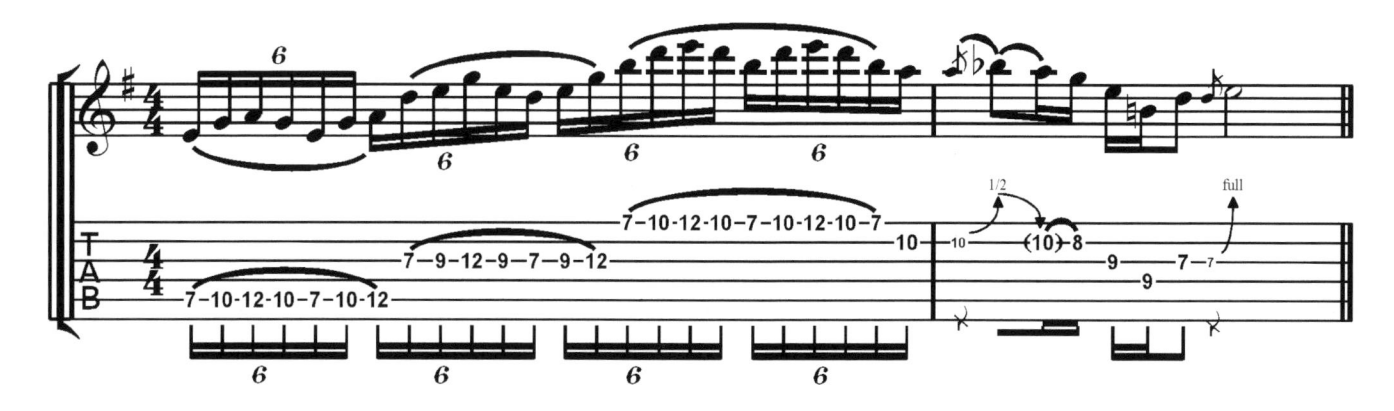

You will notice that the previous shape is not actually a complete Pentatonic scale. There is one note missing from each octave. In the context of these legato runs the wider intervals actually enhance the appeal of these licks. Naming the resultant pool of notes is not really a concern; the sound is a pleasing middle ground between Pentatonic, and minor 7 arpeggio sounds.

Despite the irregularities of the scale shape, we can still apply common sequences like this 'fours' pattern. Being confident with this pattern in a diatonic scale (such as example 3e) before attempting this stretched-out version, will make things much easier as the fingering is transferable.

Example 6g

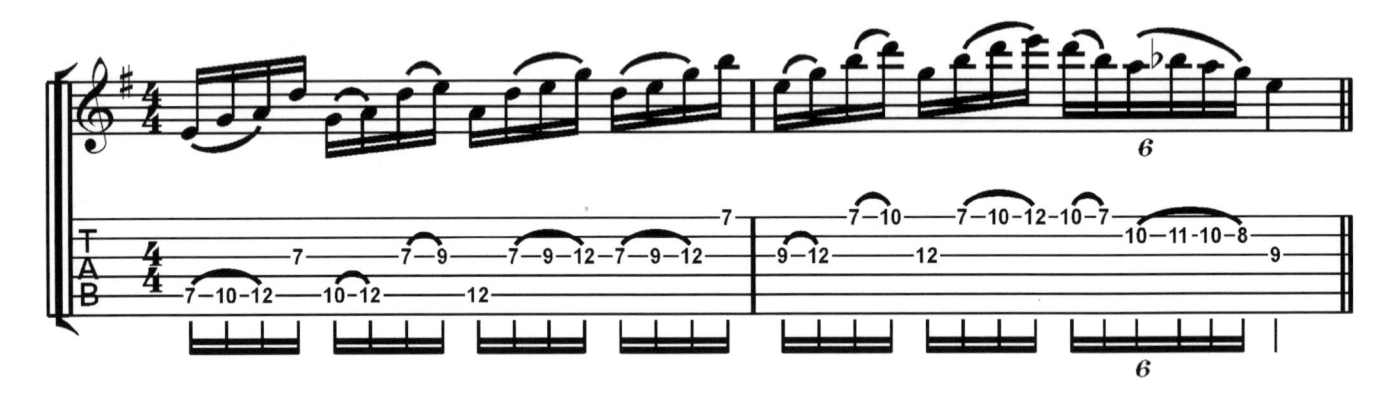

A good way to practice using this scale shape is by running between different notes, rather than rolling across all the notes on each string. This will help you to develop it from a pre-conceived lick into malleable vocabulary. In this line I've played a varied melodic contour within the shape to make the line less predictable.

Example 6h

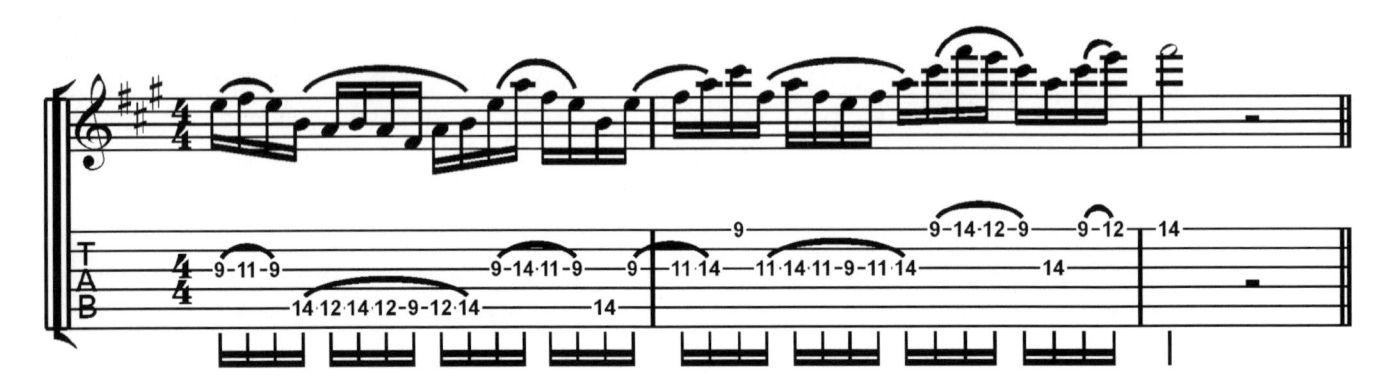

If the idea of incomplete scales offends you, then try this expanded version for size! Using a tapped note to extend along alternate completes the Pentatonic scale; this opens up potential for seamlessly legato playing.

Changing to higher strings involves using a fretting hand tap with the index finger, which you may find weak to start with. This comes as a surprise to some students, so to begin with, aim to hammer down from a distance to generate enough power.

The best way to tackle the rhythm of this lick is to practice it slowly and place emphasis on the notes that land on the beats. Once you can play it cleanly and smoothly, start trying to cram the seven notes between each beat. Your ear will guide you and the notes will space themselves out naturally.

Example 6i

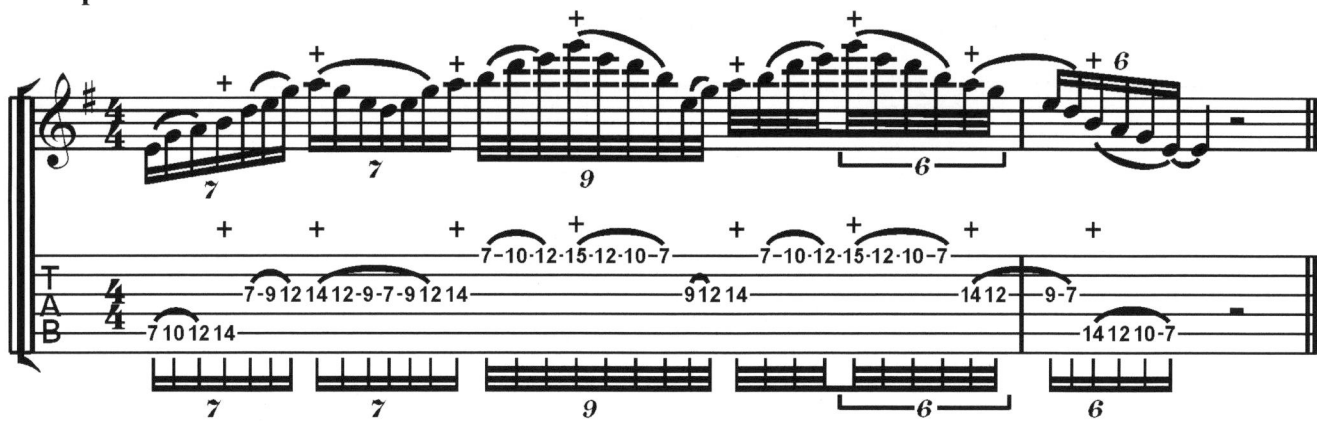

Next we add some chromatic passing tones to enhance the Pentatonic scale. This lick could, at a push, be played just with conventional legato, but bringing an extra finger into play makes the fretting hand's job much easier. Playing 'outside' the key is a topic worthy of its own book, but put simply, you can play any outside note as long as it is followed up with a rhythmically strong 'inside' phrase.

Example 6j

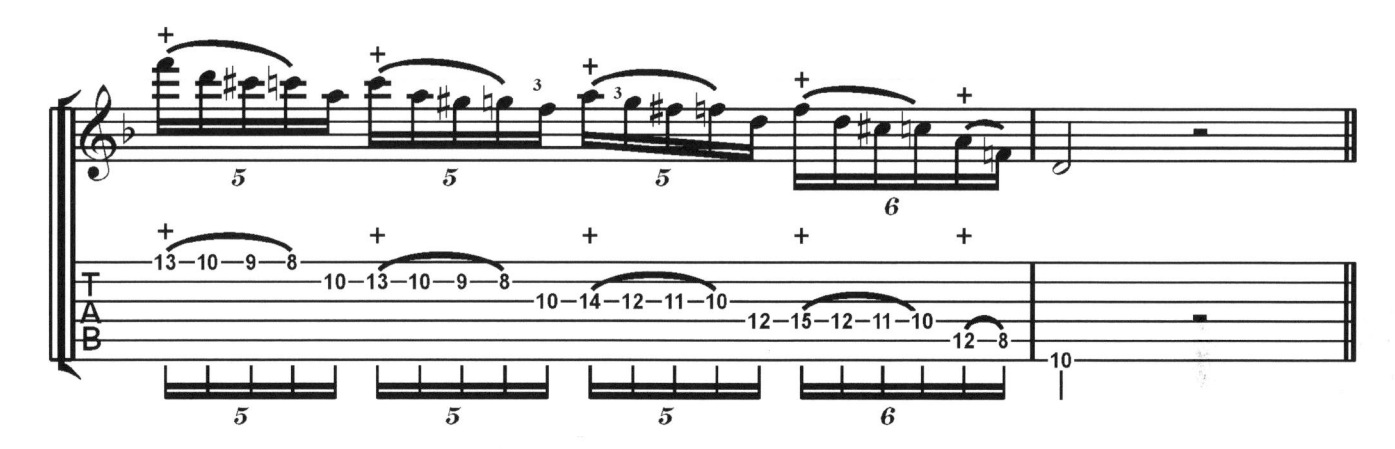

You may need to isolate different sections of the lick and practice transitioning between each string before linking the whole thing up. To hear masterful use of these phrases, listen to anything by Shawn Lane, Michael Romeo or Rusty Cooley, who all have great legato skills using these stretched out shapes.

Keep in mind the different position of the Minor Pentatonic scale as you move up the neck, moving from the 'A shape' at the 12th fret to the 'E shape' at the 17th fret.

Example 6k

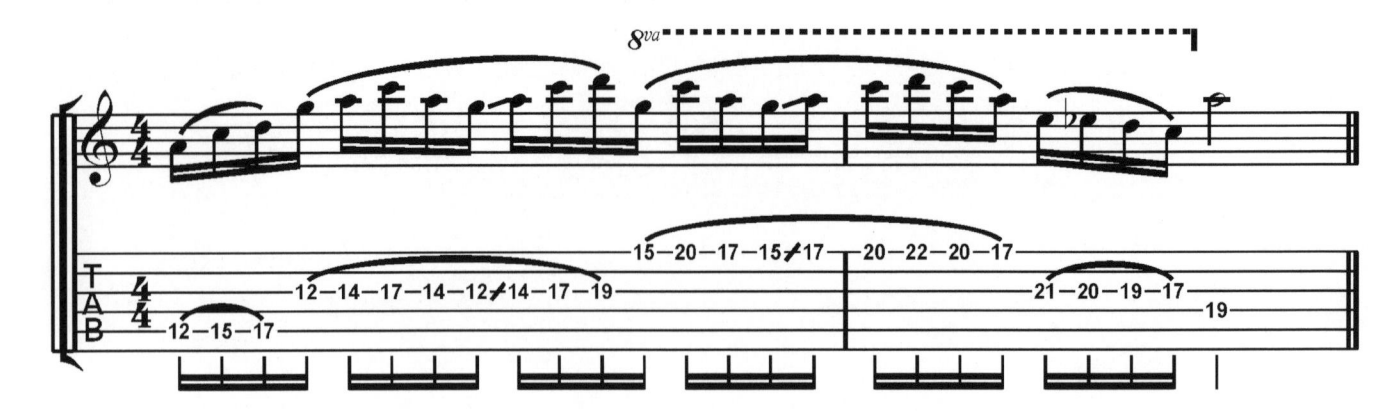

To push the envelope even further, we'll combine everything in this chapter: chromatic passing tones, Pentatonics, tapping and wide stretches. The first section of the lick may prove the hardest due to the stretching low down the neck. If you are really struggling with this, then you may want to use tapping to share the load. Good luck, and remember to get creative!

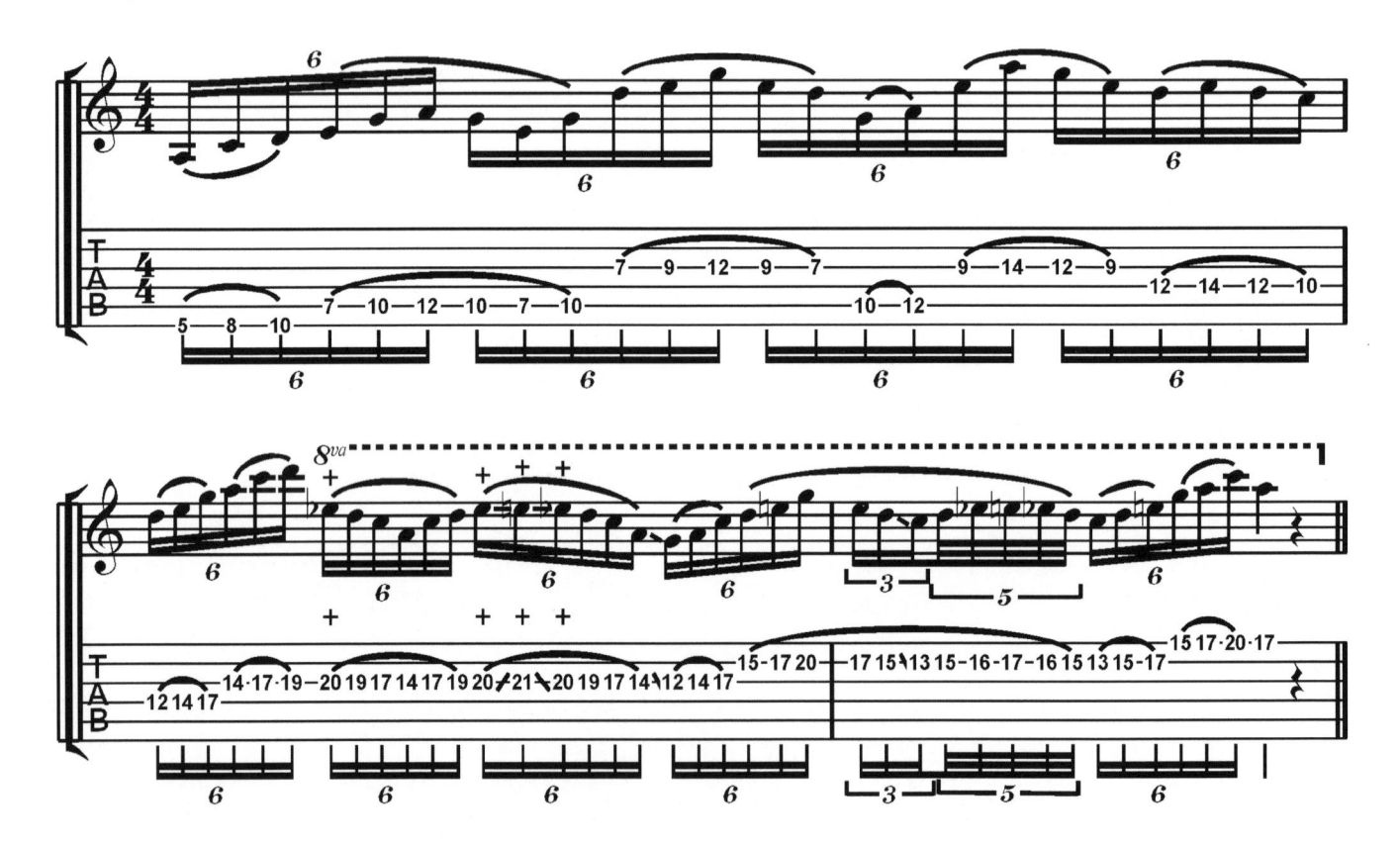

Example 6l

Recommended listening for shred Pentatonic and Blues scales:

Racer X/Paul Gilbert – *Technical Difficulties*
Mr Big – *Colorado Bulldog*
Shawn Lane – *Get You Back*
Pantera – *A New Level*
Rusty Cooley – *Hillbilly Militia*
The Aristocrats – *Ohhhh Noooo*

Chapter 7: Exotic Scales, Substitutions & Beyond

This chapter is devoted to exotic scales and harmonic tricks you can use to create new licks, including alternative Pentatonics, symmetrical scales, and unconventional phrasing ideas.

Harmonic Substitution

The substitution of scales is a massive subject that we couldn't do justice to here, but in essence it involves playing a scale or arpeggio over an alternative root note/chord to create a new flavour. In these examples we will limit ourselves to arpeggios and Pentatonics, and with a little theory, begin to understand why the resultant sound changes.

To give a simple example; if we play a major triad over its own root note, the tones would be 1st, 3rd and 5th steps of the Major scale. However, if the triad was played a tone high over the same root note, the three notes of the triad now are the 2nd, #4th and 6th (or 9, #11 and 13) steps above the root, creating a Lydian sound with just three notes.

This means that you could take your favourite sweeping and tapped arpeggio licks and achieve a new sound by playing them over of different harmonies.

We can use the same concept with Pentatonic scales. I'll show you how to derive alternative substitute Pentatonic scales and I've included a table below to act as a handy reference point for the most common substitutions.

At the risk of sounding like a maths teacher, I'll work through one example to illustrate the concept, and leave you to consider the others as much (or as little) as you care to...

Take the Aeolian mode starting on A:

A	B	C	D	E	F	G
R	2	b3	4	5	b6	b7

As well as the Minor Pentatonic scale starting on the root, A, there are two other Pentatonic scales lurking within A Aeolian:

A Minor Pentatonic:

A	B	**C**	**D**	**E**	F	**G**
R	2	**b3**	**4**	**5**	b6	**b7**

D Minor Pentatonic:

D	E	**F**	**G**	**A**	B	**C**
4	5	**b6**	**b7**	**R**	2	**b3**

E Minor Pentatonic:

E	F	**G**	**A**	**B**	C	**D**
5	b6	**b7**	**R**	**2**	b3	**4**

From at the table above you can read off which scale tones the alternative Pentatonic scales provide. Note that the scale formulas all still refer to A as the root.

For example, in the context of A minor, D Minor Pentatonic translates as the intervals 1, b3, 4, b6 and b7 while E Minor Pentatonic provides a 1, 2, 4, 5 and b7. We can then predict that playing D Minor Pentatonic over Am would give a slightly Aeolian flavour due to the b6, while E Minor Pentatonic would be more of a suspended 7th sound because of the 2, 4 and b7.

Thankfully this kind of thinking is not needed in reality, we simply need to remember the distance from the root note the scale needed to be transposed and what sound that will give us. The following table lists popular diatonic Pentatonic substitutions.

Table of Pentatonic Substitutions

Tonic chord	Substitute Minor Pentatonic	Resultant tonality
Major / major 7	1 tone up	Ionian
	Major 3rd up	Major 7 arpeggio
	1/2 tone down	Lydian
Minor / minor 7	1 tone down	Phrygian
	1 tone up	Dorian
	Perfect 4th up	Aeolian
	Perfect 5th up	7sus2/4 arpeggio
Dominant 7	Tone up	Mixolydian
	Perfect 4th up	Dom9sus4 arpeggio
	Perfect 5th up	Mixolydian b6 (Melodic minor mode)

Experiment with each Pentatonic substitution, decide which ones you like the sound of and make a note of them.

Recording a static chord vamp and playing all twelve Minor Pentatonic scales over it with help you decide which substitutions appeal to your taste. Some will sound awful, but others may give you something satisfying that you wouldn't otherwise have thought of playing. After all, the only important judge is the ear.

In the first example, the melody is based around a C major arpeggio, but we hear the combined sound as a richer minor 7 tonality when it's played over Am minor chord,. The C Major arpeggio (C, G and G) becomes the b3, 5 and b7 of the Am chord. The second phrase develops this idea further by using an E minor triad (E, G and B), to target the 5, b7 and 9 of the underlying Am chord.

Example 7a

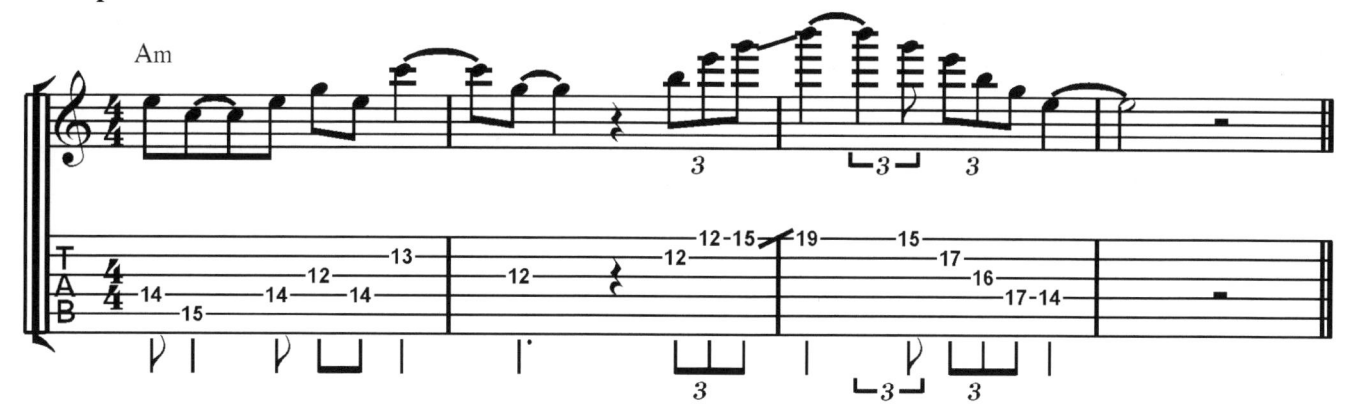

Listen to the audio for example 7a to hear how I vary the articulation to make this simple melodic phrase more expressive. There are some extra slides into notes, and also a pickup change at the end of bar two.

Superimposing arpeggios in ascending 3rds above the root results in extended tonic chords (7th, 9th, 11th, 13th) but moving up or down in 2nds or 4ths result in a more complex sound. In this next phrase we superimpose a minor arpeggio one tone below the tonic minor chord. This creates a Phrygian sound by highlighting the b2.

This kind of restless tension eventually requires resolution, so notice after the C minor arpeggio how we step back 'inside' to the tonic Dm arpeggio.

Example 7b

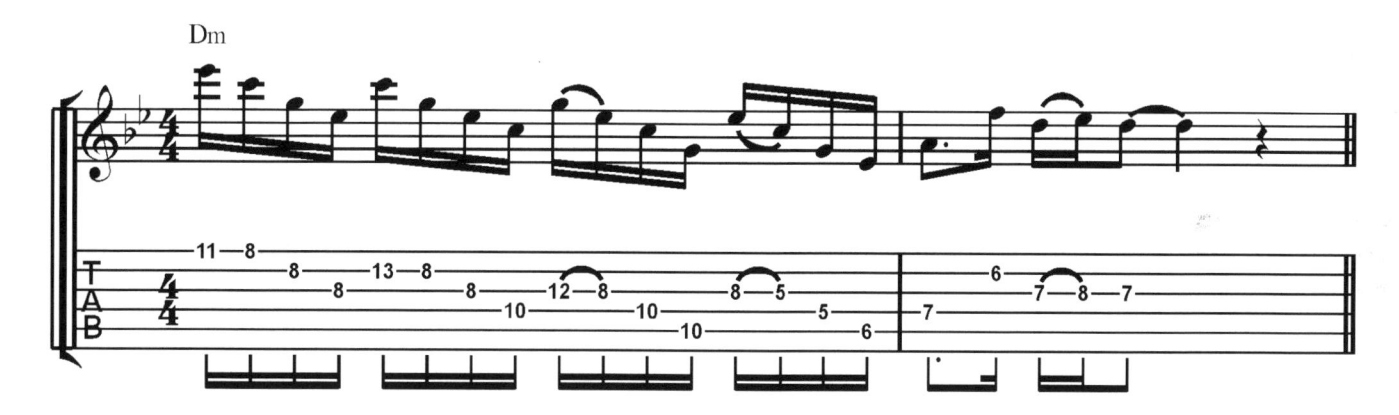

The Minor Pentatonic scale phrasing's inherent bluesiness is paired with the enchanting sound of the Lydian mode thanks to its being superimposed over a maj7 chord. Playing the Minor Pentatonic a half step below the chord provides us with the #4th and major7th steps, the two notes needed to evoke Lydian.

Steve Vai is a big fan of the Lydian mode and the slides within the Pentatonic scale here is characteristic of his style.

Example 7c

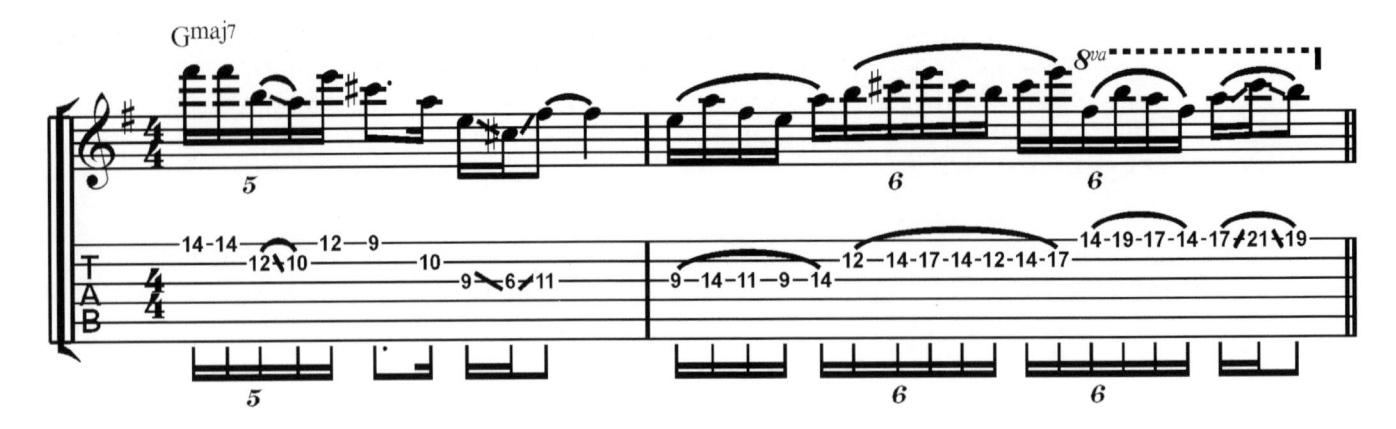

To clearly show the effect of superimposition, a short motif is transposed between the three Pentatonic scales within the Aeolian mode, those formed from the i, iv and v (Am, Dm and Em). Notice how the 'flavour' of the lick changes with each version. In the second phrase I've stayed in the same range but adjusting the notes to fit each scale rather than transposing.

This has the effect of morphing between Pentatonics in a smoother manner.

Example 7d

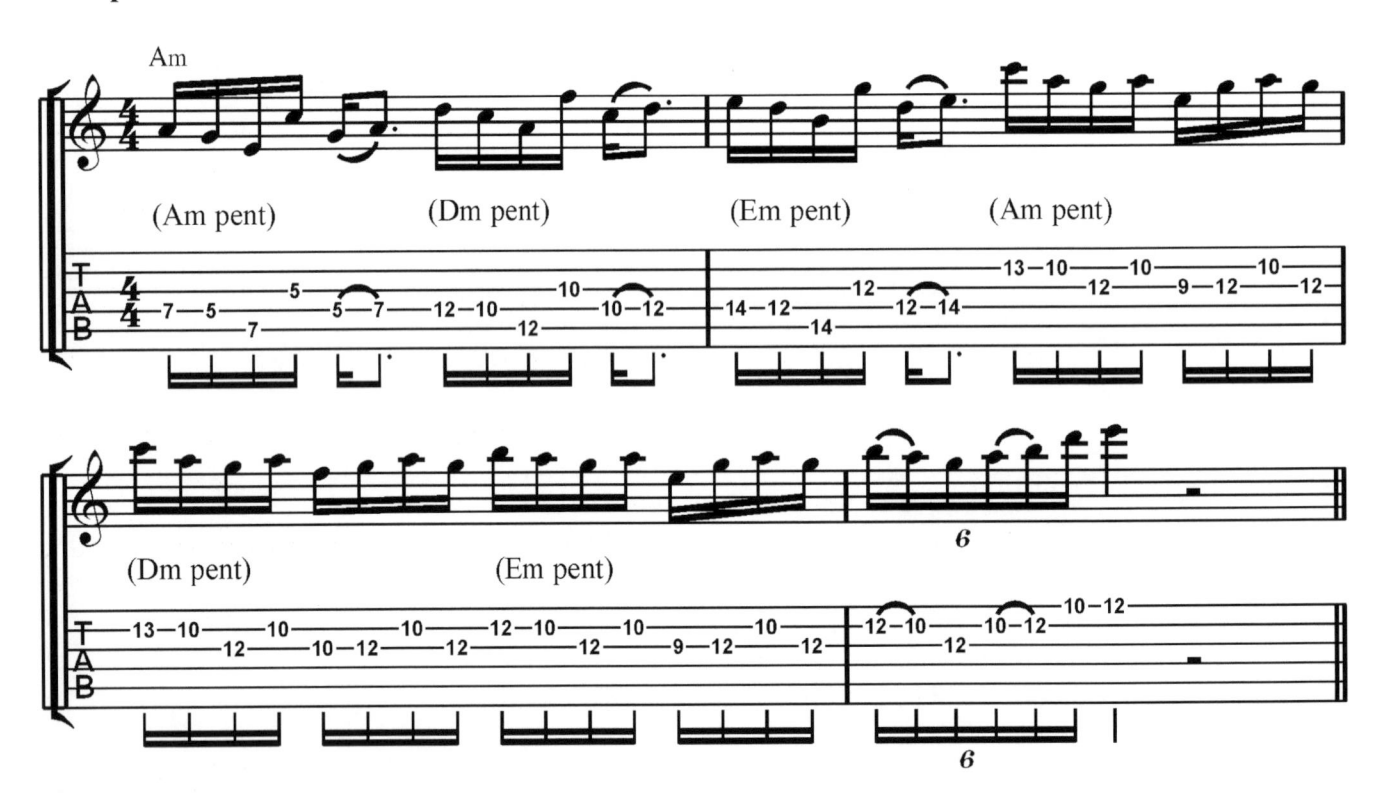

Exotic Scales

Although we tend to think of the Pentatonic scale as the 1 b3 4 5 b7 of The Blues, any group of five notes is a Pentatonic scale. Studies of Indian and Far-Eastern musical traditions reveal that just about any combination of pitches has already been explored by one musical culture or another. Several of these scales are used in the guitar styles of Marty Friedman, Jason Becker and Steve Vai.

We will look at a few named scales in the musical examples, but just as with everything else we've covered, I encourage you to perform your own musical experiments to discover more for yourself. Try taking a seven note scale and remove any two notes to create many different groups of five notes to explore

'Kumoi' Pentatonic scale

The collection of notes in example 7e is known in Japanese music as the Kumoi or Hirajoshi scale. The formula is 1 2 b3 5 b6. It can be more user-friendly to see it as a truncated version of the familiar D Natural Minor scale. Whatever way you choose to look at it, the wider intervals combined with the semitones brings out a distinctly oriental sound not present in the western Pentatonic scale.

Example 7e

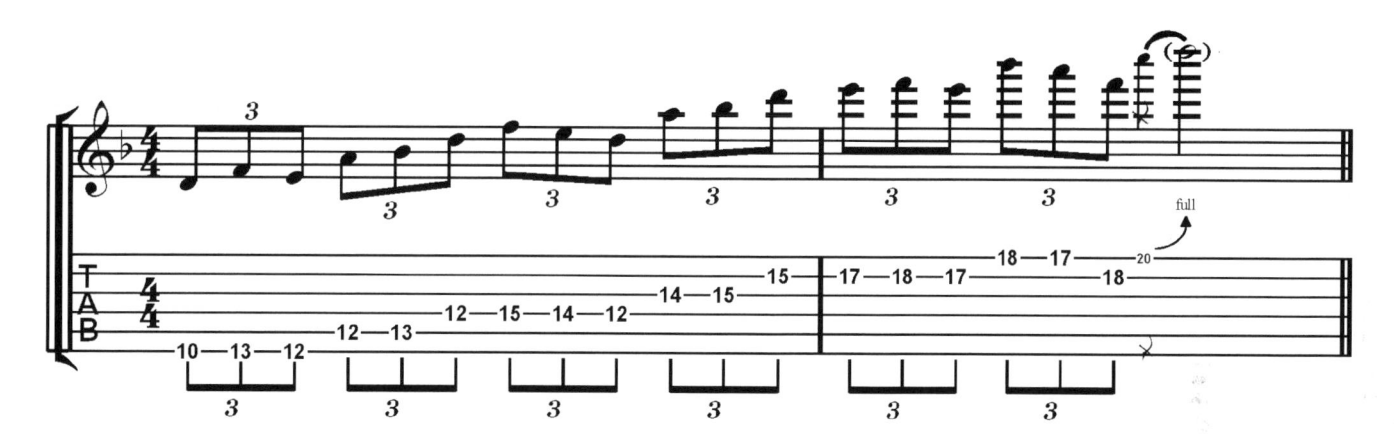

The semitones make fingering the D Kumoi scale with alternating groups of two and three notes per string the easiest option. However, as an interesting blend of the exotic with the familiar it's arranged into two-note-per-string groups below which allows you to apply your favourite Pentatonic patterns easily to the new scale. As a result, some of the shapes can, at first, be a little awkward to get your fingers around. Here we have a typical Zakk Wylde ascending Pentatonic run, albeit with the exotic flavour of the Kumoi scale.

Example 7f

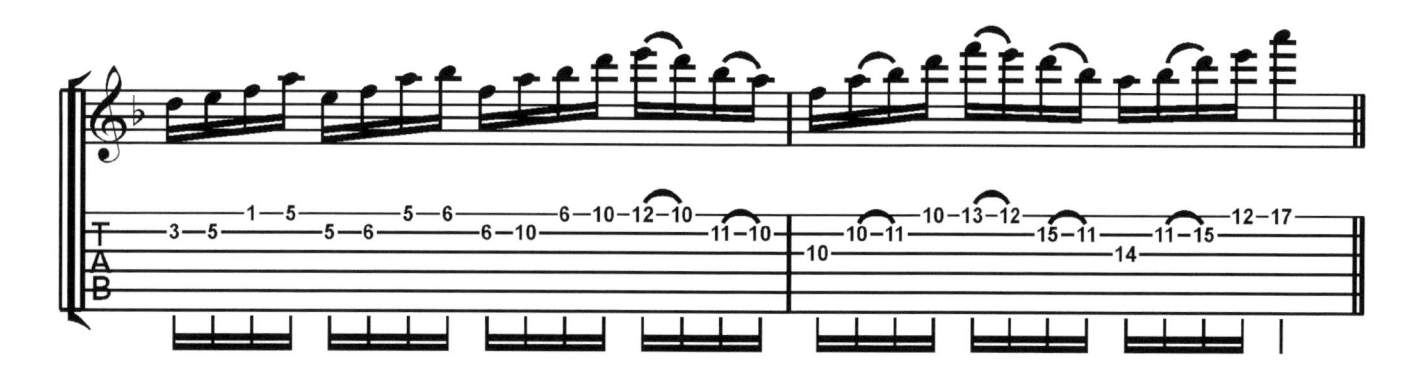

Next is another take on the same idea but this time moving across the strings in one position. You could alternate pick the whole lick for an abrasive sound, but the hammer-on between the first of each group of six notes varies the texture, as well as simplifying the picking.

Example 7g

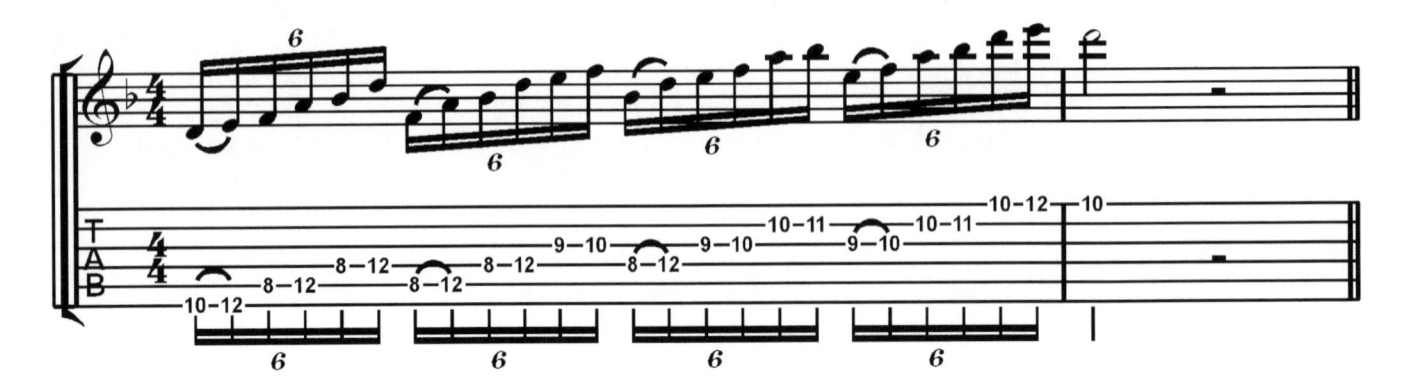

'Indian' Pentatonic scale

The formula of 1 3 4 5 b7 is a more interesting alternative to the Major Pentatonic scale for dominant 7th and major chords where a sense of tension is not required. Known as the 'Indian' Pentatonic, this is not commonly found in rock and pop playing, but provides an interesting alternative to the Major Pentatonic for those rare major chords in metal.

In this lick we start with a hooky melodic fragment then descend through a slippery legato and slide phrase based on an F#7 arpeggio with the addition of the 4th to complete the Pentatonic scale. The bends in bar one should just be a flick of the wrist to give the note a little bounce. These 'curl' bends can be heard in Marty Friedman's playing and are inspired by Japanese Koto music.

Example 7h

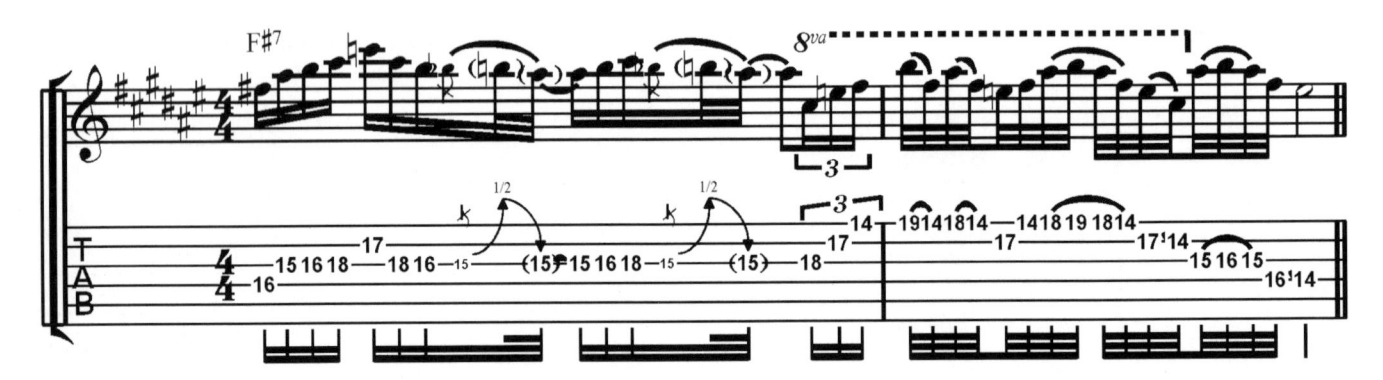

Symmetrical Scales

Finally, some scales are composed of repeating intervals. These are known as symmetrical scales because they contain the same intervals wherever you start in the pattern (unlike the Major scale for example which forms a different mode from each of its notes).

These scales have less "gravitational pull" towards a tonal centre, since in the scale any note could be considered the tonic. This gives them a 'floating' and unsettled quality. For this reason, you will often hear their distinctive tonalities used in film scores to represent unearthly or mysterious themes.

The French composer Olivier Messiaen catalogued many symmetrical scales which are known as his '*modes of limited transposition*', but we will only feature the most common ones in rock, the **Wholetone scale**, and the **Diminished** scale.

As the name suggests, the Wholetone scale is a sequence of six whole tones, and as such, can be seen as two Augmented triads a tone apart. This means that there are only two possible scales to learn (A B C# Eb F G, and Bb C D E F# G#), hence '*limited transposition*'.

Before we look at some licks, here's the Wholetone scale laid out on the fretboard. This fingering tries to remain at the fifth position across all the strings, but you can also arrange it with three notes per string.

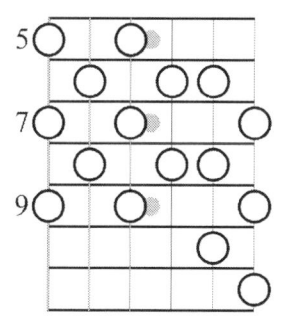

A Wholetone Scale

To show how less-conventional scales can easily be integrated into your existing musical vocabulary, the following Wholetone lick derives from a commonly-used metal lick with the fingering adapting to accommodate the appropriate scale tones. If you weren't already acquainted with this scale, you will recognise the sound immediately from dramatic film and video game music, as well as from the work of the more progressive modern metal players.

Example 7i

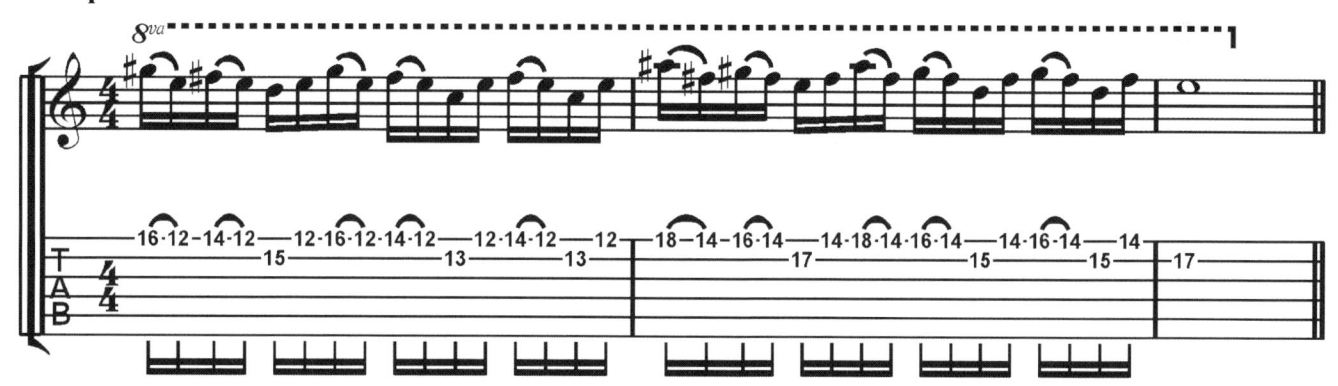

To remain within the Wholetone scale when using a three-note-per-string pattern, we have to keep moving up the fretboard. This continual position shifting adds a challenge to what would otherwise be a straight forward legato exercise.

Example 7j

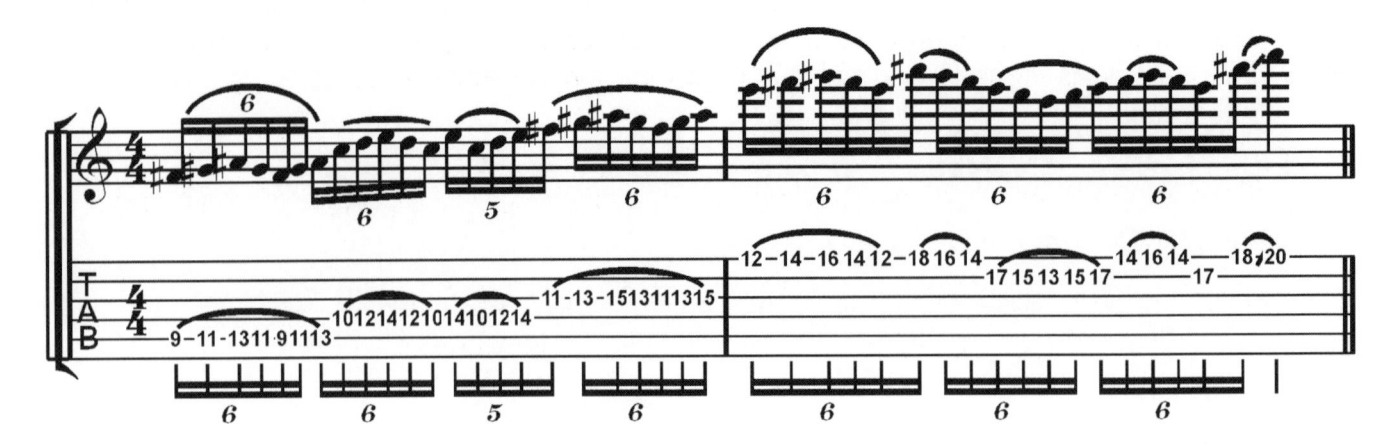

As I said in the introduction to this chapter, the Wholetone scale can be broken down into two Augmented triads (triads composed of stacked major 3rd intervals). A great way to get the Wholetone tonality while using a more 'open' intervallic sound is to alternate between these two triads. This approach offers unlimited variation, so you can adapt any arpeggio approach we've discussed to the Augmented triad, and get creative!

The diagram below shows the Wholetone scale shape with the two triads coloured in black and white. Play all the black notes followed by all the white notes to hear the way the two triads slot together.

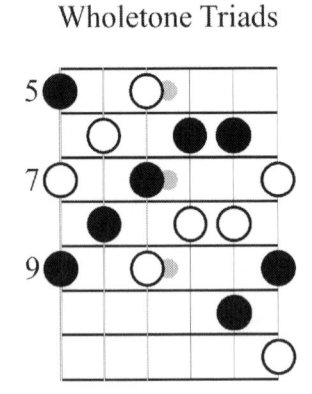

Wholetone Triads

The next phrase moves the same triad shape along the middle strings before developing onto the top strings on beat 2 of bar 2. Analyse the triads used here to help you see how the phrase is constructed.

Example 7k

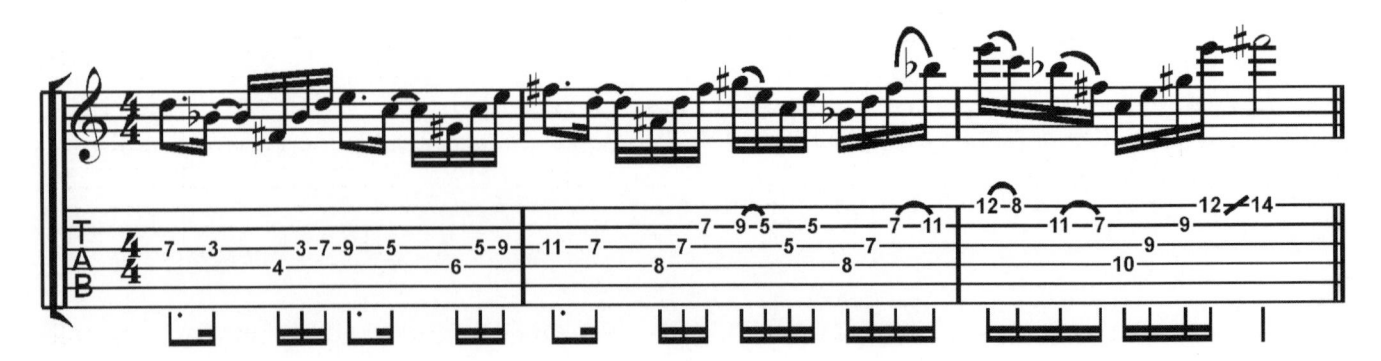

60

It's worth noting that due to their strongly recognisable flavour, the Wholetone and Diminished scales can be used over harmony where they may not be 'theoretically' correct. As long as the resolution to a more conventional scale is convincing, the audience can accept almost any temporary departure. This is especially true for metal, where the backing is often power chords or single note riffs.

The Diminished scale is a repeating pattern of semitones and tones. (It's sometimes called 'the Half-Whole scale'). It is symmetrical in minor 3rds, so there are only two different starting notes before the pattern repeats itself.

The Diminished scale also requires some position shifting for the fretting hand, and there are a number of different ways to finger it. I've suggested one option here that remains as static as possible you can assimilate it more easily into your existing knowledge of scale and chord shapes.

A Diminished Scale

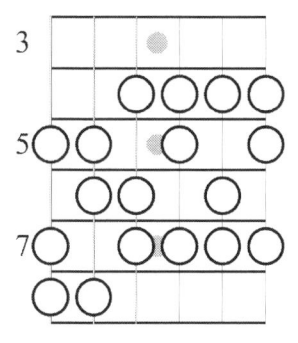

In the following idea, we ascend using a repeating two-string shape before finishing with a string skipping phrase between the G and E strings.

Example 71

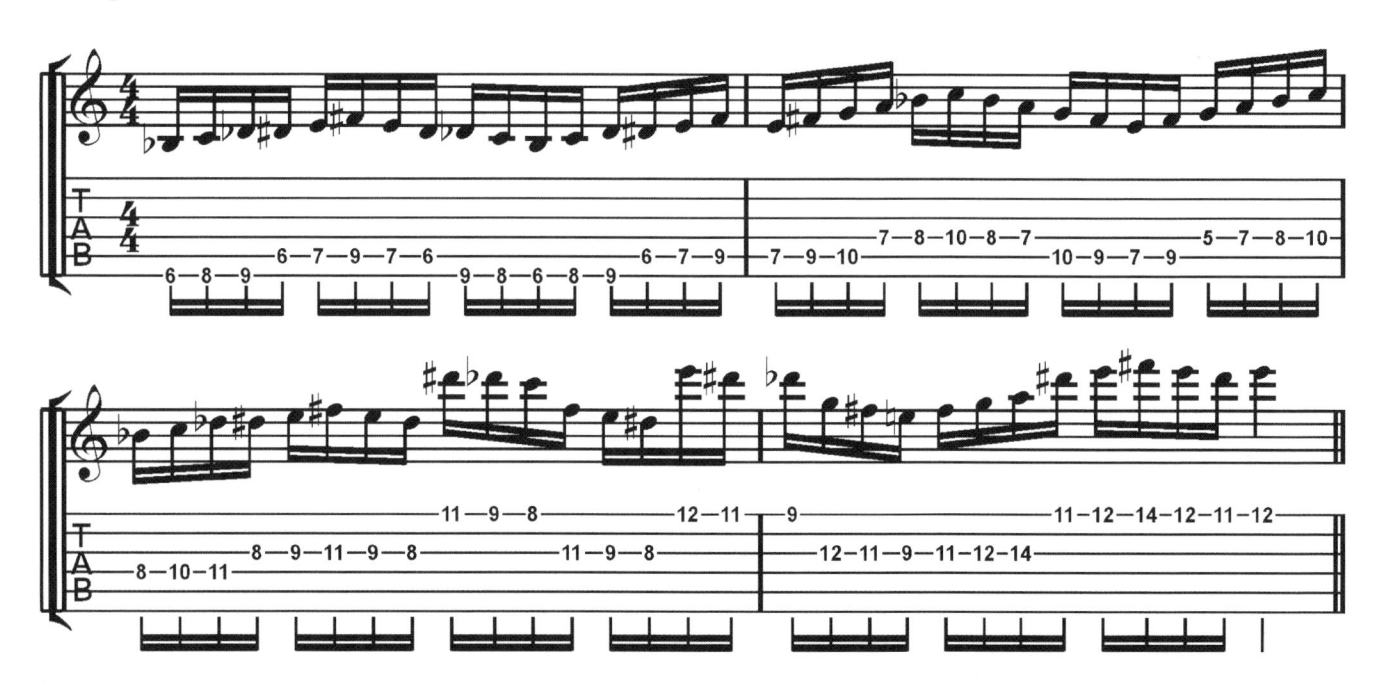

Next, we exploit the repeating semitones found throughout the Diminished scale. In the previous example we started with a tone/semitone, which suggested a Diminished triad, but here we start semitone/tone.

Example 7m

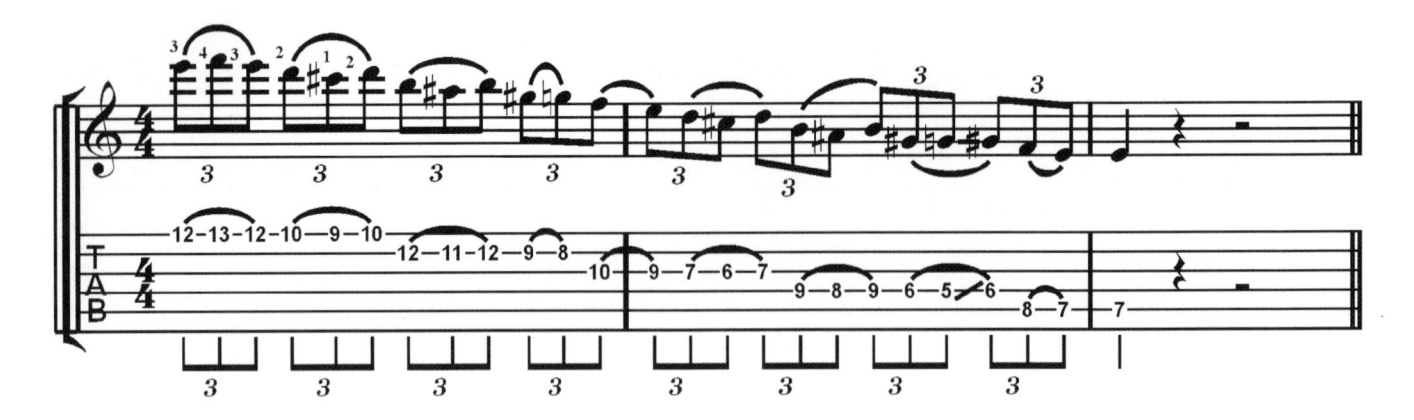

The eight notes of the Diminished scale can be broken down into two Diminished 7th arpeggios a semitone apart. Just as with our Wholetone diagrams, I've illustrated these arpeggios within the scale shape.

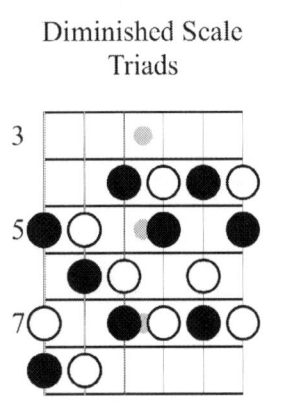

Diminished Scale
Triads

Any phrases that you may use with a single Diminished arpeggio can be shifted up or down by a scale step inside the Diminished scale. In the following example, I move away from predictable patterns by varying the length of time on each arpeggio.

Example 7n

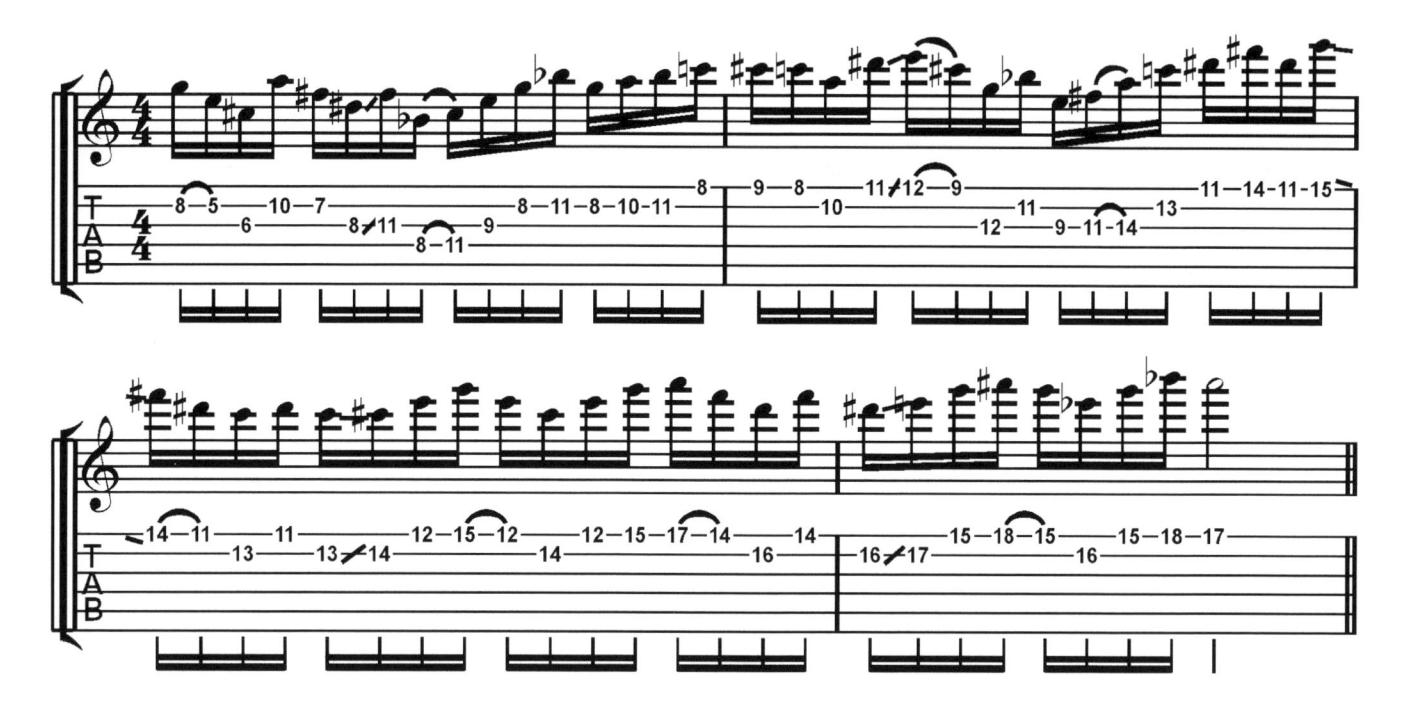

Once again, we use our trend of recycling familiar licks with unfamiliar note choices by incorporating bends and slides from a more traditional blues lick. This time creating the unsettled feeling with first the Harmonic Minor and then the Diminished Scale.

The more bluesy you can make the timing here the better.

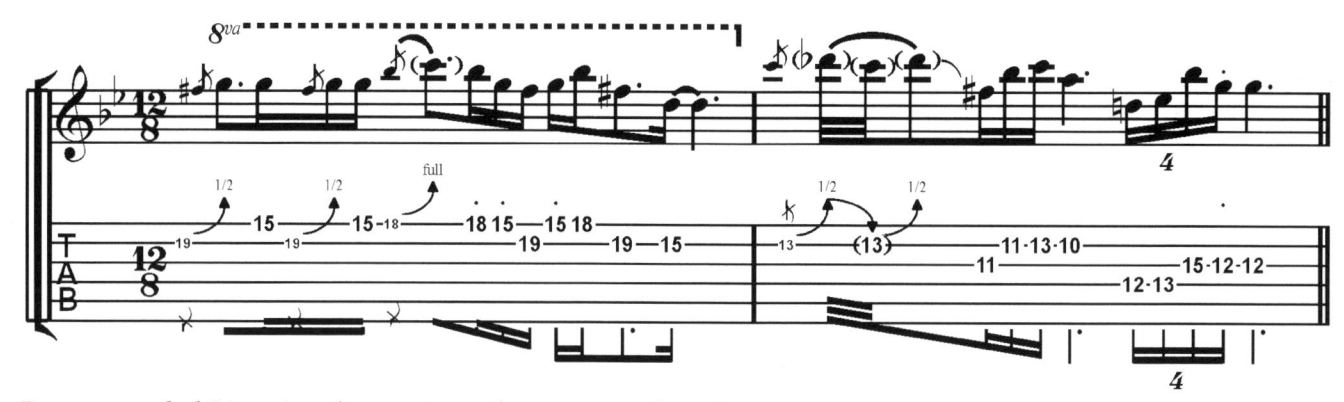

Example 7o

Recommended Listening for exotic and symmetrical scales:

Megadeth - *Tornado of Souls*
Dream Theater – *Octavarium*
Trivium – *Gunshot to the Head of Trepidation*
Opeth – *The Eternal Rains Come*
Bumblefoot – *Mafalda*

Chapter 8: Harmony Guitar

After all that soloing, we'll now devote a few chapters to topics that will benefit your writing, arranging and overall musicianship.

We will begin by looking at how to write guitar harmonies. Starting with classic rock bands like Thin Lizzy and Wishbone Ash sharing lead guitar spots, and later with Judas Priest, Iron Maiden and Metallica, there are lots of colourful textures that have been applied in metal song arrangements.

Progressive rock bands that incorporate keyboards have been able to enhance their musical palette even further, often drawing on classical influence too.

We'll move chronologically through a range of musical examples to show different ways that multiple guitar parts can complement each other.

To help us understand what's going on, let's blow the cobwebs off some chord theory. Building common chords always involves stacking notes a 3rd apart from within a scale.

The figure below shows the C Major scale harmonised in triads. C is harmonised by the 3rd (E) and 5th (G) to create a major triad. The note D is harmonised with notes a 3rd and 5th above it (F and A), but the pattern of tones and semitones that make up the Major scale causes this to a minor triad.

The triad harmonisations of the C Major scale are shown below.

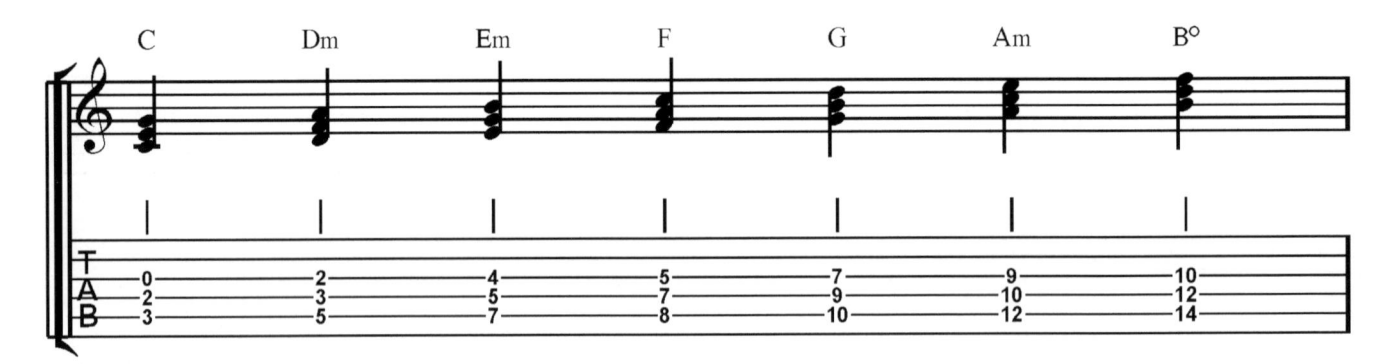

```
    C        Dm       Em       F        G        Am       B°

T  -0------- -2------ -4------ -5------ -7------ -9------ -10------
A  -2------- -3------ -5------ -7------ -9------ -10----- -12------
B  -3------- -5------ -7------ -8------ -10----- -12----- -14------
```

For our first example we're examining the sweet-sounding harmonised melodies of Iron Maiden. In the top line of tablature there is a simple melody in E minor, and in the bottom line we have the harmony part.

To create the harmony part, I moved each note from Gtr A up by two notes in the E Natural Minor (E Aeolian) scale. The top line of the notation contains both parts and you can see that they remain separated by a 3rd throughout.

Each harmony note is either a minor 3rd (three frets) or a major 3rd (four frets) higher than Part A. Your ear will quickly tell you whether you've selected the right note or not when writing parts like this.

To practice the ideas in this chapter, I suggest recording the melody part to a click track and then playing the harmony parts in time with the recording.

Example 8a

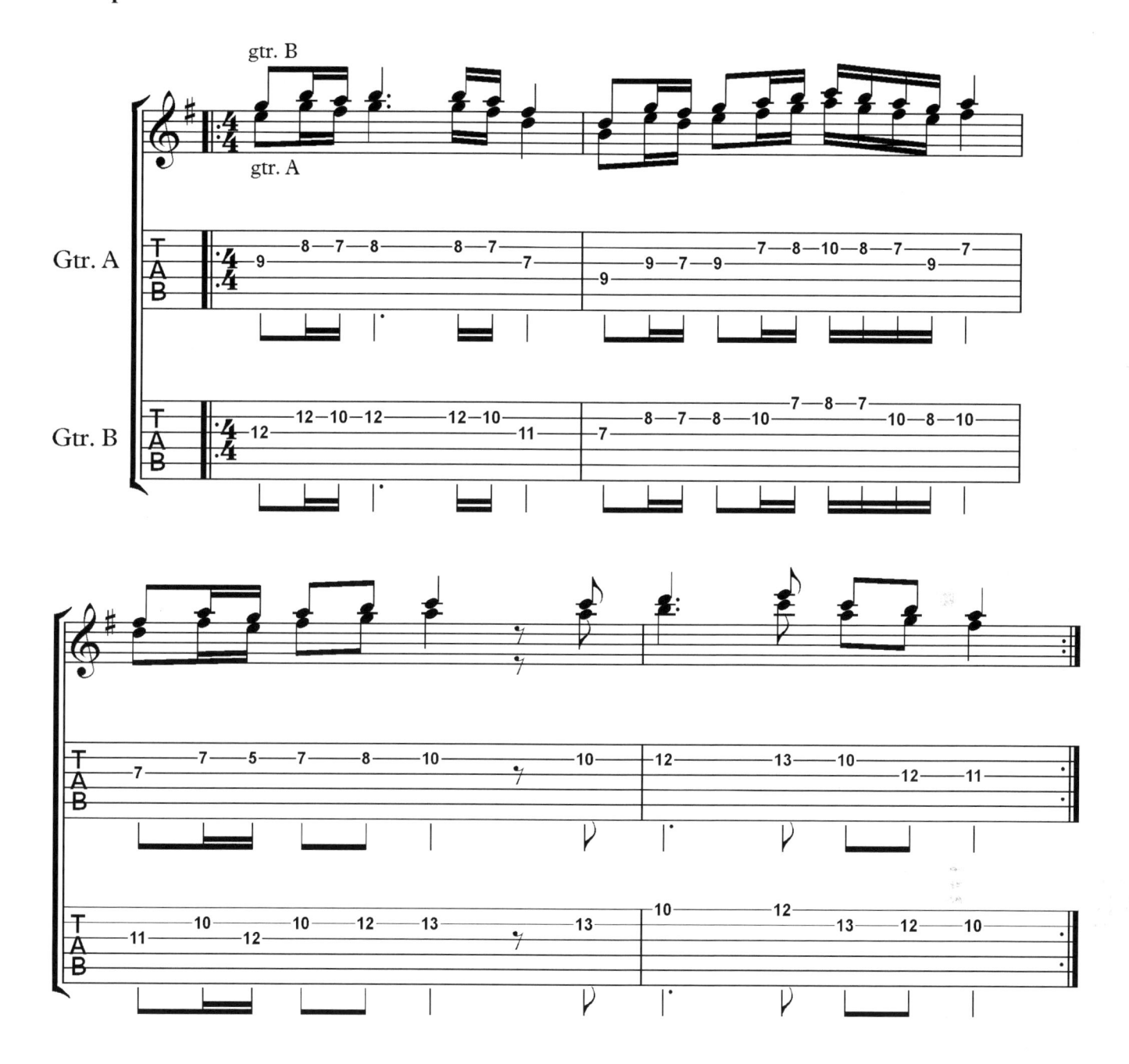

If you are familiar with the different positions of the Major scale and its modes, there's an easy way to work out harmony in 3rds (as well as using your ears!). Start by playing Part A in a three-note-per-string scale shape, and then play the same fingering using the shape two positions higher of the same scale to create the harmony part.

The next example contains more scalic playing.

If you and a fellow guitarist are planning on performing twin harmonies, it's worth setting aside special practice time away from the band to make sure you gel together. Paying attention to the speed of vibrato and string bends will make you sound slick and professional.

Example 8b

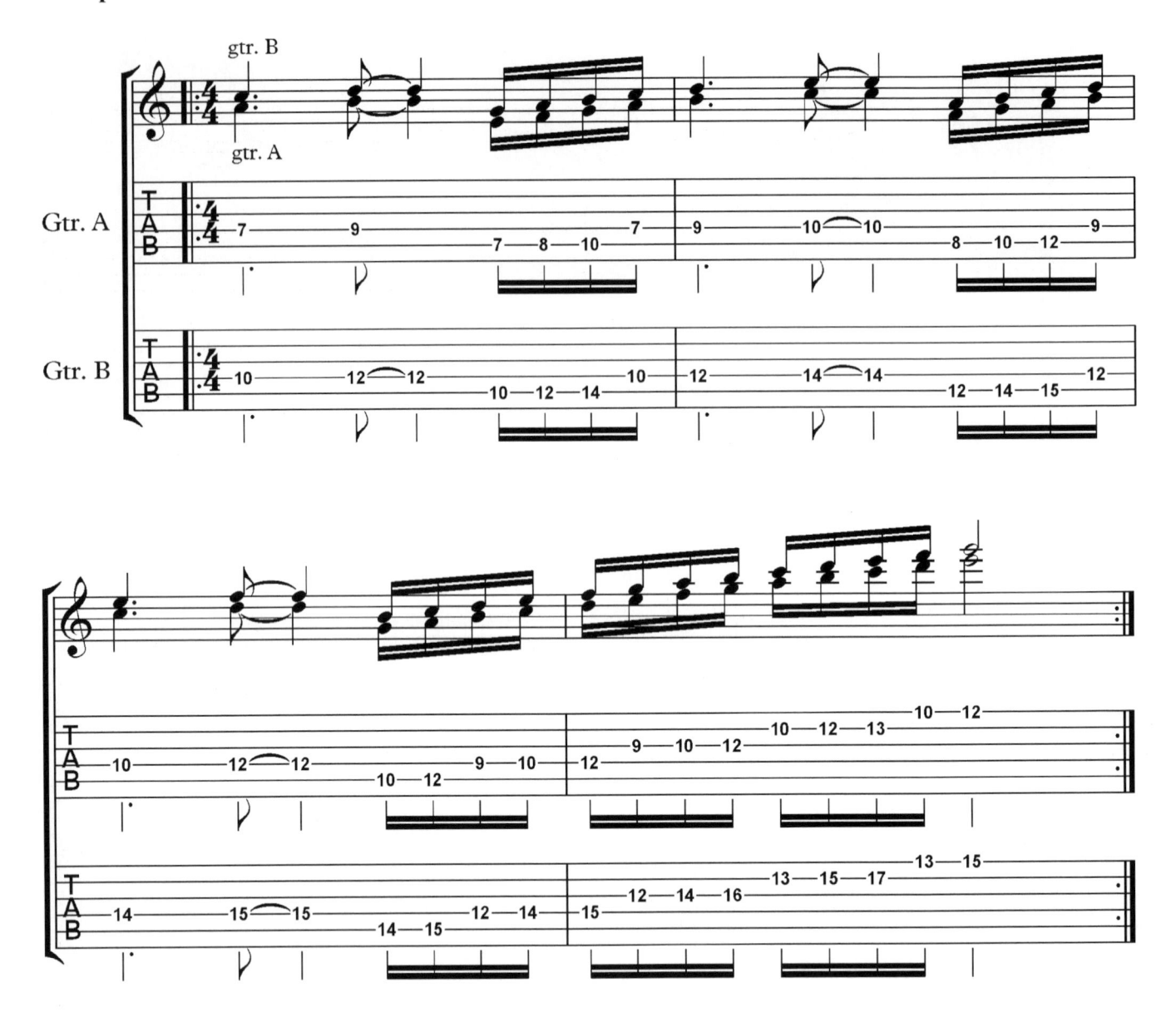

The next passage develops the 3rds harmony by adding a degree of sophistication. Instead of sticking doggedly to diatonic 3rds, we're going to adjust the harmony to better fit the accompanying. Most of the harmony part remains as 3rds but occasionally a 4th or a 2nd is a more appropriate note choice.

For example, in bar two when Part A plays the 5th of the chord, it would be better to have Part B add a 4th above to hit the root, rather than a 3rd which would have given us the less consonant 7th. In bar three we pass over the b7 of the chord, and the harmony is the root rather than the 9th which would be slightly dissonant in this context.

Example 8c

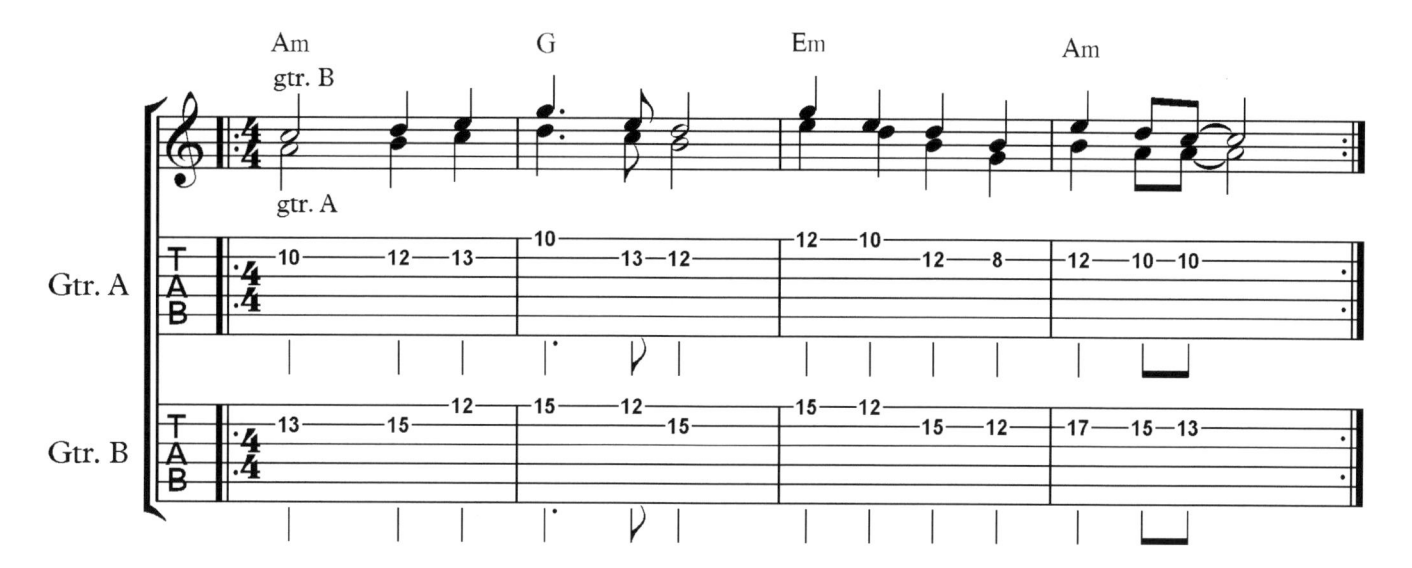

The third example demonstrates how we can invert intervals.

Every interval can be inverted, for example, moving from C to A is a major 6th, but moving from A to C is a minor 3rd. (Top tip: inverted intervals always add up to 9: 3rds become 6ths, 4ths become 5ths and 7ths become 2nds). The inversion of a 3rd is a 6th, therefore playing Part B a 6th below Part A will give us the same notes as playing them a 3rd above Part A.

One advantage of playing your harmony a 6th below is that the original A part will remain the top melody (and therefore more clearly audible), while at the same time being thickened and supported by a harmony underneath.

Feel free to experiment with 3rds below your A part, although this is less commonly done as the harmony part is less likely to compliment the overall harmony. 6ths below does a better job of automatically matching the chords.

Example 8c

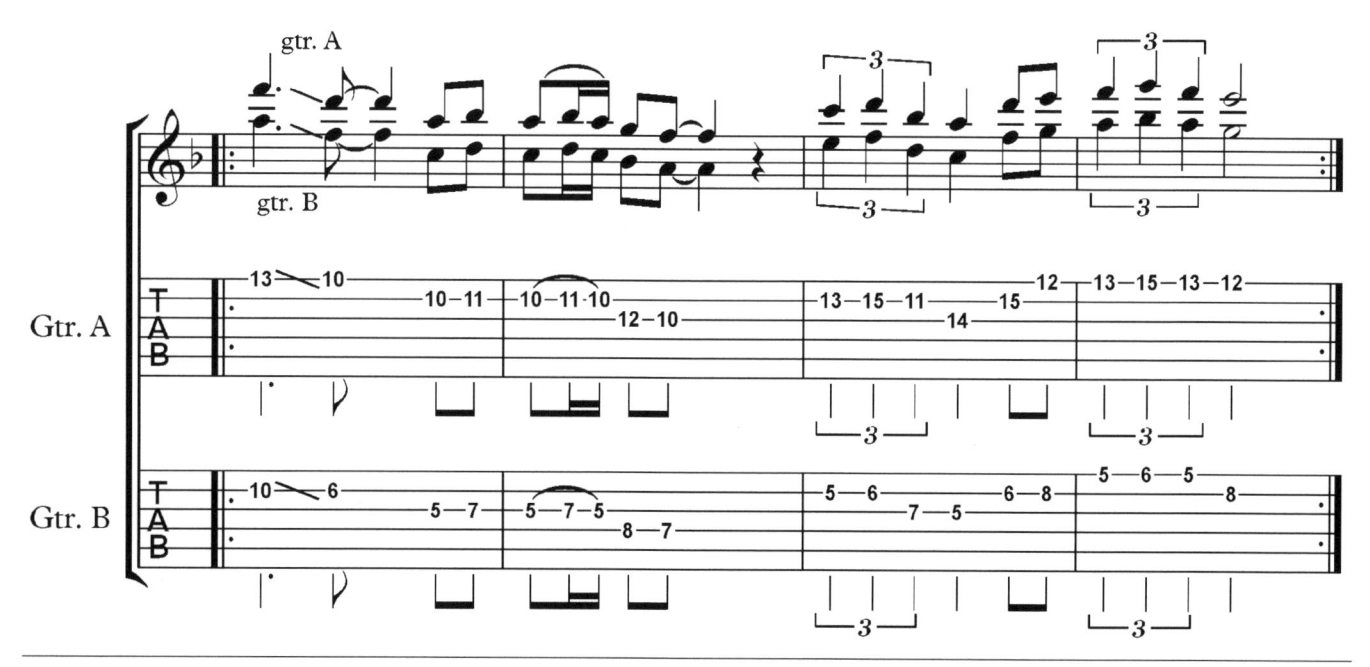

The next passage develops the 3rds harmony by adding a degree of sophistication. Instead of sticking doggedly to diatonic 3rds, we're going to adjust the harmony to better fit the accompanying. Most of the harmony part remains as 3rds but occasionally a 4th or a 2nd is a more appropriate note choice.

For example, in bar two when Part A plays the 5th of the chord, it would be better to have Part B add a 4th above to hit the root, rather than a 3rd which would have given us the less consonant 7th. In bar three we pass over the b7 of the chord, and the harmony is the root rather than the 9th which would be slightly dissonant in this context.

Example 8d

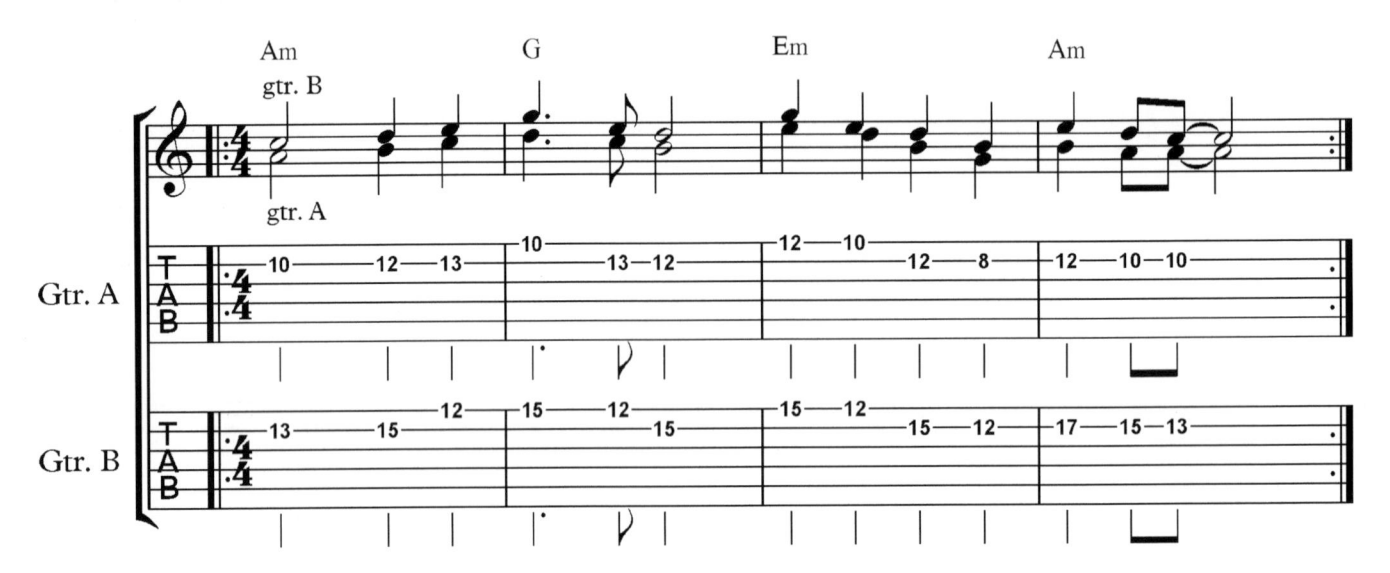

```
        Am              G              Em             Am
        gtr. B

Gtr. A
        gtr. A
       |--10-----12--13--|--10-----13--12--|--12--10-----12---8--|--12--10--10--|
       |-----------------|-----------------|---------------------|--------------|

Gtr. B
       |--13-----15------|--12--15--12-----|--15--12-----15--12--|--17--15--13--|
       |-----------15----|-----------15----|---------------------|--------------|
```

Now for some more technical shred ideas inspired by bands like Racer X, Cacophony and more recently, Trivium.

First we have some fast arpeggios to be harmonised. Trying to synchronise this with another player will really test your rhythmic accuracy. Recording both parts together can be revealing of any sloppy time keeping, but it is a great way to monitor your progress.

We could have harmonised each melody note a 3rd above, however this time I repeated each arpeggio shape in the next inversion up. This way, each one is still limited to the notes of that chord and thus maintains the clarity of harmonic progression initially provided by the use of arpeggios.

Learn each shape slowly to start with, preferably using a metronome that can count individual subdivisions, to help you lock in with the time. Try playing with a friend, or recording yourself when you practice. Record the melody part and then play the harmony part in time.

Example 8e

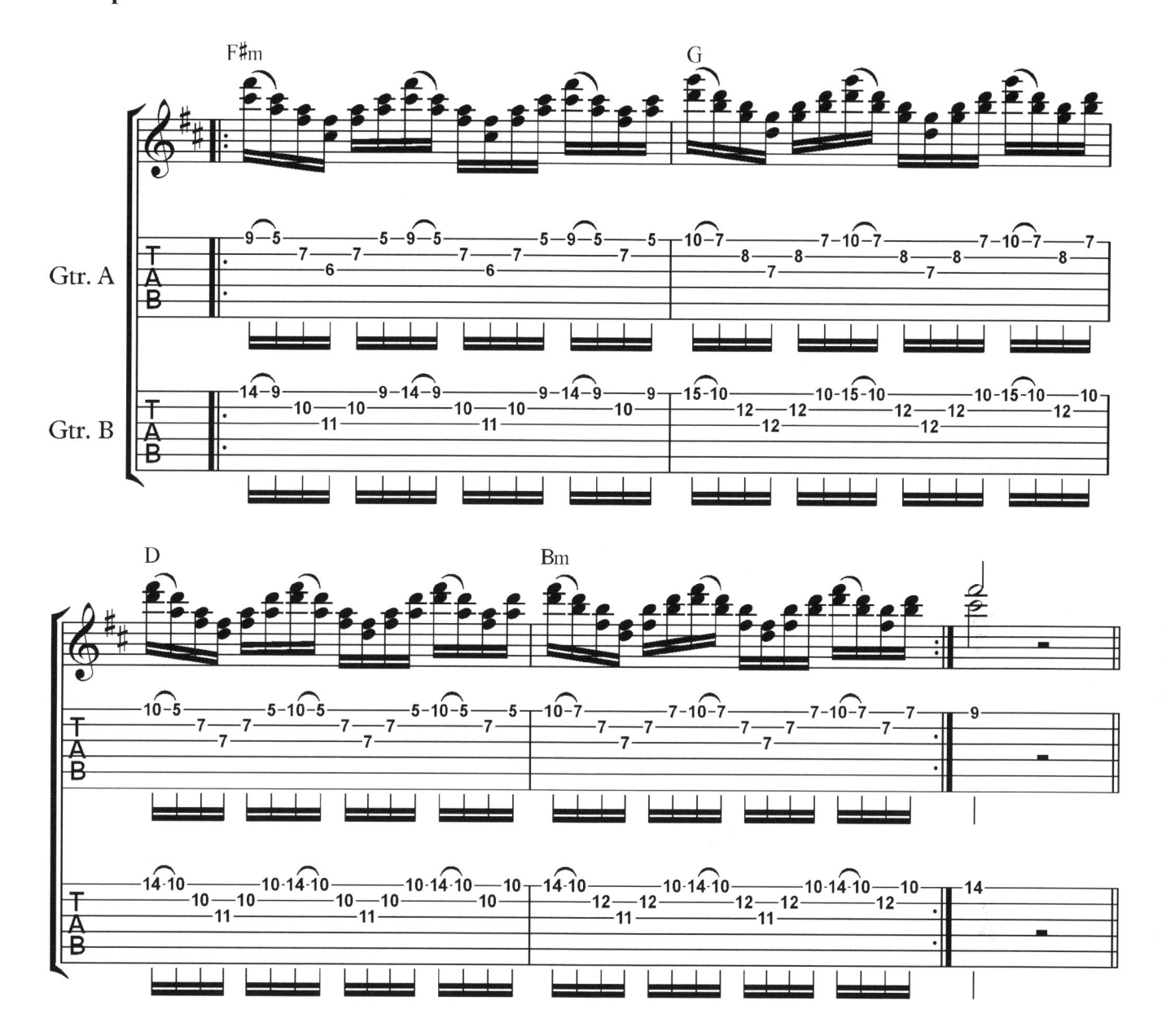

In the next example we combine arpeggios and a scale run to create a more exciting and varied contour. It's impossible to overstate the need for accuracy when playing such material. Practicing with the other player at slow tempos is the only way to really get it properly synchronised. Remaining in time when moving between different picking techniques takes a lot of coordination.

The first bar uses B major and C major arpeggios, but unlike example 8e, the two parts are *contrapuntal* (each line moving in an independent direction) to avoid being too predictable. When coming up with your own arpeggio ideas you can confidently explore different shapes knowing that, with there only being three notes to choose from, it will always be consonant.

The scale run in the second bar begins in diatonic 3rds (just as in example 8b), but then splits into 6ths and ends up a 10th (Major 3rd) apart. Look at the notation to clearly see how the directions of the two lines split.

Example 8f

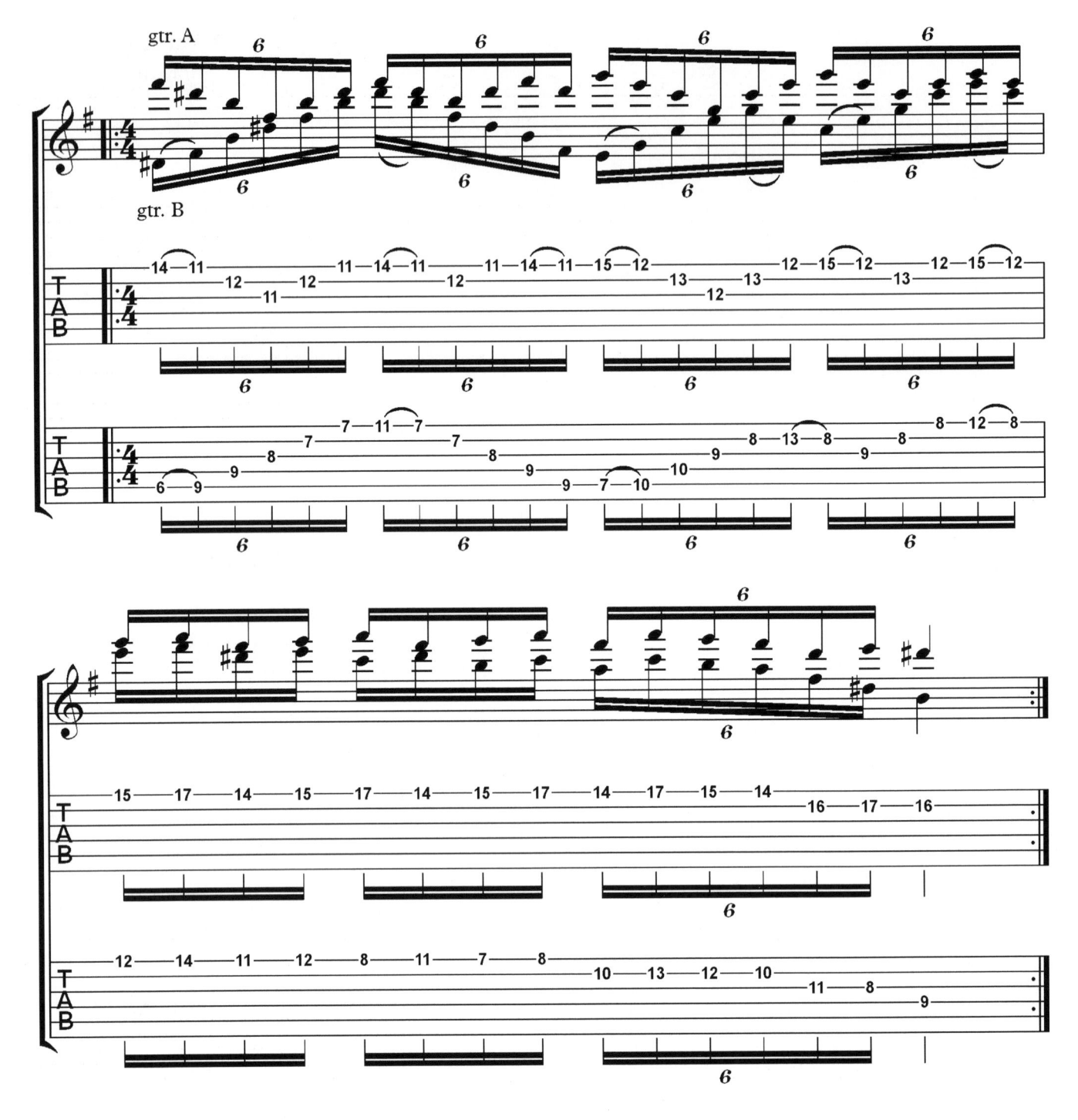

Now we'll move away from the pleasing but rather 'saccharine' sound of 3rds and chord-based harmonies, and look at quartal (4th-based) and parallel harmonies. As I mentioned before, inverting a 4th will give you a 5th which creates a similar sound to harmonising the melody with power chords.

The following example harmonises a melody entirely in 4ths. Listen and compare it with the sound that we achieved when using 3rds. I've kept a perfect 4th between parts A and B, even though the diatonic scale has one Augmented 4th. The Augmented 4th is so dissonant that by comparison the ear accepts the non-scale tone more readily than it does the 'correct' in-key harmony.

Example 8g

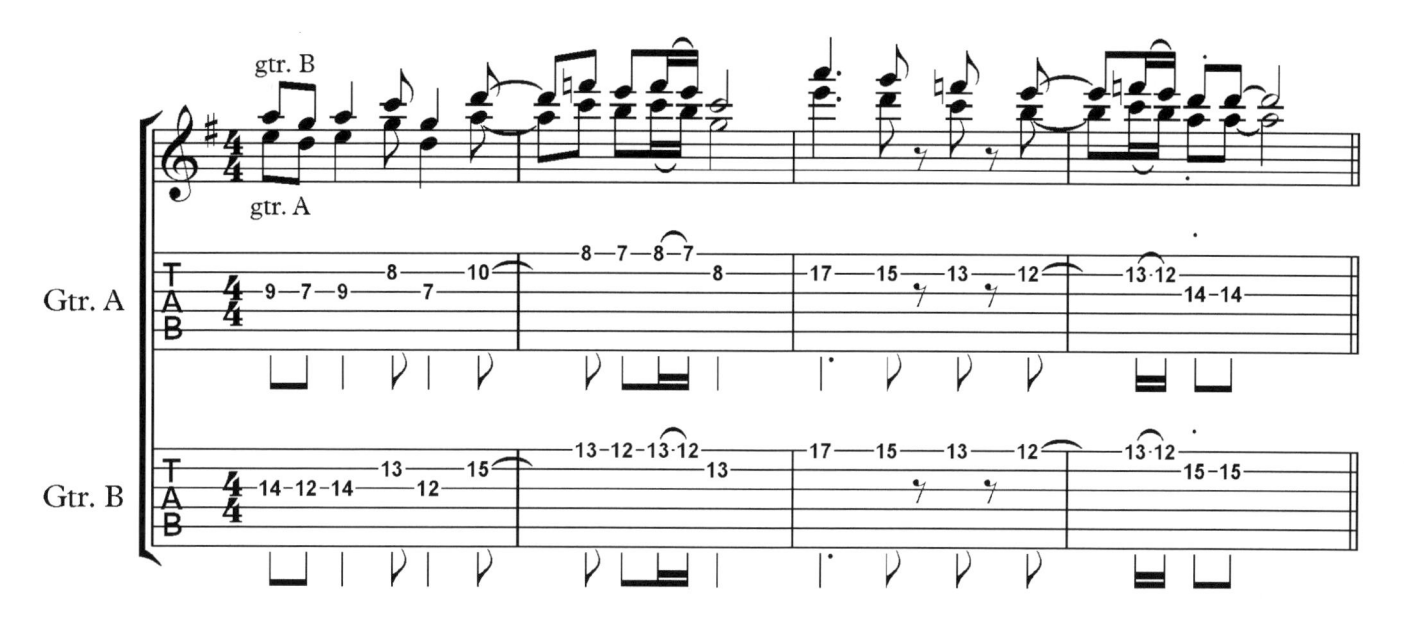

This time we're not going to use the notes of a specific scale to form the harmony part. Instead we will select a fixed interval and stick with it. I've written a harmony part that always stays a major 3rd up from Part A at all times.

The listener is happily lead by the consistency of the pattern whilst the use of non-diatonic notes provides a type of dissonance known as *bitonality*. Bitonality refers to playing in two keys simultaneously. While our Part A lick is in E Phrygian, the harmony, if heard in isolation, would be G# Phrygian. (The same scale a major 3rd above)

Example 8h

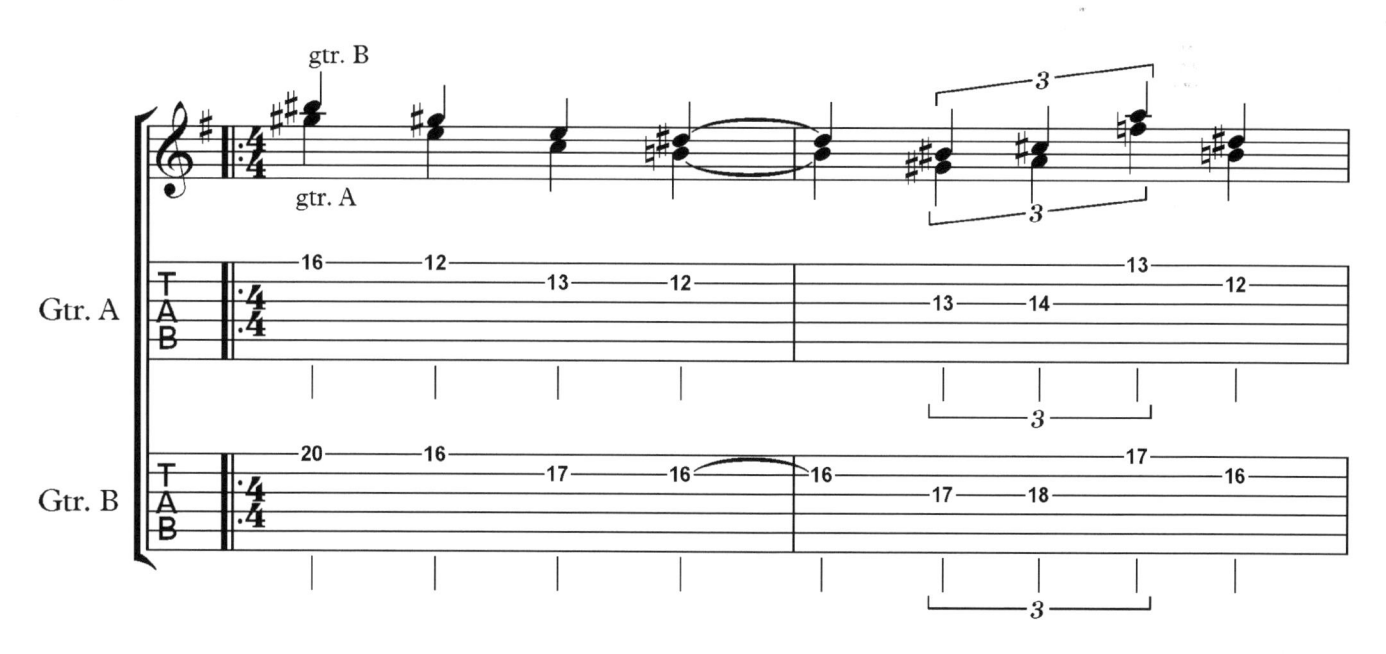

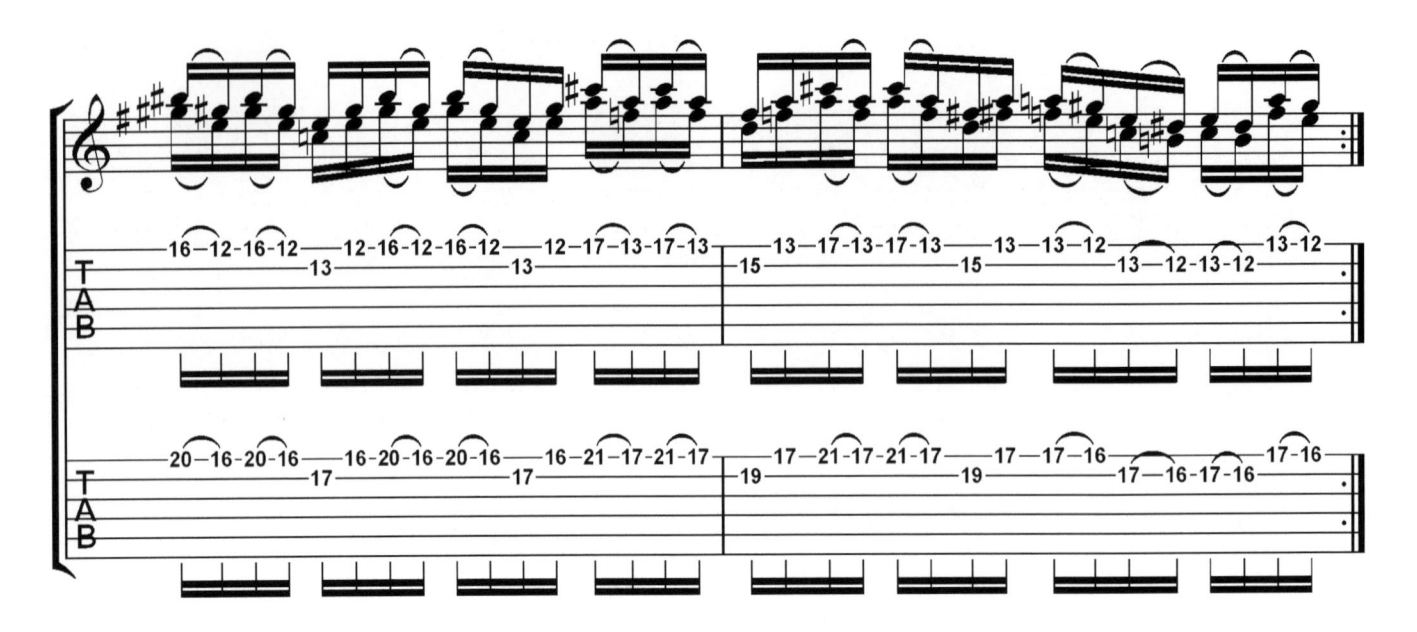

Compared to other styles of music, modern metal's lack of harmonic richness allows us to layer more dissonant note combinations that wouldn't work over conventional pop harmony.

Parallel harmonies can add a quite jarring effect to any passage.

Rhythm Guitar Harmony Riffs

We can take the same techniques and also apply them to rhythm guitar parts.

Drop D tuning is used in the first example to add some extra meat to the low notes. The energy and movement comes from the contrasting bursts of high harmonised notes between the chugging D's and power chords. Listen carefully to the audio to hear how some are palm-muted while others ring out.

This modern-sounding riff is inspired by metalcore bands like Killswitch Engage and The Ocean. This style is characterised by the chunky riffs and huge production. Bolstering the melodic fragments with octaves and then harmonising them guarantees a fatter sound, as does the big open-string power chord made possible by the drop D tuning.

Example 8i

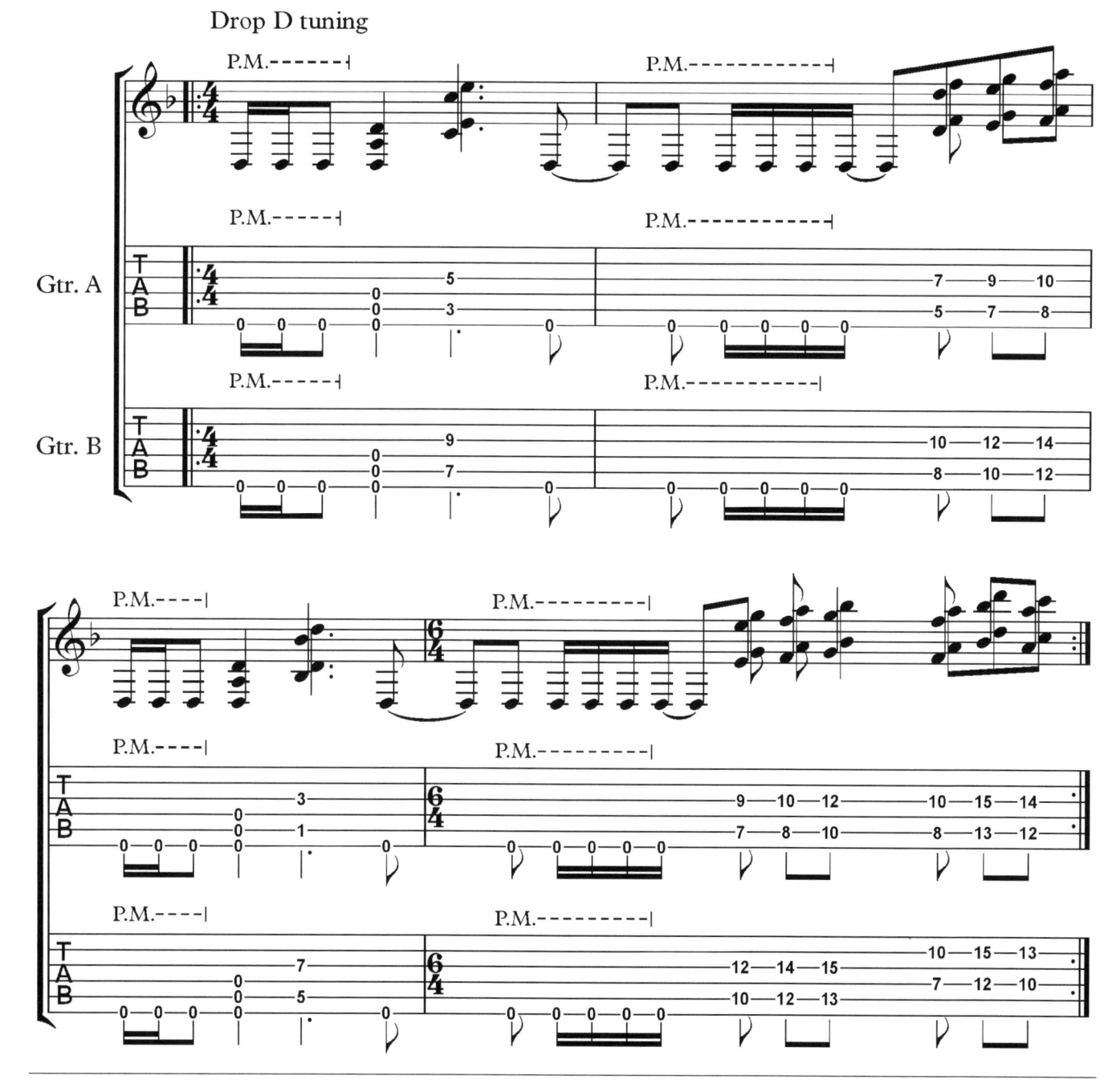

The second harmonised riff is quite intricate, so you may have to slow it right down in order to get the constant 1/16th notes even while balancing the picking and legato. We harmonise within the E Harmonic Minor scale, to give a definite neoclassical slant. The driving rhythmic feel draws on bands as diverse as Megadeth, Yngwie Malmsteen, and Symphony X.

The second bar ends with a Diminished arpeggio that is harmonised by simply moving the same pattern up by three frets. (See Chapter Seven for more detail on symmetrical scales.)

Example 8j

Our third riff uses a much more dissonant harmony. Both guitars bounce off the low E string, but the accented notes are a tritone (b5) apart. The result an alarm bell-like percussive sound effect.

One guitar could play both high notes as a chord, but using two guitars delivers a more focussed result, avoiding the mushiness of playing a chord through a distorted amp.

Example 8k

So far, all of the harmony licks have been in rhythmic unison, but the final two riffs give each guitar a contrasting rhythm. The first of which uses a panning trick to make the same phrase bounce back and forth across the stereo field. When playing stop-start rhythmic fragments it is easy rush or delay on the subdivisions, even more so than when playing a constant stream of notes.

The technical music theory term for this shifting back and forth between two musical voices is *hocketing*.

Example 81

The final riff develops the previous two concepts by having one guitar concentrate on low chugging power chords while the other guitar intersperses with a clashing semitone in between. Break down the syncopated rhythm carefully and listen to the audio.

We're back in Drop-D tuning for a heavier sound and to also make the moving power chords in Gtr. B easier to finger.

In theory, one guitar could once again play both parts, but the sound is much cleaner and relaxed when split between two players: both can focus on making their phrases as clean and detached as possible. To help you both lock in with the rhythm, Part A should listen to the snare drum accents and Part B should focus on the kick drums. The cymbals outline the overall 4/4 pulse.

Listen to Sikth's *Skies of Millennium Night* for a fantastic example of this idea, with each guitar panned hard left and right – the song also ends with a great harmonised tapping riff.

Example 8m

We've barely scratched the surface of how we can orchestrate and arrange rhythm and lead guitar parts. To develop your awareness and creativity in this area, I suggest you experiment writing harmonies using different intervals, both diatonic and parallel. Furthermore, listening to other musicians, starting with the bands I've suggested below, will give you plenty of inspiration.

Recommended listening for creative twin guitar playing:

Iron Maiden – *Revelations*
Judas Priest - Exciter
Metallica – *And Justice for All...*
Racer X – *Technical Difficulties*
Cacophony – *Speed Metal Symphony*
Trivium – *Ascendancy*
Dream Theater – *Never Enough*
Arch Enemy – *Nemesis*

Chapter 9: Meter and Cross-Rhythm

This chapter introduces some rhythmic concepts found in modern metal that build upon on those discussed in my first book, Heavy Metal Rhythm Guitar. We'll examine more uses of odd time signatures and then we'll look at cross-rhythmic effects that can be achieved by overlaying different meters.

The first group of riffs feature combinations of different time signatures one after another. The way to approach them is to feel the whole phrase as a repeating block. You'll probably need to begin by counting carefully to get your head around their feel, but once you're confident with each meter in the progression, sequencing them shouldn't prove too challenging.

Since the '90s, metal has developed a high degree of rhythmic complexity. Following thrash metal, the Death Metal genre exemplified by Death and Cannibal Corpse often featured dramatic changes of tempo during the course of a song, as well as switching between triplet and straight pulses. A little later Fear Factory and Meshuggah introduced very precise syncopated rhythms, almost always played in unison with the kick drum.

The legacy of these bands, particularly Meshuggah, is clear in many current bands of the so-called 'djent' sub-genre. It's become the norm in this style to use extended range 7 and 8 string guitars, but in the interest of accessibility I've written all the examples for 6 strings, however, these concepts are transferable to any tuning.

I often hear it said that modern metal employs *polyrhythms*. This is slightly incorrect, so before we dive-in I'd like quickly to clarify some terminology. *Polyrhythms* and *crossrhythms* are subtly different methods of combining two or more layers of rhythm, and it is crossrhythm that is commonly found in metal. With the exception of Frank Zappa's compositions, polyrhythmic ideas are rarely used in rock music.

A polyrhythm divides a single length of time in two different ways. If you look at the following figure you'll see we have one bar of 4/4 divided into eight 1/8ths in voice 1. In voice 2 the bar has been divided into six equal notes using 1/4 note triplets which cannot be subdivided to fit into the 1/8th note grid. The audible effect of this is that two tempi appear to be occurring simultaneously, providing a disorientating, ambiguous pulse.

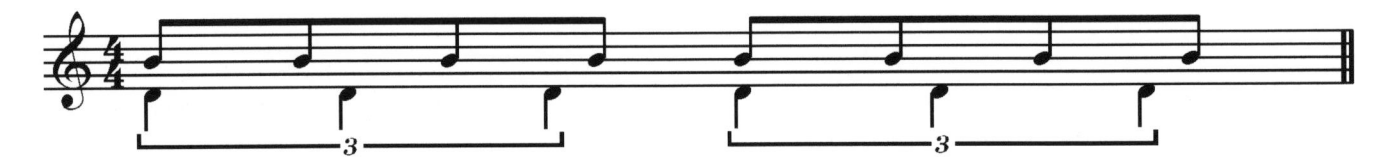

By comparison, the second figure illustrates a crossrhythm, which is easier to play and understand. Here, both voices fit into the same structure of subdivisions, but while the top voice is playing on every second 1/8th note, the lower voice is playing on every third 1/8th note. This means that the pattern does not repeat within one bar. In fact, it takes three bars before the two voices sync up again on the first beat of a bar.

In the second half of this chapter we'll be taking the concept of crossrhythm to more advanced levels. If you're interested in hearing examples of polyrhythm in use, listen to the classical music of Frank Zappa, Charles Ives, or Elliot Carter, as well as traditional African drumming. Charles Ives' polyrhythms are so conflicting that his fourth symphony requires two conductors!

Combining Odd Time Signatures

The first riff links together three bars of 3/4 and one bar of 2/4. Although neither are considered 'odd' on their own, the combined effect may need to be heard several times before you get a feel for what's going on.

Reduce the gain slightly to give clarity to the sustained chords in the first half of the example. The notes should be breaking up without becoming muddy and indistinct.

Example 9a

The second riff is built from a fairly straight-ahead 4/4 one-bar riff, interspersed with odd fills that disrupt the groove. The fills are short and constructed from a constant stream of notes, so once the fingerings are memorised they should take care of themselves.

To help to you feel the length of different note groupings, try improvising new fills in the odd-time bars. Either follow the meters I've written here, or just pick one grouping and alternate it with the 4/4 riff.

Example 9b

Next we have an example of *metric modulation*. Metric modulation is when we change between tempi or feels in a controlled way instead of just jumping from one to the other. If the two tempi have something in common then there will be a better sense of flow and continuity to the transition.

In this example we're moving from 140bpm to 105bpm, but the triplets in the first riff are actually the same speed as the semiquavers in the second riff. So in reality we're just changing from accenting every third note, to accenting every fourth note.

Death used this idea a lot to link between contrasting sections of a song, but if you listen to contemporary bands like Tesseract, the music will often shift back and forth between the two feels rapidly, spending only a couple of beats on each.

Example 9c

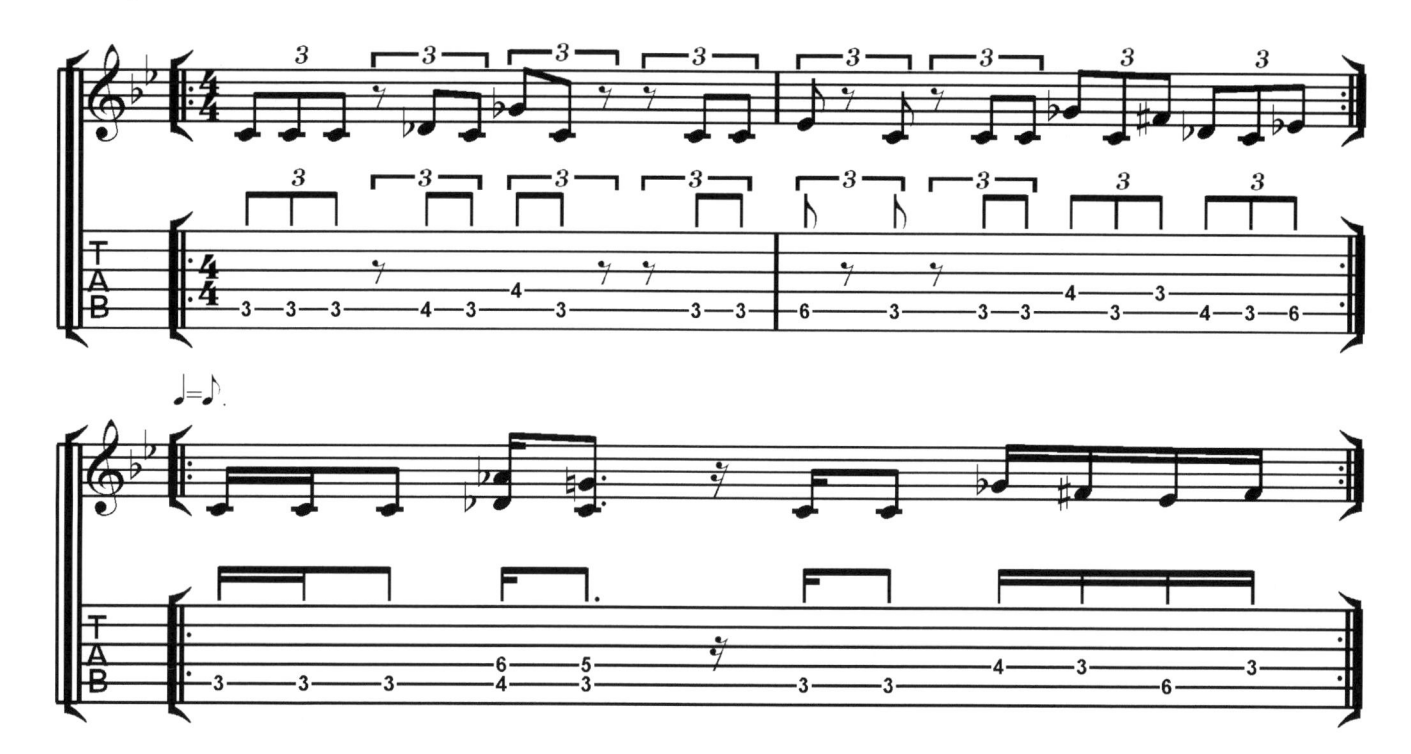

In the following example, the tempo is constant but the beat is subdivided differently. The main division is straight 1/16th notes but is interspersed with bursts of 1/16th triplets. It can be a challenge to gauge how much to speed up by, in order to get the triplets accurately in time.

It's worth practicing this quite slowly as it'll really help your overall timekeeping and awareness of subdividing the beat. You will probably find it hardest at slow tempos because the longer spaces between notes allow for a wider margin of error.

Example 9d

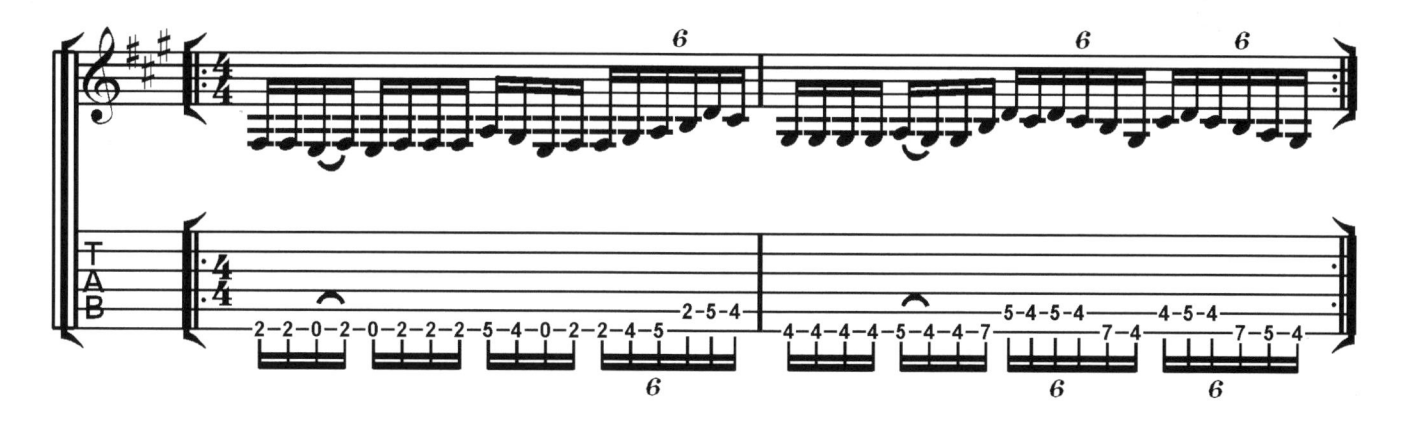

We dipped a toe into 1/16th-based time signatures in Heavy Metal Rhythm Guitar, but next up we have a more daunting example. Although the long notes make the phrase look easier to play, it actually requires much more awareness of the rhythm, this is because we can't simply play a stream of notes and 'meet up' at the finish line as before.

A good way to approach this riff is to count how many 1/16th notes each note is sustained for, and then count in those groupings. Rather than furiously counting numbers, it's easier to have words for different groups. For instance: monkey = 2, elephant =3, alligator = 4 and hippopotamus = 5. You might feel a bit daft, but try them and see if it helps. For colossal sounding riffs in such meters, check out doomy French Prog-metallers Gojira.

Example 9e

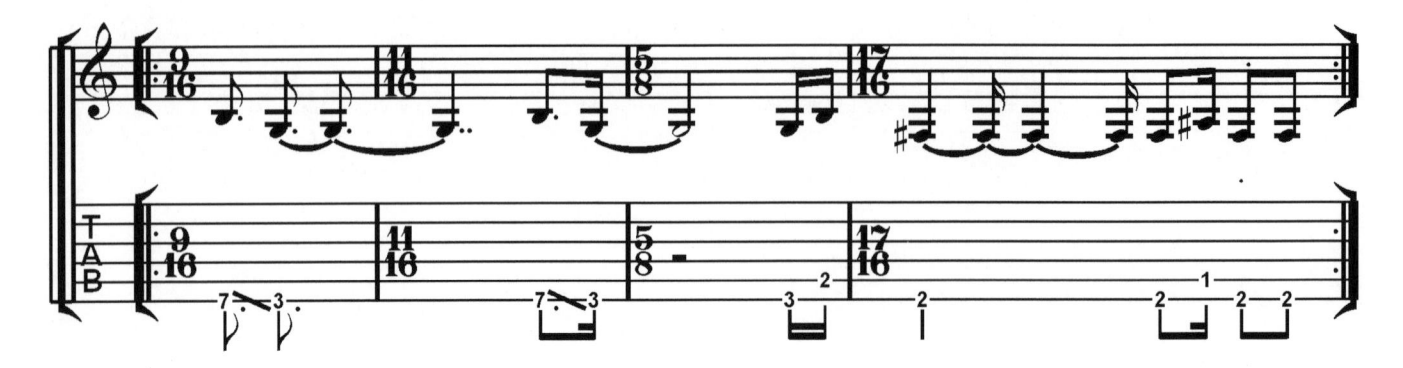

To end the first half of this chapter, here's something a little different.

In this common rhythm, the guitar and bass drums keep a constant tremolo note against a rock beat. The difference is that we cram in five notes per beat (quintuplets) rather than four 1/16ths. Listen carefully to the audio at both speeds to get the sound of fives into your head. This idea will only feel secure once five-note groups feel as comfortable as playing 1/16th notes and triplets

Example 9f

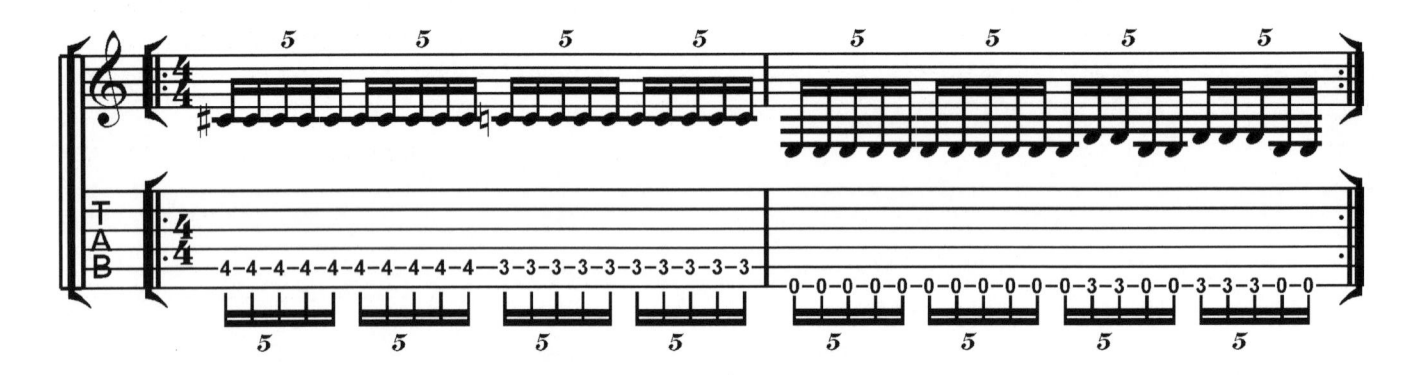

Cross Rhythmic Riffs

By superimposing odd meters over a familiar 4/4 rock feel we can combine interesting, intricate syncopation with a solid sense of groove. Although uneven rhythms can be very effective at the right moment, they can disengage the listener if they're too difficult to follow. The cross rhythmic style that has developed in recent years allows for both cerebral interest *and* the almost-danceable groove that is familiar to most people.

To develop the split sense of time that allows you to be expressive with this technique try clapping the cross rhythm while tapping your foot to the 1/4 note pulse. Tapping your foot is very important because it lets you test whether you are actually balancing both parts.

With practice, you'll start to let the 4/4 pulse carry on subconsciously while you really feel the odd phrase lengths. Once this has clicked, test your skill by moving your foot to half time by only tapping your foot on beasts one and three.

I've used a dotted line to 'box off' each cell in the displaced layer across the main pulse so you can easily observe how the rhythms interact

The first riff uses a feel that you've probably come across before - a three-notes pattern played as straight 1/8th notes. After listening to the audio it should be quite easy to play, but the challenge comes in being able to keep track of the 4/4 pattern and not to get lost in endless repetitions of the 3/8 phrase.

As the displaced part is easy to memorise, you can focus your attention on the drum part when playing along with the track. The cymbals and snare drum remain in 4/4 to help you keep track of where you are. Three bars of 4/4 pass before the crossrhythm returns to start on beat one of the bar again.

Example 9g

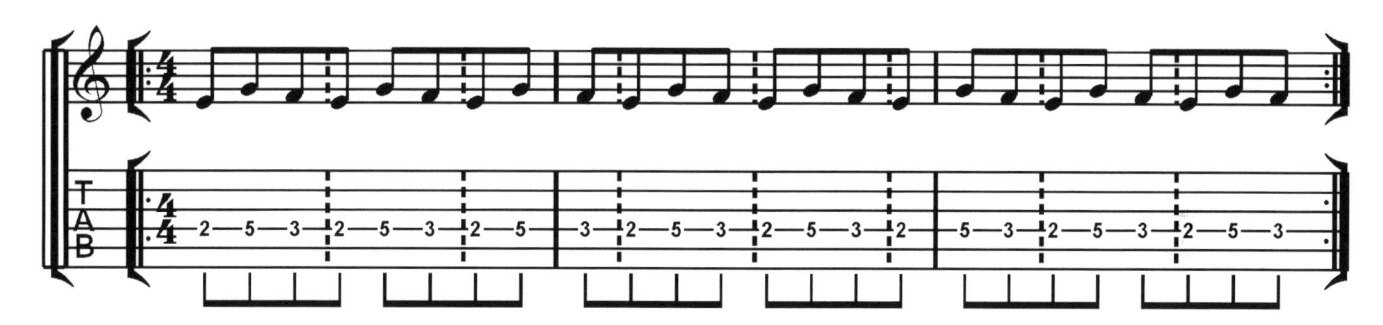

It isn't complicated to explore the possibility of these cross rhythms. If you have a sequencer, program a basic rock beat and try play different odd-note phrases against it. Start by playing every notes, until you can hear the phrase repeating, and then start to include held notes or rests within the phrase.

Example 9h repeats a phrase that lasts eleven 1/8th notes and also includes a more diverse rhythm within the superimposed part. **Example 9h**

Next we up the pace to 1/16th-note-based phrases by essentially halving the phrase-length of example 9g.

To start with you'll find it helpful to keep the picking hand moving in constant 1/16ths, although we're only hitting the first beat of each three semiquaver group. Any repetition of an odd-metered phrase will start on alternate down and up strokes. This can also give you a helpful physical point of reference to keep in time.

Example 9i

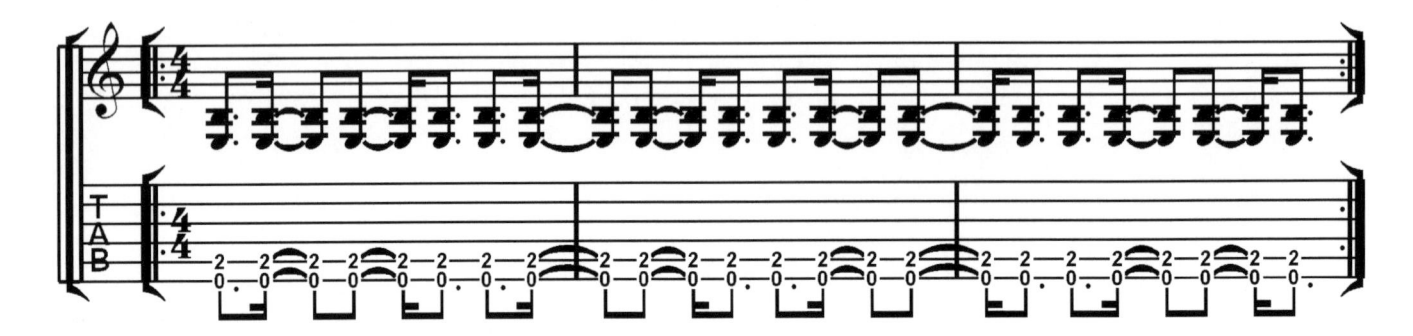

The same advice stands for 7/16, if you keep the picking hand moving consistently throughout. The first cell will be four downstrokes, the second will be four upstrokes and so on.

The first couple of cross rhythms have included enough bars of 4/4 for the downbeats to sync up again, but in reality it's much more common to maintain the familiar structure of four bar phrases, and the melodic and harmonic structure will often remain in 4/4 too. The cross rhythmic texture really provides a way of generating interesting and logical syncopation within a conventional framework. To show this in the next example we allow the 7/16 cell to repeat until four bars are nearly complete, then just add an extra 1/16th note to complete the bar.

Example 9j

Time to stretch ourselves: This next example is inspired by Meshuggah, the kings of this sub-genre. Our overlaid cell is in 25/16. Though this sounds intimidating there are a couple of ways that you can to tackle it. Firstly, try playing the 25/16 cell in isolation, without worrying about the 4/4 element. It is best felt as five straight beats, and then a group of five 1/16ths (i.e. 5/4 + 5/16).

Just as in the previous riff, we use a shorter variation in the final bar to 'close the loop' of the underlying 'standard' eight-bar phrase.

Another approach is to ignore the 25/16, and work through the notated part and memorise each bar of 4/4 in turn, dealing with the syncopated rhythms as they occur. With the riff memorised, try playing along to the audio file. By hacking away at it slowly, the feel of the whole riff will start to make sense.

Using both these approaches together should give you an awareness of how the two parts interact. Perform it accurately and you will be able to step back to observe the repetitions of the cell.

Example 9k

In the following Tool-inspired riff we combine meters with an extra degree of complexity. You can look at this riff as having two parts to it. In the 'bass' part we use a similar 7/16 rhythm to example 9j, while in the top part we play a two-note chord on beat three of each 4/4 bar. This is a real test of how well you're tuned into the underlying 4/4 pulse.

Learn this idea this first as a drumming pattern. Clap out the 7/16 while tapping the 1/4 note pulse with your foot. Next, try counting aloud '1,2,3,4'. When that's okay, catching beat three should be achievable. Otherwise, break it down, bar by bar until you've memorised the whole passage.

Example 91

All of our riffs so far have been in 4/4, but to inspire you to explore more possibilities, here's a pattern that is overlaid onto 12/8 time. The triple feel gives an added dimension of interest, and helps to keep the imposed 5/8 pattern less predictable than when heard straight.

Finding an appropriate picking pattern can be tricky as down and upstrokes both fall on the beats when playing triplets, so just practice it carefully and be sure to avoid consecutive down strokes without a 1/8th rest between them.

Example 9m

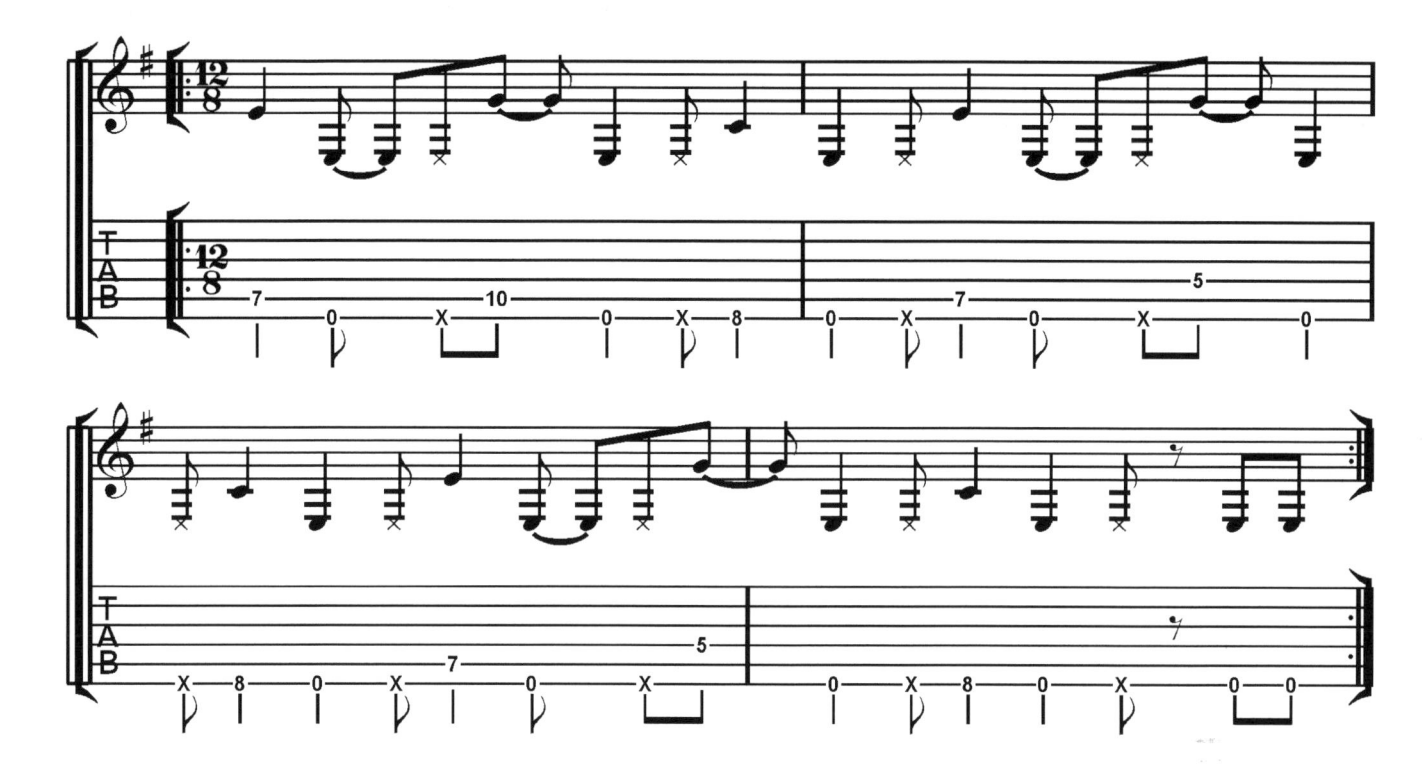

There is boundless scope for experimentation and exploration in this style of music, much of it still untapped. This gives you a good chance of coming up with completely new ideas by combining rhythms and meters in different ways.

The more familiar you are with the sound and 'shape' of each meter, the easier it will be to overlay them. However, there's nothing wrong with programming ideas using a sequencer to 'audition' new ideas quickly. As there is almost infinite scope for experimentation, I advise that you only explore ideas you immediately like the sound of.

Recommended listening for time signatures, groupings and cross rhythm:

Death – *Overactive Imagination*
Cynic – *Textures*
Meshuggah – *Rational Gaze*
Sixth – *Bland Street Bloom*
Tool – *Right in Two*
Panzerballett – *M.w.M.i.O.f.R.*
Animals as Leaders – *Infinite Regression*
Karnivool – *Deadman*
Stimpy Lockjaw – *Shrimpy*

Chapter 10: Demo Solos

This chapter gives you some longer solo studies to learn, and demonstrates how you can construct solos using some of the ideas we've covered.

I have included four separate solos, each over a different backing track so you can play along as well as writing your own solos.

They cover a range of metal styles from '80s Neoclassical rock to modern Progressive and Death metal.

Example 10a

The first solo study takes its inspiration from the Neoclassical shred movement of the late '70s and '80s by Richie Blackmore, Uli Jon Roth, and of course Yngwie Malmsteen. Many other players explored this style, defined a whole genre of instrumental rock guitar music. Shrapnel Records became the home of many of these artists, and their catalogue of albums shows how populous and diverse the scene became.

The solo is sixteen bars long and follows a common chord progression in the key of A minor. The slow ballad feel is performed using clean picked guitars and synth strings, both of which imply a subtle, classically-influenced feel.

Example 10a – Chord Progression

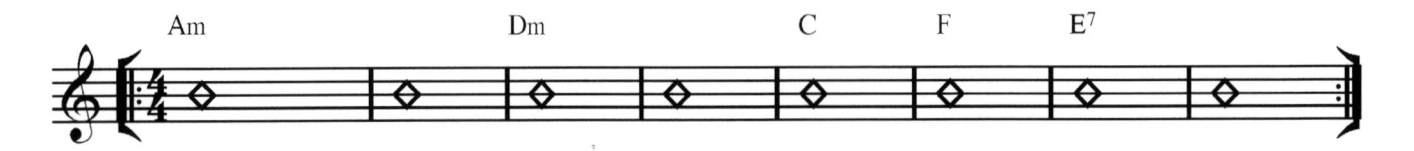

The solo uses several of the ideas from Chapter One, including pedal point, sequences and arpeggios. I Keep things interesting by varying the tone of the guitar and using a mixture of techniques.

Many of these ideas are technically demanding and combine several different techniques in a single phrase, so be patient and start slowly before building up to performing the entire solo. Alternatively, listen to the audio and cherry pick any licks that you particularly like.

The Neoclassical style creates a strong sense of melody by closely following the harmony. Licks often target chord tones or use arpeggios which help to keep them memorable and musical, even when playing faster licks.

If you listen to different guitarists in this style you'll notice that while they are all very technical, each will favour different techniques and patterns. Becoming a unique, individual musician can be as much about missing things out as including everything. So, while pushing yourself to learn more and more, it's also important to play to your strengths and focus on the ideas with which you really connect. For example, if you favour legato or tapping rather than sweep picking or alternate picking, then go ahead and modify the solo to suit your style. After all, don't waste time learning things you would never want to use!

Bars 1-2: The opening section of the solo features an Am arpeggio, but with each of the notes embellished with a chromatic passing tone. The second phrases begins in the same way an octave higher but is interrupted with a tapped bend before descending to target the D note in the next chord...

Bars 3-6: As expected, we now play a D minor arpeggio. Hybrid picking could help you here if you are struggling to alternate pick all string crossing in the pattern.

After the slippery legato embellishment, slide up to a held string bend. Sliding into a bend gives the impression of a much wider and more dramatic change in pitch. You'll frequently hear this type of articulation at the end of licks in Malmsteen's playing.

One of Yngwie's trademarks is his floating and expressive sense of rhythm when playing fast runs. Rather than sticking to strict 1/16ths, he will float across the beats, before landing in time on the downbeat.

The descending arpeggio over the F major chord will take some time to get clean as it's very fast. The speed will only come when the shape feels completely familiar and effortless at slower tempos. The 11-tuplet rhythm may look daunting on the page, but the important thing is to land on the next beat in time; the notes are just crammed in as needed.

Bars 7-8: As the solo builds to its first climax over the E7 chord, we hit the first of our long scalic runs drawn from E Phrygian Dominant. I've used alternate picking throughout, but you could try economy picking or legato according to your taste and technical strengths. The second bar of the run accelerates from sextuplets to demisemiquavers (1/32nd notes, or 8 notes per beat). However, given that our tempo is a sedate 70bpm, this is not quite as scary as it looks.

Bars 9-12: As we resolve back to A minor, we keep the intensity of the speed picking but apply it to a melodic phrase down through the arpeggio.

The second bar is a pedal point lick and was examined in detail in our Neoclassical chapter. Vinnie Moore in particular is known for pedal point licks, executed with spellbinding speed and accuracy. However, to give the solo a sense of pace and dynamics, this one is much slower, with a bluesy, staccato articulation at the end.

After that short lull, the gas is reapplied with an ascending three-note-per-string legato sequence reminiscent of Randy Rhoads. The nine-tuplets are fast, but again it's a case of cramming in the notes and landing on the beat. The picking hand only plays the first note on every string, so actually picks 1/8th note triplets. With repeated listens trying to hear the underlying triplet, the '3x3'ness of the full nine-note grouping might be easier to play than you think.

Bars 13-14: The next dose of shred calls upon Tony MacAlpine and Greg Howe, both of whom possess a wide range of legato and tapping licks that make use of tapping. Familiarity with fretting-hand tapping enables us to be free from clichés by being able to start on any note.

Muting with both hands wherever possible will help to ensure a clean execution, as unwanted ringing can happen when tapping with both hands. When performing the two fingered tap with the picking hand at the end of the run, I actually flatten my fretting hand across all the strings slightly before it's needed again, to fret the last three notes.

Bars 15-17: Finally, we 'unleash the fury' with a long E major and Diminished sweep arpeggio phrase typical of the mighty Swede! Yngwie has absolute fluency with this vocabulary, and rather than simply ascend and descend through the E arpeggio, we take a more varied and interesting contour that also draws on the occasional scale tone. This lick is fast and technically challenging so be disciplined in ironing out any technical issues to reach the level of control demanded by this style.

To finish, we have a descending A Harmonic Minor run. The timing is free here, so aim for a gradual and expressive slowing down towards the last note.

Example 10a – Lead Guitar

91

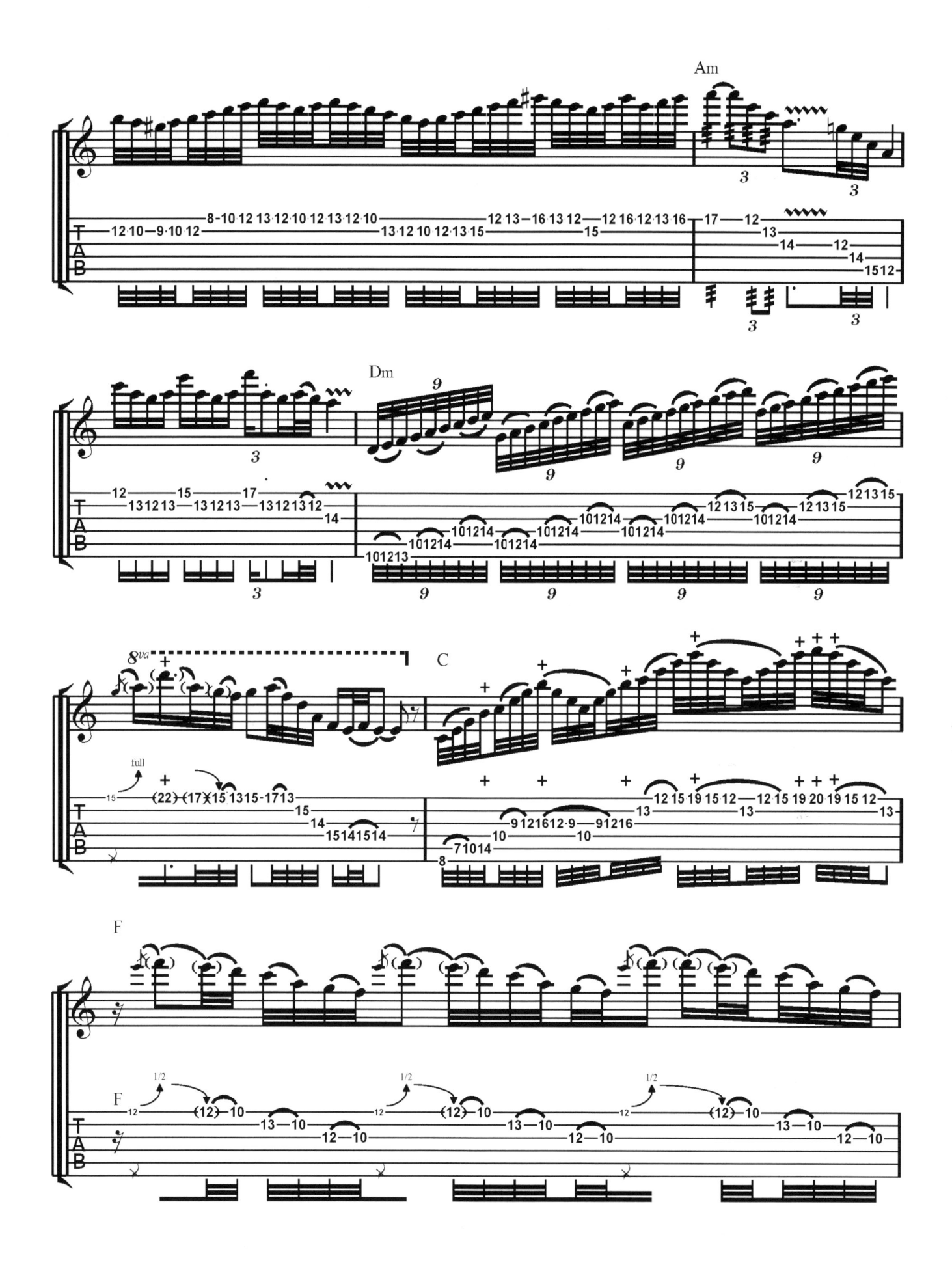

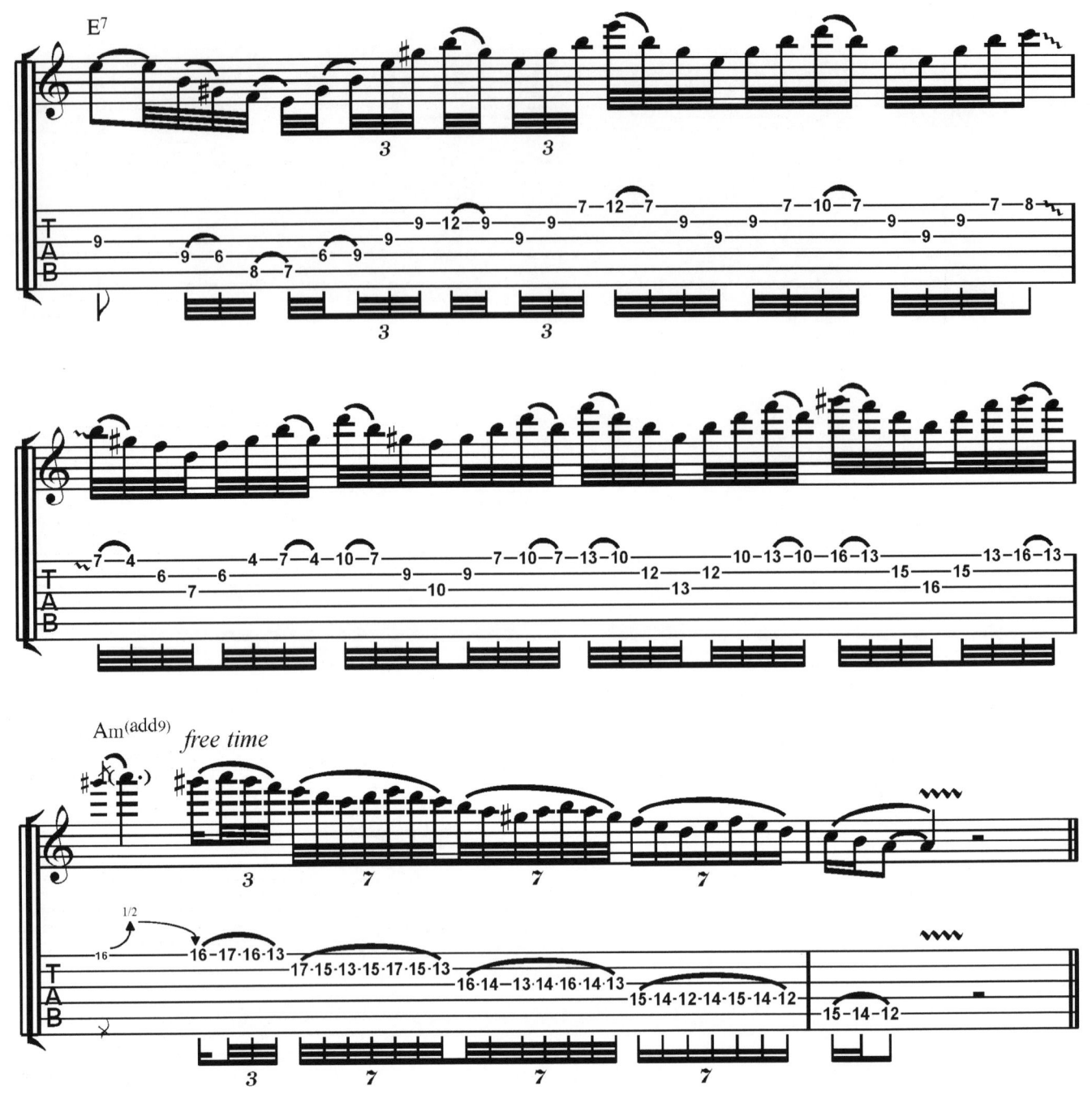

Example 10b

Our second solo features a more contemporary backing part based in F# minor, and draws on the F# Phrygian mode to create a dark tonality. This is more reminiscent of the more Progressive Death Metal bands like Cynic or modern acts like Nevermore and Between the Buried and Me.

Although the licks aren't any faster than the first solo, the technical challenges are a little more involved as we're drawing on a combination of advanced techniques, including hybrid picking, wide legato stretches, string skipping, alternate picking and sweep picking. The melodic phrasing is a lot less blues influenced and owes more to angular jazz fusion.

Example 10b - Rhythm Part

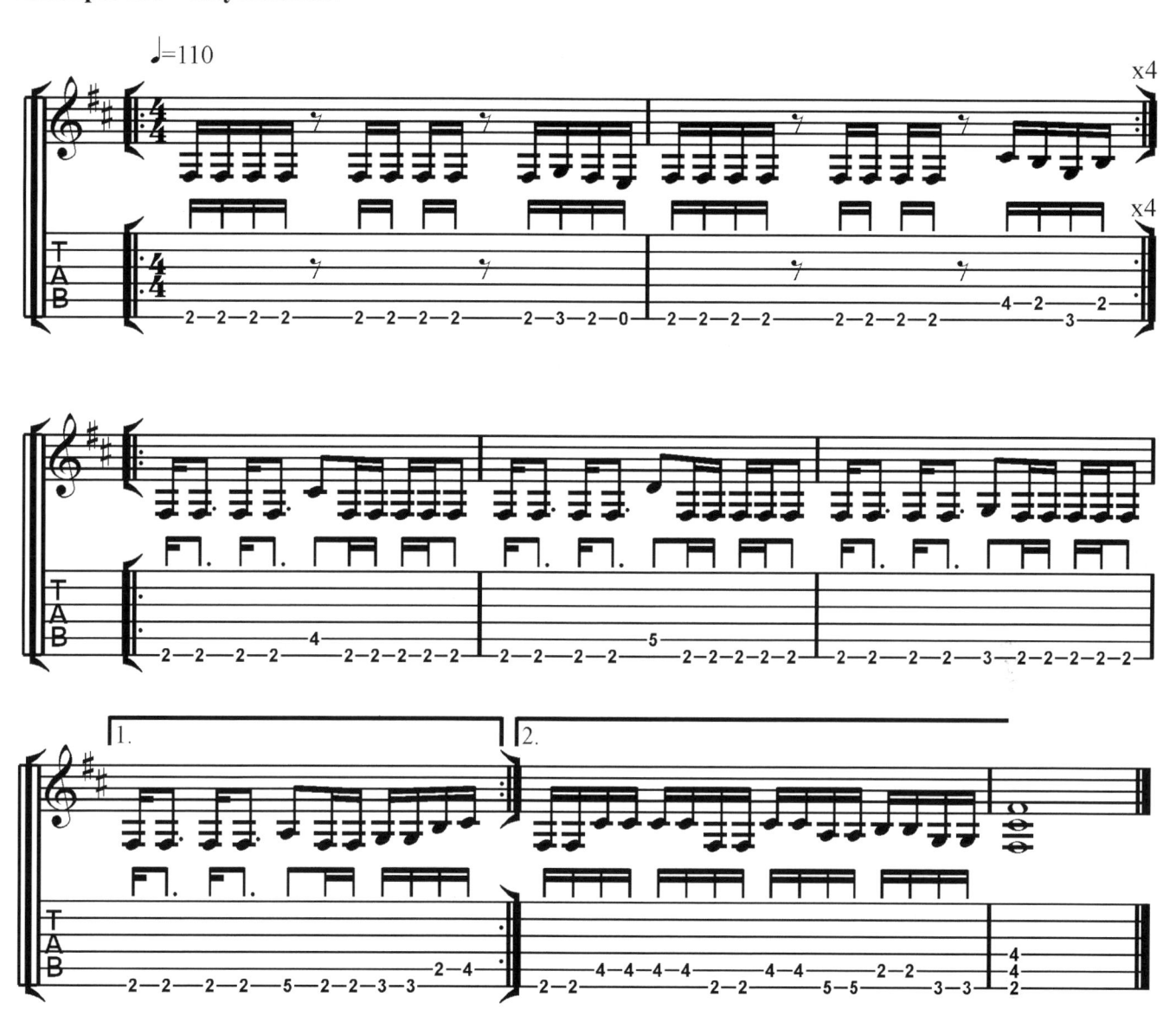

Bars 1-4: Although metal soloing had shaken off much of The Blues and hard rock influence by this period, we start with some unison bends. Listen to the way the first bend is articulated. I purposely released the bend slightly to produce a jarring effect as the bent note moves out of tune with the other. The melody in bars three and four is based around semitone intervals found in F# Phrygian (F#-G, and C#-D) to bring the dark Phrygian tonality to the fore.

Bars 5-8: Use hybrid picking to play the mutated country lick. It begins with a banjo roll pattern applied to a Dsus2 shape. The A# comes from Phrygian Dominant, which can be used interchangeably with the normal Phrygian mode here. The descending lick again picks out diatonic semitone pairs and alternates them with the open strings to get an appealingly dissonant result. Country guitar is usually played with a clean sound so notes can ring together, but with a high gain distortion it's worth applying some palm muting to give the notes more definition and prevent them becoming a sloppy mess. John 5 imports bluegrass ideas seamlessly into his shred metal solo albums.

Bars 9-12: Here the underlying groove changes and the solo uses some longer notes to allow the music to breathe again for a moment. 5ths give an angular modern sound compared to 3rds and 6ths. Here we have two perfect 5ths a tritone apart, resulting in two consonant intervals dissonant with one another. The fast sliding melody in bar ten requires accurate timing in the fretting hand, but makes the solo more expressive and varied. The disjoined phrase in bars eleven to twelve works against the rhythmic flow of the music, but confident execution and a solid sense of time will make it convincing.

Bars 13-16: Here's a long picking run in the style of Chuck Schuldiner or Andy LaRocque. It starts off in straight 1/16ths but then accelerates to 1/16th-note triplets. I've notated the groupings exactly as played, but aim to keep your sense of pulse and simply land in the right place. The final two bars are quite demanding and use some Diminished arpeggios and an F#7 arpeggio (with both the 5 and b5).

The majority of bar fifteen uses legato and picking combined, but the speed and the note choice give it a new flavour. We looked at a longer version final sweep picked Diminished arpeggio lick back in Chapter Six.

Example 10b – Lead Guitar

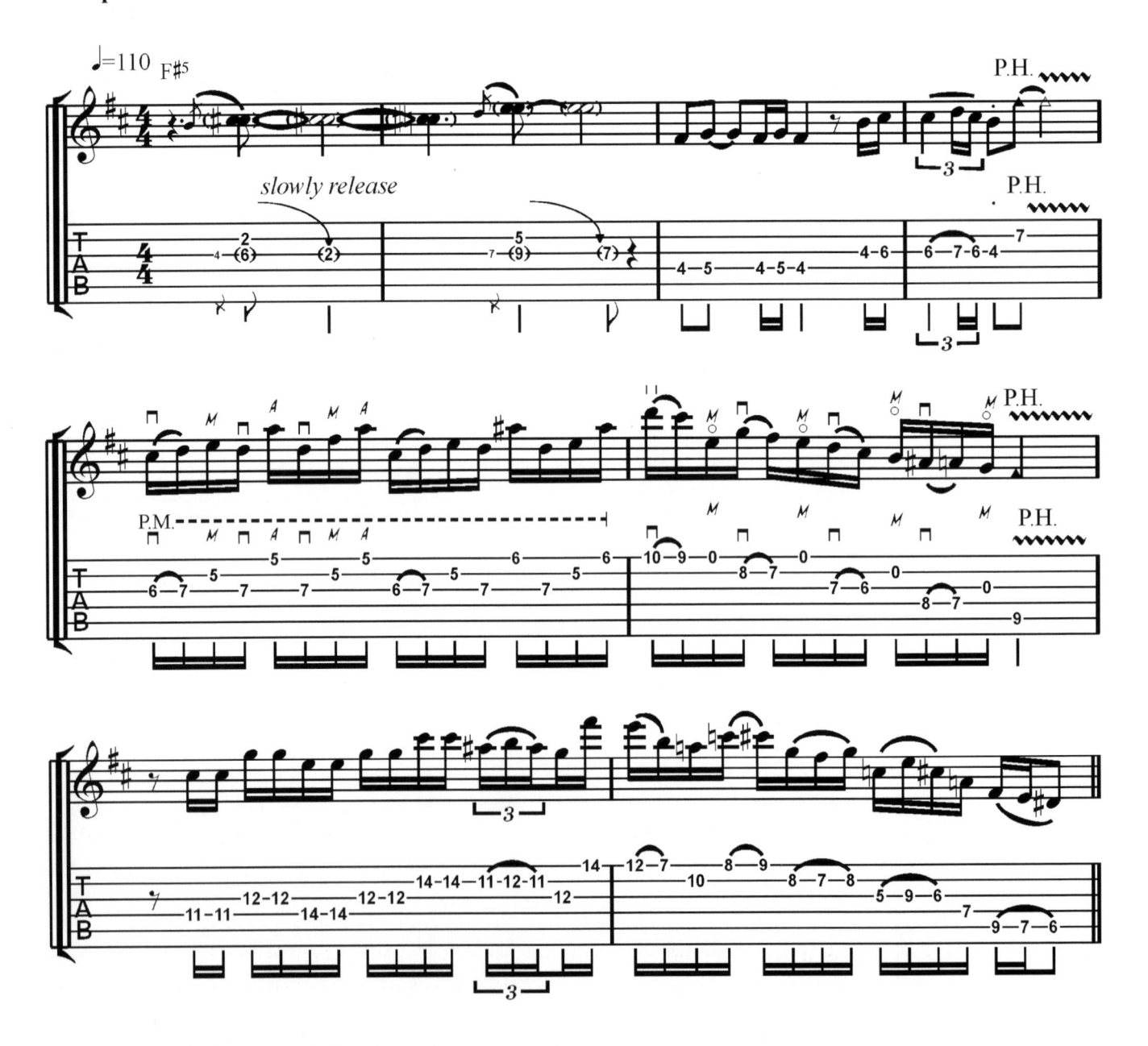

Example 10c

Our third solo is in the style of progressive metal bands like Dream Theater and Symphony X. There are several technical moments in this solo, but the main feature is the time signature. Even when you've played many riffs in 7/8 or other odd time signatures, phrasing the lead guitar melodically can still pose a challenge.

When creating your own ideas in odd meters the best approach is to set up a loop and improvising simply with only a few notes per bar, then gradually explore different rhythmic permutations. Try off-beat ideas too, to give yourself the most freedom, but remember to focus on the underlying pulse.

It's common to mix several different meters to enhance the musical impact of passages such as this. Unbalancing the rhythm can provide a sensation a bit like dissonance in harmony, which can be 'resolved' to a more regular time signature. However, for the purposes of this study, we remaining in 7/8 throughout.

After the first section of alternating G minor and Eb major chords, there is a short unison riff shared between organ, synth, bass and guitar which is common in this style. Rhythmic precision is of concern in all aspects of heavy metal, but never more so than unison parts, which should all sound like a single voice to blend the different timbres seamlessly. When repeated, this is transposed up an octave to add intensity. In the final two bars we use the tense F Diminished scale (half/whole) to bring the music to a climax before landing on a big Fsus4 chord.

Example 10c – Rhythm Part

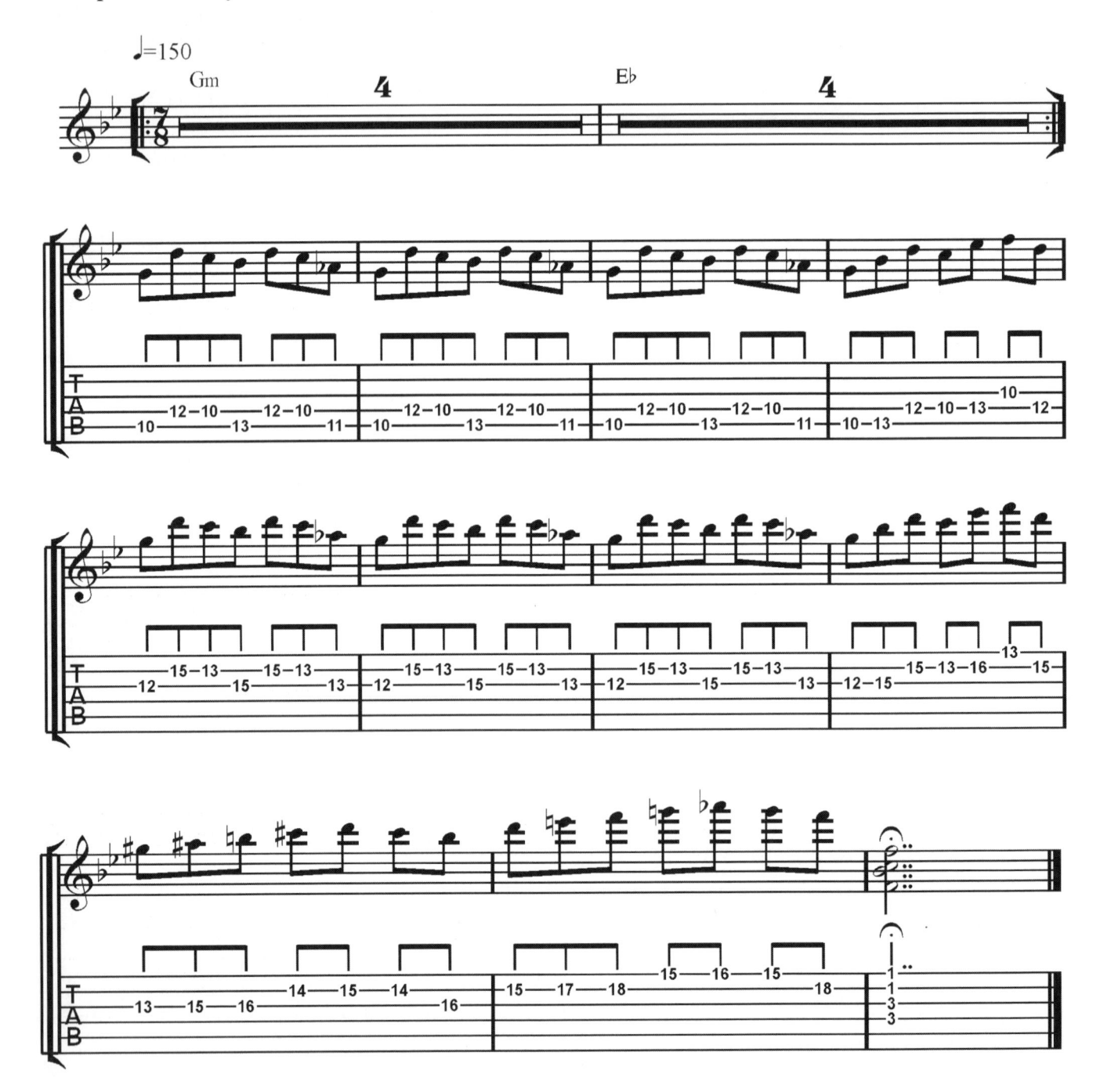

Bars 1-4: We kick things off with an intervallic idea that slides up the fretboard. Notice how the intervals get bigger over the course of the phrase, starting with 3rds, and then 6ths, and finally a minor 7th. Use the second finger for the first bar, with the first finger muting behind it to prevent unwanted noise.
Keep the same fingering for each section of the descending lick starting in bar three. The bends should be a quick curl rather than being strictly in time as notated.

Bars 5-8: The harmony has now moved to Eb with a more melodic phrase that involves tapped bends. Although the use of odd time in rock was mostly inspired by 20th century classical music, the origin is in the folk music of Eastern Europe and North Africa; so explore music from those cultures to get more inspiration for melodic ideas in meters in five and seven.

More intervallic ideas next, starting with ascending 5ths which lead into a fast sus2 arpeggio. Prog keyboard players like Keith Emerson and Jordan Rudess can often be heard using sus2/4 arpeggios in their solos, as they create an exciting modern tonality and work over both major and minor harmony.

Bars 9-12: A defining feature of John Petrucci and Dimebag Darrel's playing styles (which helped them both stand out from the rather bloated shred scene in the early '90s), is a bluesy slant to their solos. This was in part influenced Stevie Ray Vaughan and Steve Morse. This four-bar phrase makes a nod to that approach with Hendrix-esque sliding doublestops and a chromatic passing tone.

Bars 13-16: We conclude with a long alternate picking run. After using Ab's in the preceding the solo to imply G Phrygian, we switch here to A naturals, giving the more colourful sound of Eb Lydian. Notice how the run is divided into groups of seven notes. Accent the first note of each seven note grouping, every other one of which will begin with an upstroke.

Example 10c – Lead Guitar

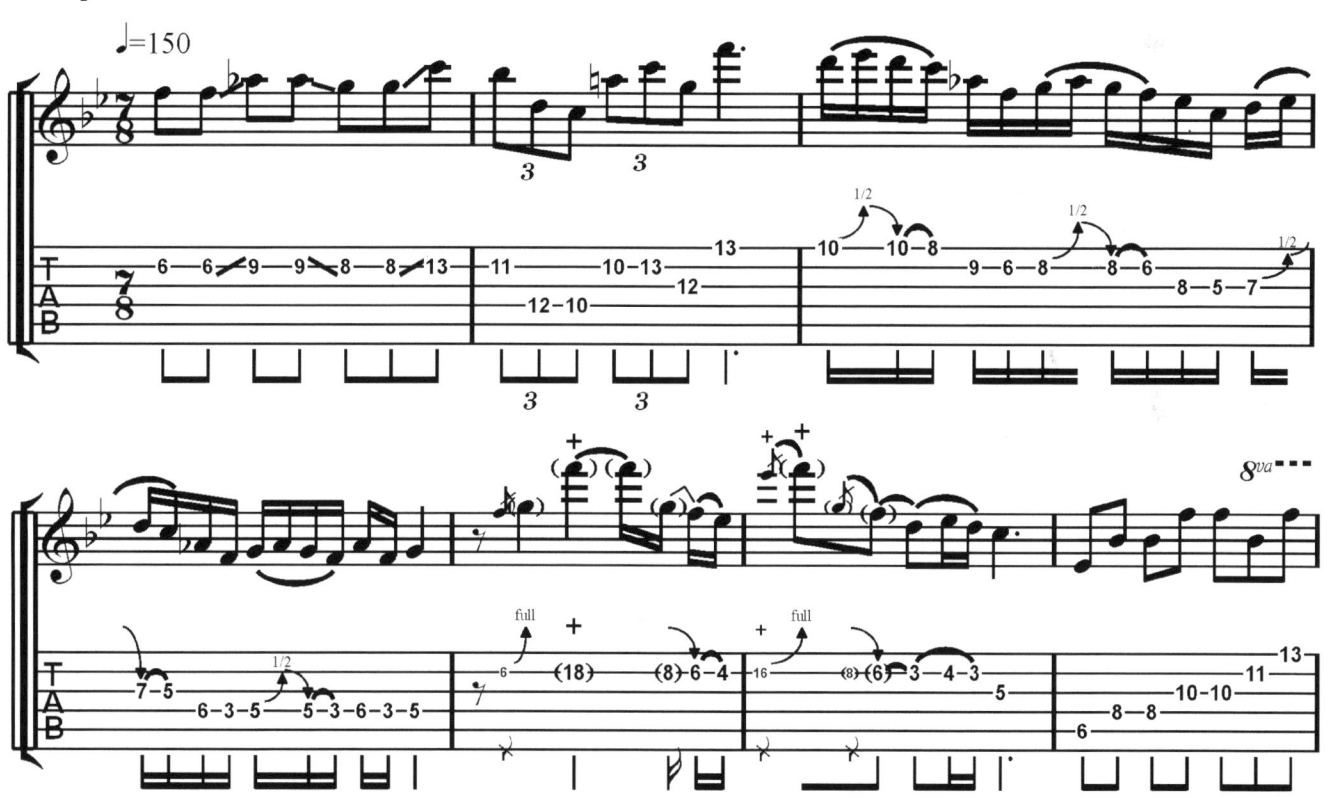

Example 10d

Our final metal solo study draws on the most experimental avant guard players in heavy music such as Buckethead, Bumble Foot, Ron Jarzombek and Mattias Eklund. These players often use unusual and dissonant note choices, odd rhythmic groupings, and complex combinations of various rock techniques to push the boundaries of metal and make original and individual music.

The rhythm part here is inspired by bands like Meshuggah and Animals as Leaders. It is a chromatic vamp around a B pedal tone. (To get a modern heavy sound I tuned down to B for the riff, but you could get a similar result by playing an octave higher.) Rhythmically, the guitar is divided into five semiquaver cells, and repeats a sequence of five groups of five notes, followed by a group of three before repeating. This cross-rhythm played against the main pulse of the track creates a constantly changing syncopation.

The second half of the track follows the same rhythmic grouping, but with a constant stream of notes. If you're learning the rhythm guitar part, then tackling this part (after working through the examples in the cross rhythm sub-chapter) is easier than the A section riff, as getting the notes in the right order means the rhythmic phrasing takes care of itself.

In an attempt to escape clichés, a lot of experimental metal is atonal, or contains great dissonance. Your note choice when soloing is therefore wide open. All twelve notes add a different colour over the B tonal centre, but we still have a sense of tension and release if we see these colours in a spectrum from consonant to most dissonant.

As a creative listening exercise, try ordering all twelve notes against a held drone in what, to you, sounds like increasing dissonance.

Example 10d – Rhythm Part

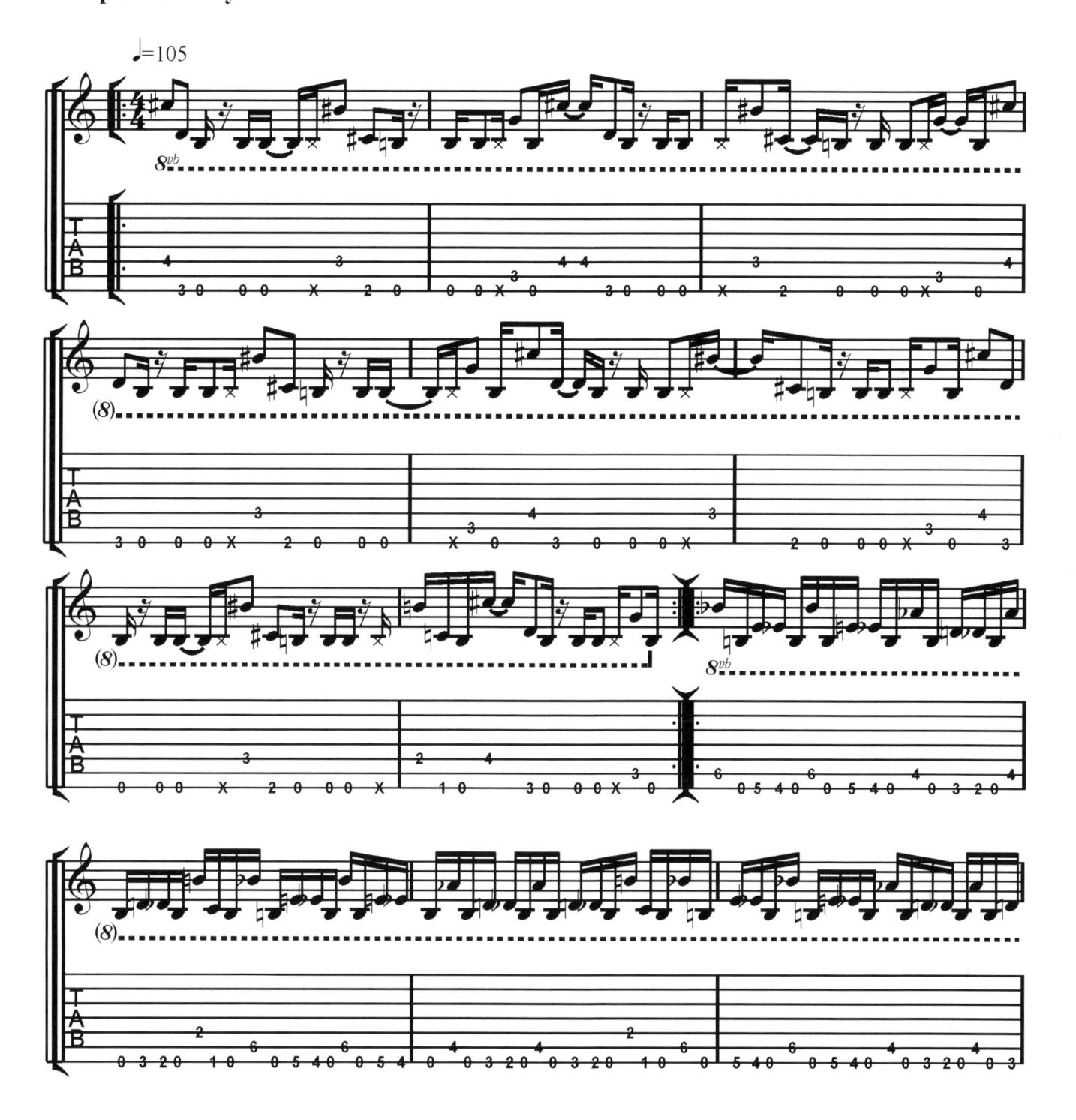

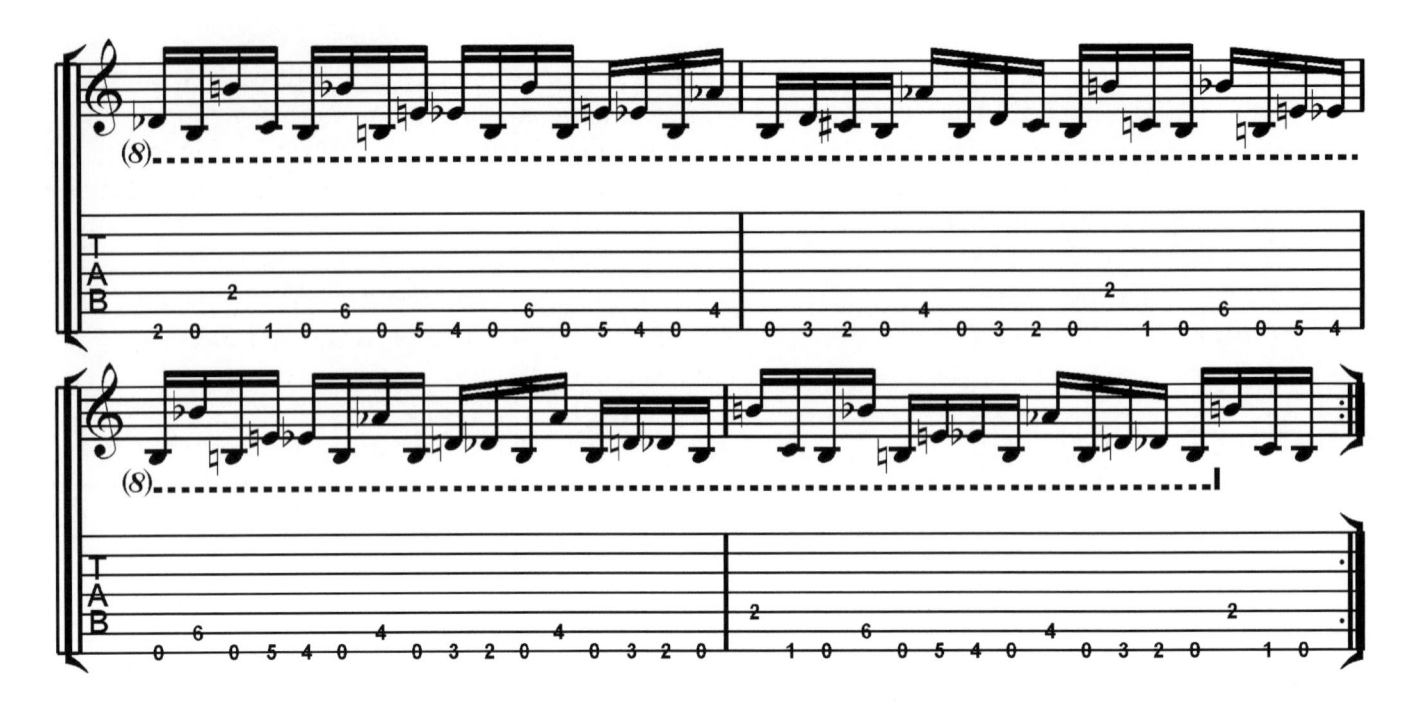

Bars 1-8: The first section starts with a slow melody comprising several tritone intervals, before developing into short bursts of legato. The long slide in bar five gives the effect of a whammy pedal. The position shift for the fretting hand should be made during duration of the tapped note. If you need to look at the fretboard, keep your eyes ahead of your hands by looking at the destination fret.

The legato phrase in bar eight loosely targets the notes of D minor with a lot of chromatic notes surrounding them. Jazz fusion guitarist Allan Holdsworth has had a great influence on metal guitarists. His virtuosic legato technique and outside note choice has been approximated by many metal guitarists, introducing a fusion influenced sound to their lead licks. Players as diverse as Van Halen and Frederik Thordendal have acknowledged his influence.

Bars 9-12: An atonal backing track doesn't dictate any particular mode or key as being 'inside'. So it is entirely down to you to use your ear to find melodies that sound 'correct' to you. Any note is fair game any groups of different intervals can be put together or transposed to help give your ideas more cohesion.

To illustrate this, our next line expands the legato texture to include both tapping, and open strings to achieve longer arpeggio-like contours. We start with a D Augmented triad, before repeating the same note cluster on the B string. The intervals along each string are then altered but the repetition of the overall shape gives the listener something to hang on to.

There is more fusion-influenced vocabulary as we continue, with an ascending and descending line of perfect 4ths. Cleanly articulating the 4ths takes a careful barre-roll with the first and second fingers of the fretting hand. This phrase concludes with a mixture of perfect 5th and 4th intervals and a short sliding melody.

The 4ths and 5ths still have a recognisable flavour even in the dissonant context. Superimposing a line with some internal logic will work even when they are 'wrong notes', so long as they are resolved tactfully.

Bars 13-16: Accent every fifth note in the first part of this lick to help convey the cross-rhythmic pulse. The string-skipping octaves will probably take some slow practice to master, but will really help your overall picking dexterity.

Bars 17-20: These four bars all follow the same two-beat sextuplet tapping pattern. If this is new to you, get confident with the first two beats before moving on to the different positions. Many players use a hair band or string mute to prevent unwanted string noise, but keeping the noise down is manageable by carefully placing the heel of the picking hand over the lower strings and muting the B string with the tip of the fretting hand's first finger.

Bars 21-25: Here's where things get a little more unorthodox. If you've ever experimented playing with a bottleneck, or making sound effects by tapping the strings with the whammy bar a la Tom Morello, you'll know that notes can continue up the string after the fretboard ends. Inspired by Ron Thal (aka Bumblefoot) I used a thimble on my picking hand pinkie to tap notes over the neck pickup area. Use the lower part of the neck to reference the lower octave to find the accurate pitches and remember where they occur over the pickups. For example, on my guitar the G natural ('28th fret') is just higher than the middle of my neck pickup)

Again, take each section of this lick very slowly so you can be sure that the thimble tapped notes are in tune and in time. You'll need to be use the bridge pickup here so that the pickup is still behind the active portion of the string.

Some sound effects round of this piece: The cascade of slides is done by alternately sliding up the fretboard, hand over hand. The second part is done by rubbing the thimble across the strings starting on the high E close to the bridge, and moving towards the lower strings over the neck. Finally, we end on a ringing dissonant semitone interval. To get some more interest into the sustaining notes, I rapidly switched between the two pickups to give a filter-sweep effect.

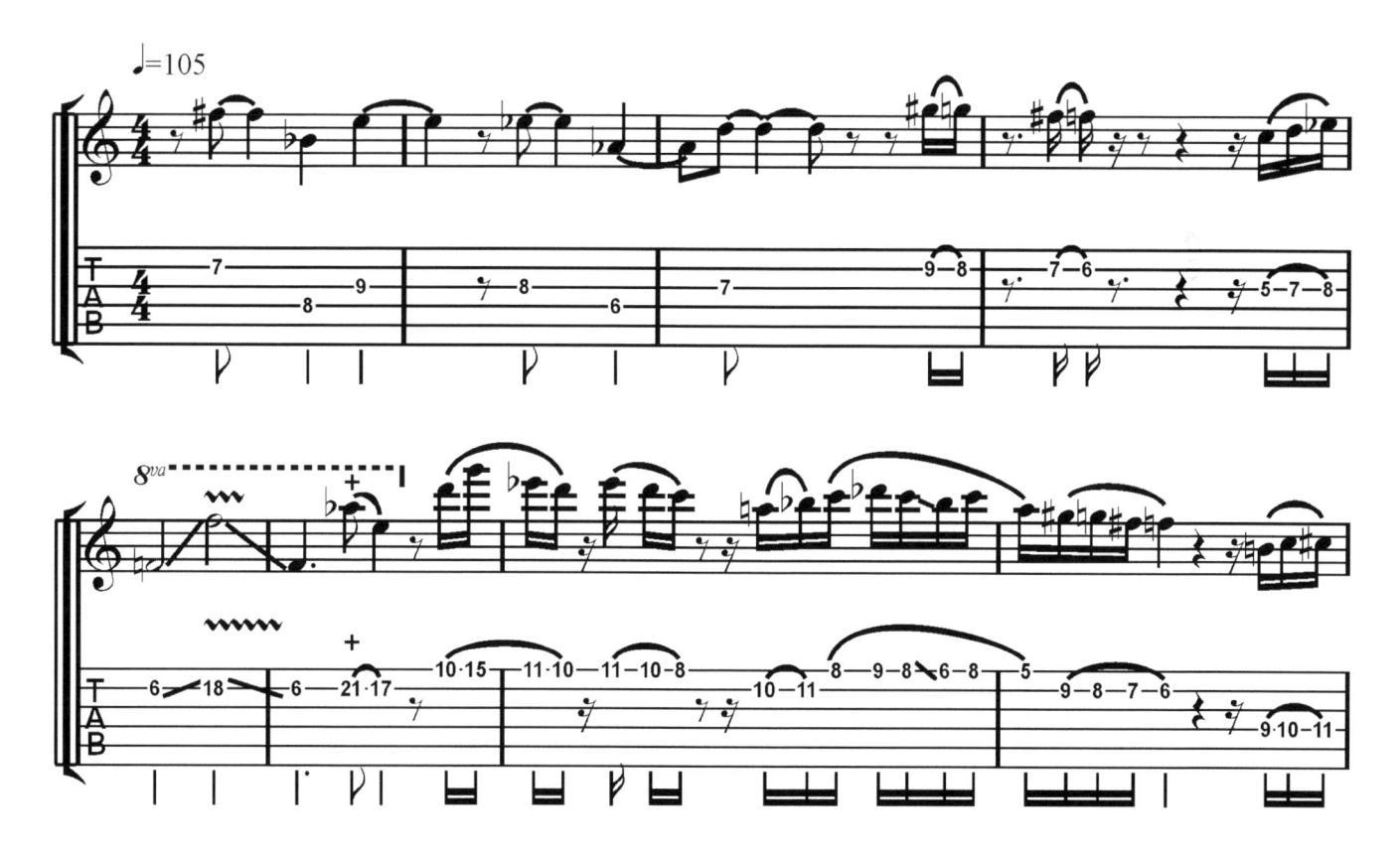

102

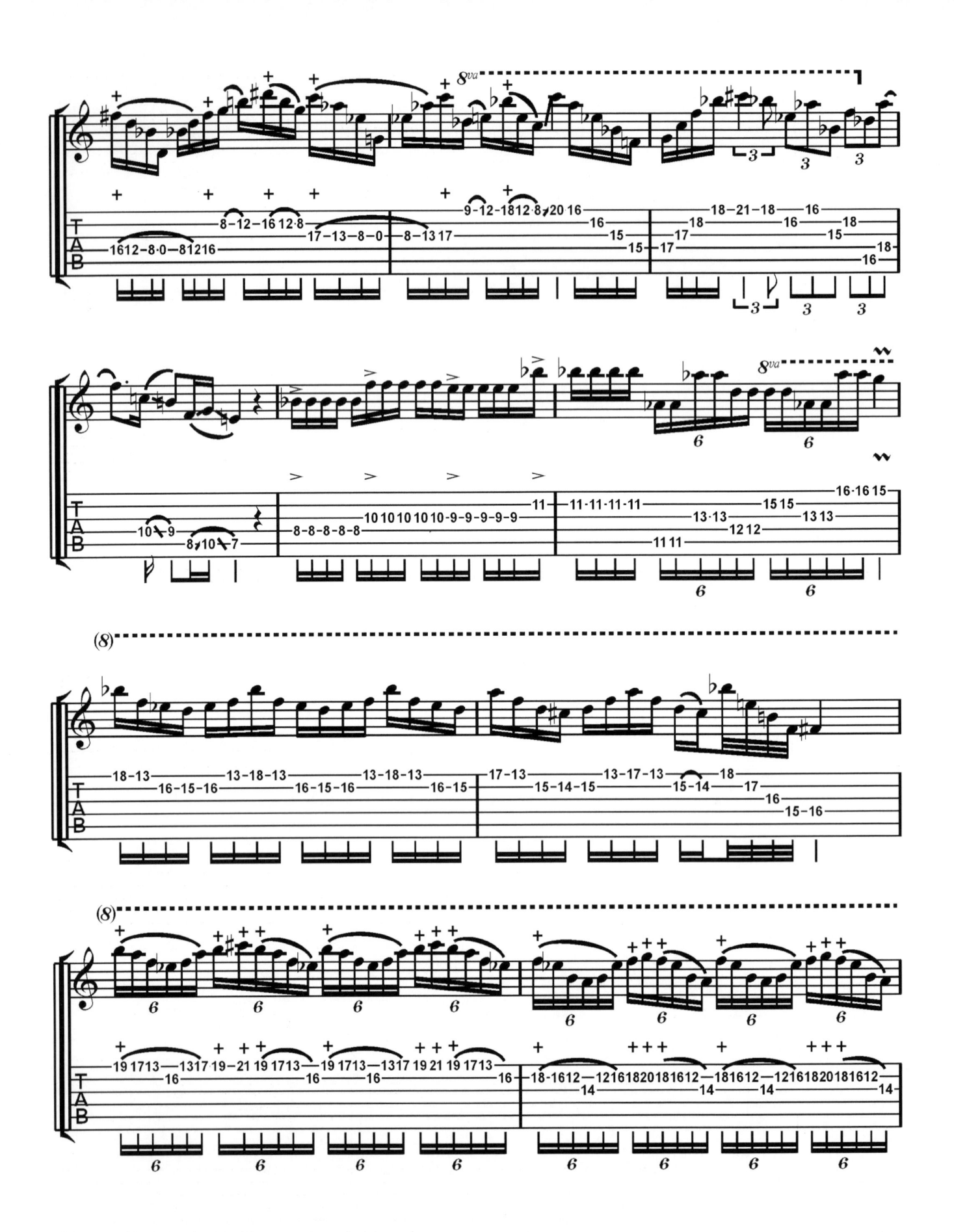

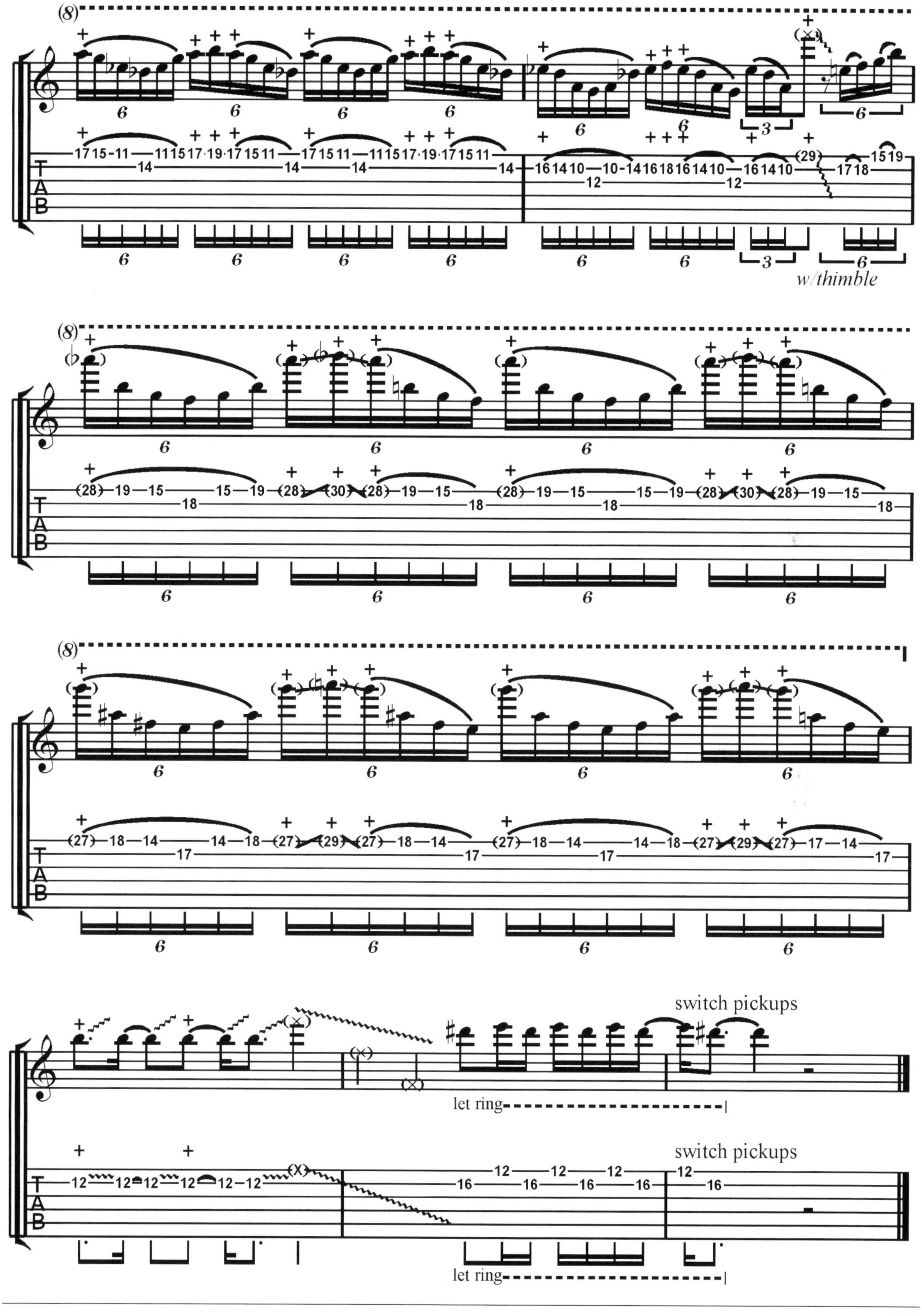
w/thimble
let ring
switch pickups
switch pickups
let ring

Neoclassical unaccompanied performance piece – Paganini's Caprice No. 16 in G minor

Among violin virtuoso Nicolo Paganini's (1782-1840) best known compositions are a set of twenty-four caprices. Here we'll be looking at the 16th Caprice in G minor.

The final study is a transcription of Paganini's Caprice No. 16 originally composed for unaccompanied violin. Adapting such pieces provides us with the rare opportunity to play a rewarding and highly musical solo item. Violins are tuned in 5ths which, coupled with the much shorter scale length, allows for wider intervallic leaps to fall easily under the fingers. To keep up with 'The Devil's Violinist' the transcription uses a mixture of several advanced rock guitar techniques including sweep picking, hybrid picking, legato and two-handed tapping.

Paganini was one of the main sources of inspiration for the neoclassical shred movement as a composer, but also because of his reputation as a virtuosic instrumentalist and flamboyant performer, just like his contemporary, the pianist Franz Liszt, and of course the master, J.S. Bach.

As well as being internationally known as a master of the violin and a flamboyant performer, Paganini also played guitar, and I'd like to think he'd approve of the direction in which electric guitar playing has developed to be able to perform his violin music.

We don't have room to analyse the whole of this piece from a harmonic perspective so to get the most out of learning this work you should keep track of the compositional devices used as you work through the music phrase by phrase.

Paganini's masterful use of arpeggios and chord tone targeting allows the solo melody to clearly imply a chord progression. Visualising the chord shapes that each phrases draws upon will help you to memorise it and also carry over the ideas into your own vocabulary.

Before playing, listen to the audio and isolate any sections that particularly appeal to you and work on those first. Come up with different versions and practice using them over metal backing tracks to really develop your neoclassical style. Of course, learning the whole piece will give you a beautiful and impressive piece of solo guitar music to add to your repertoire.

Bars 1-8: The opening section covers many of the ideas that recur throughout the piece so it's worth spending a good period of time memorising and practicing this chunk before tackling the rest of the tune.

If you've been practicing your arpeggio shapes, then the patterns will be recognisable. The first bar outlines the tonic G minor triad with a short embellishment around the root before descending. Bar two moves to D7, and, after a short pedal point lick, the line leaps up to start a descending dominant 7 arpeggio from the root, before switching to a Diminished idea in bar three.

After another brief recycling of bar two's pedal point motif on beat one of bar five, the harmony changes direction towards Cm, setting up the change with a G7 arpeggio to signal C as the new tonic. However, this is immediately undermined by the following arpeggios which outline F and Bb chords, revealing a II-V-I sequence in Bb major, the relative major of G minor. This might sound like a lot of theory but the musical effect is a confounding of our expectation as listeners as to where the piece is heading, all done by the use of chords shared by two keys.

Bars: 12-13: After more hybrid picking, we reach one of the fiddliest moments in the whole piece. We are juggling two note fragments in different registers of the instrument - similar to some of the twin guitar ideas we looked at towards the end of Chapter Eight. Follow the picking directions very carefully to ensure you have the most economic approach, and memorise the shifts slowly. Combining sweep and hybrid picking like this requires a compromise of hand position, so experiment until you find a comfortable balance.

Bars 15-20: This passage uses a lot of chromatic notes to target different chord tones, but should prove technically easier than the gymnastics of the previous few bars. Using legato here can provide a nice break from the pick attack, both for you and for the listener!

Bars 21-26: Back for more sweep/hybrid picking action. Paganini has combined an arpeggio with some chromatic passing notes and answered it with a pedal point lick over the next chord. We're moving from Bb – F7 then Adim back to Bb in the second two bars. The A Diminished triad functions here as an F7 which resolves to Bb.

Bars 46-49: A flurry of descending chromatic notes finishes the piece. I've kept things as legato as possible from the start of the section to help transition into the tapping used at the end. Damping the strings will be an issue when making such wide string skips as this. The wide jumps up to the high D and F# in bars 48-49 are best handled by tapping with the middle and ring fingers.

Bars 50-51: The motif we saw introduced in the previous bars of jumping to a pair of high chord tones in D major is now recycled on the tonic chord of G minor in order to resolve harmonically. Both hands are tapping here. Keep the fingers of the fretting hand flat against the strings in between hammering onto the low G notes to clean up the left hand tapping.

Bar 52-End: If you're playing this track with distortion the final chord will sound unclear, so during the preceding legato phrase leading use your picking hand to roll off the volume pot a little. This will bring out a pleasingly warm G minor chord, and will leave the listener with a much nicer final impression than if you ended on a muddy distorted noise.

Niccolò Paganini (1782-1840)

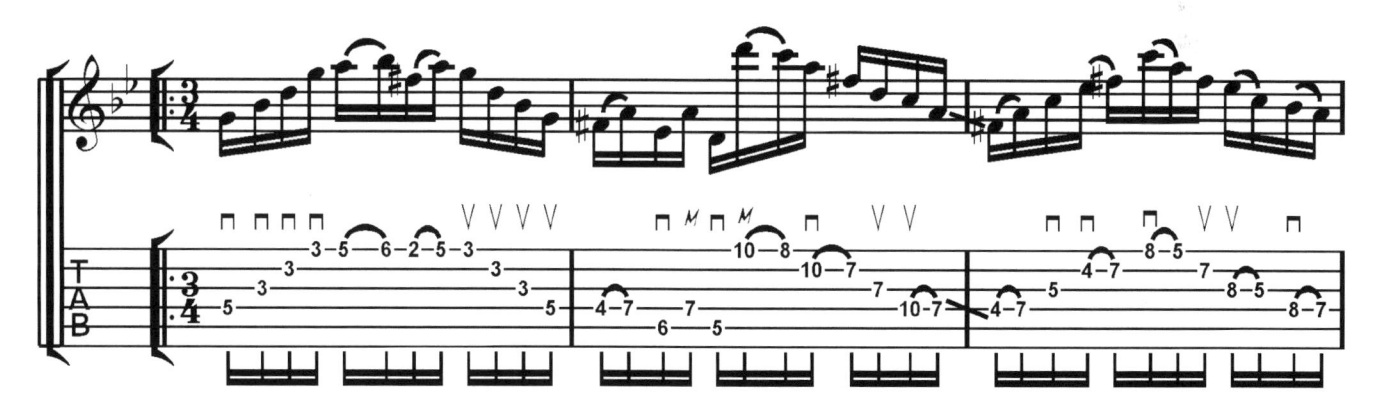

106

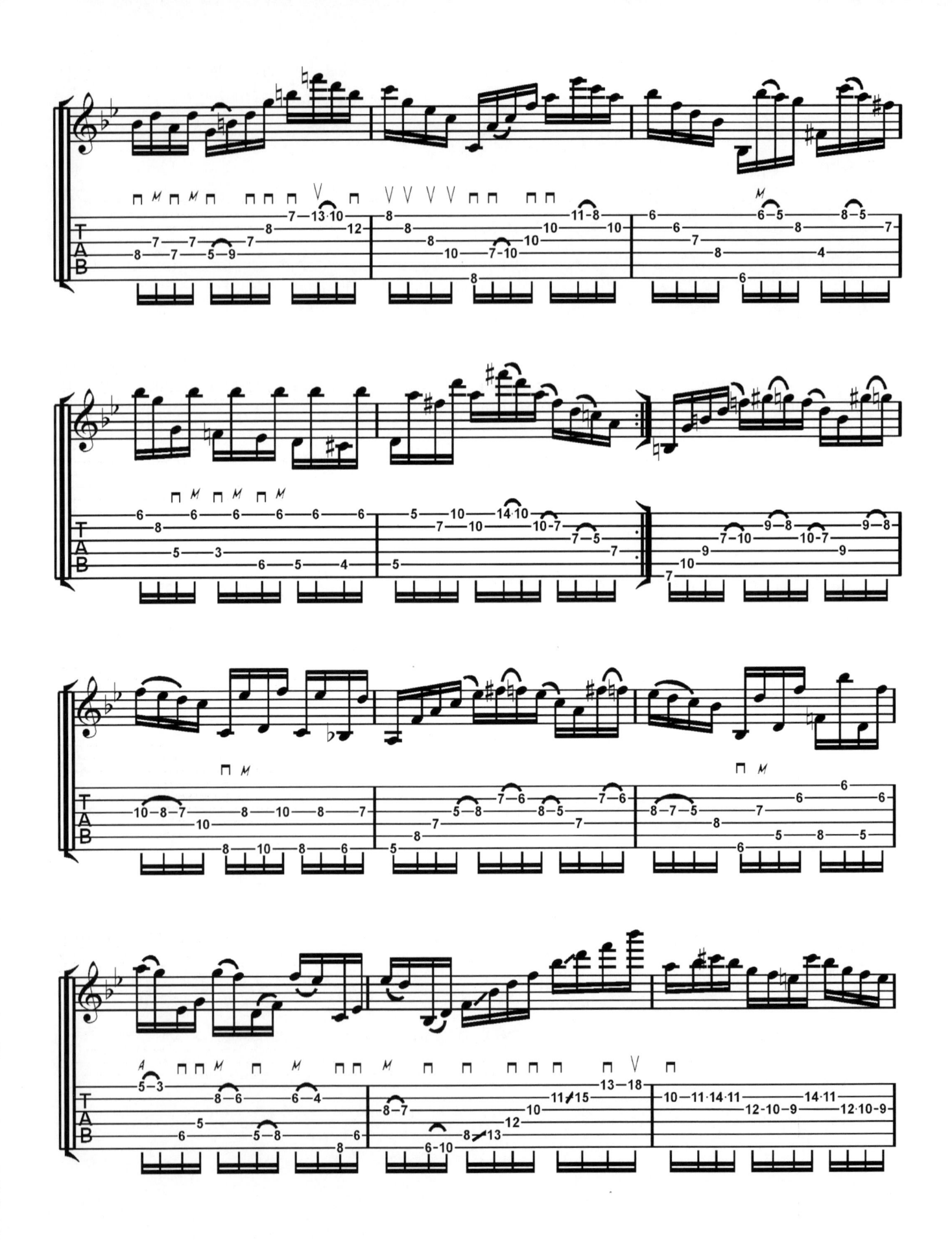

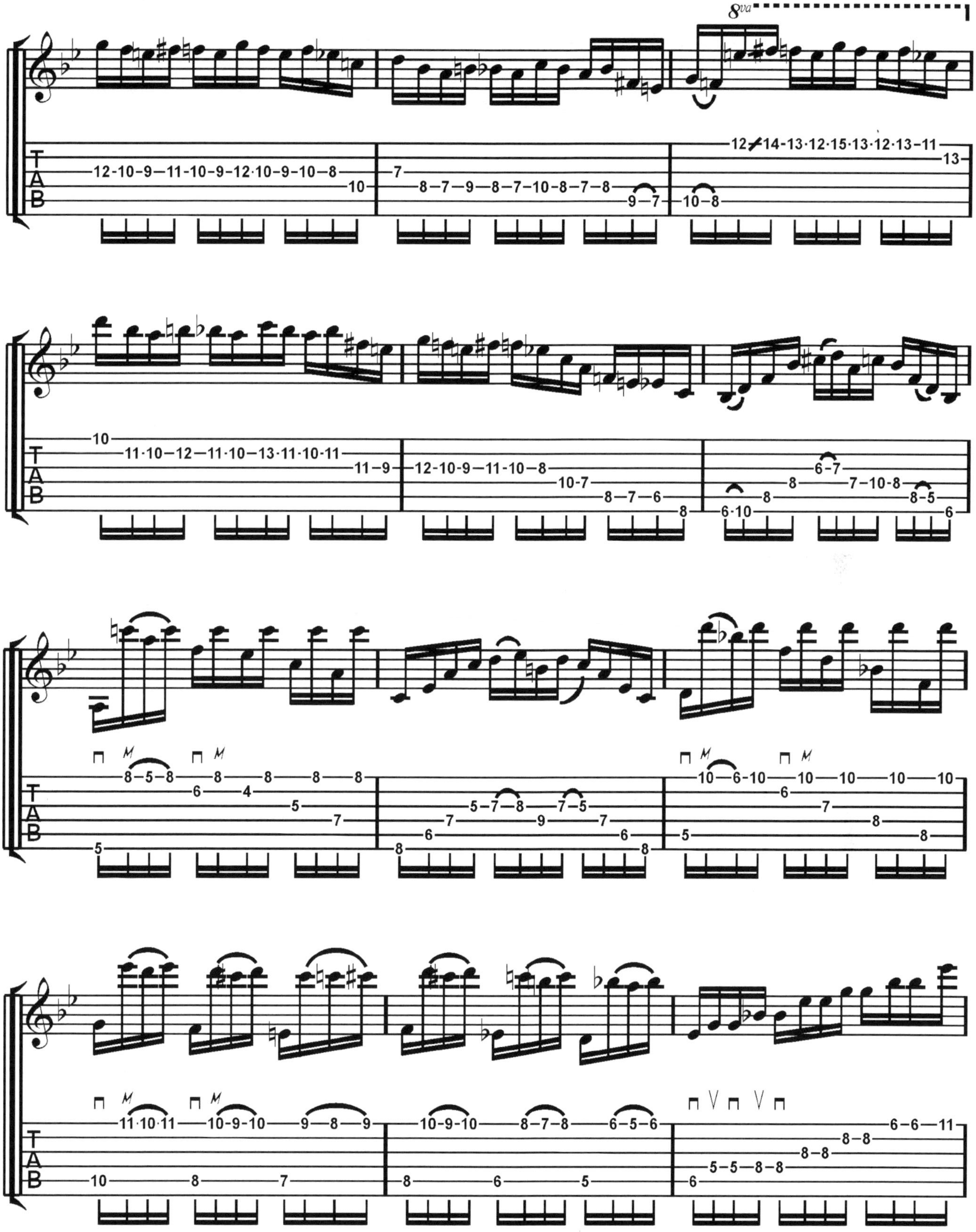
8va
TAB

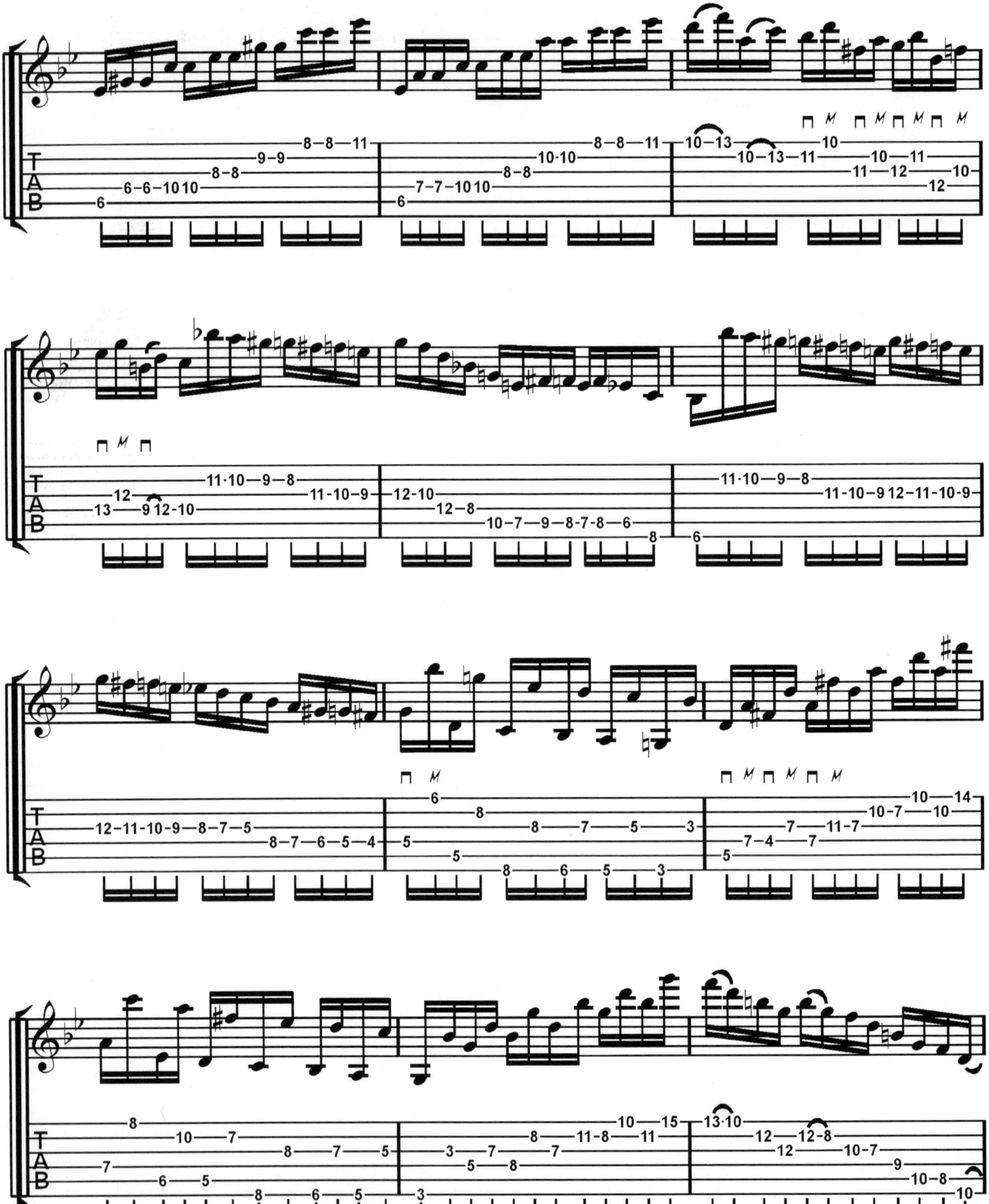

109

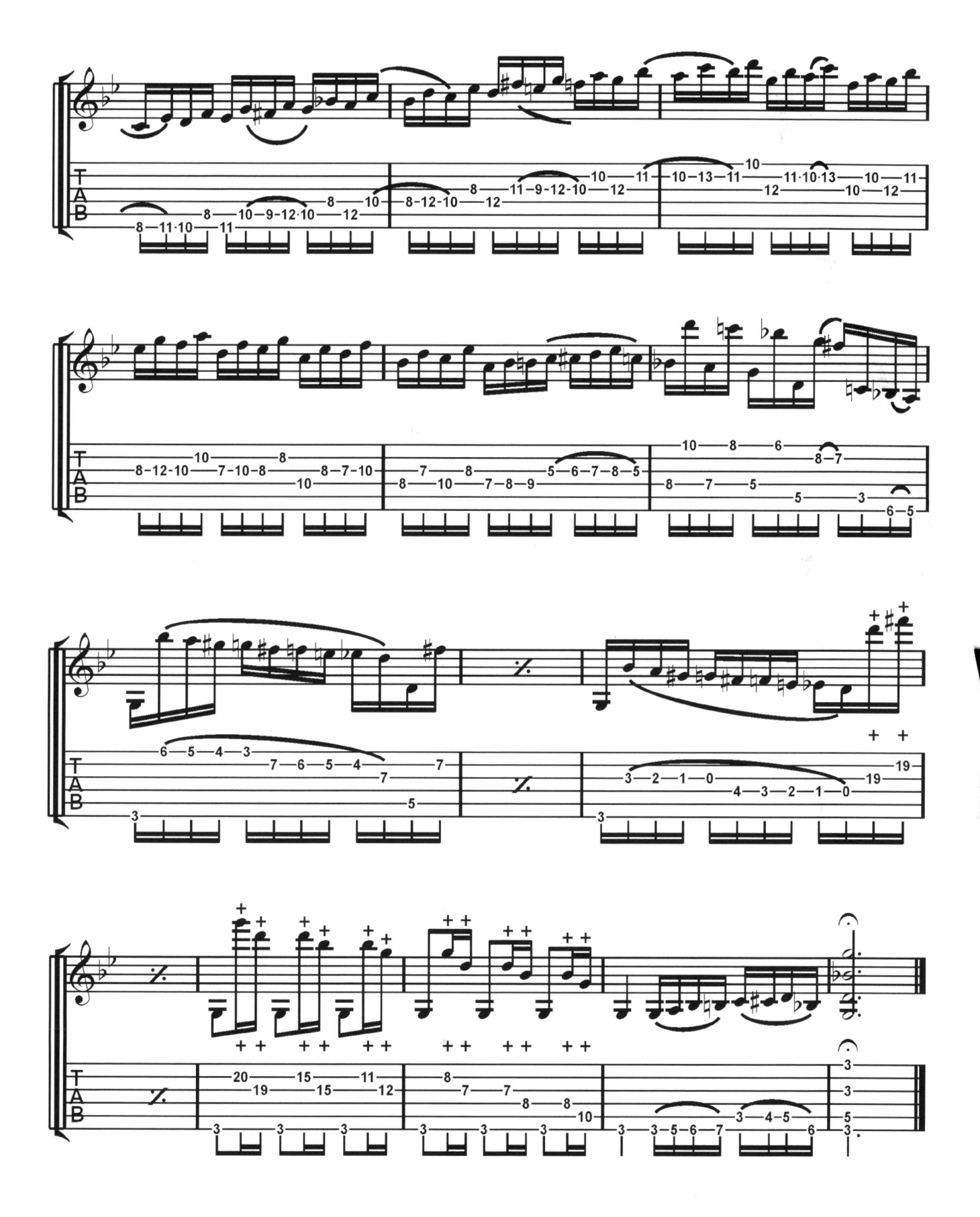

Chapter 11: Forging Your Own Style - You Can Do It!

To close, I'd like to offer some suggestions to help you develop your own unique voice on the instrument. As creative musicians the ultimate goal is surely to be expressive on the guitar. All too often however, we feel that our progress is sluggish, or that we are just regurgitating the ideas of other players without saying anything new.

It may be a lofty dream to achieve the mastery of the most famous and respected players (and unrealistic as we all have busy lives in which practice is limited) but I believe there are some logical steps you can employ to help drive your playing in a more personal and expressive direction.

A player with a strong individual musical identity can usually be recognised from hearing only a few phrases. For many of these players, their style is defined as much by the ideas they don't use as by those they do. By narrowing the focus of their vocabulary they are highlighting those elements of their playing that are unique to them.

It's worth noting that while some players distance themselves from the pack by employing unusual or very complicated ideas, (Buckethead and Ron Thal spring immediately to mind) an expressive voice can be a fresh or slightly progressed take on the conventions of the style. After all, many clichés end up such because they are great! Think of Kirk Hammett's solos on the early Metallica recordings – he is employing mainly bending and repeating Pentatonic licks, but with his own patterns, phrasing and wah pedal use, it is recognisably 'Kirk Hammett'.

Expanding Your Vocabulary

All of us draw inspiration from other people's music in the same way that language is learnt by listening to, and copying others. There is no shame is taking the licks of players whose style resonates with you, but after imitating them the creative guitarist will take those inherited ideas and break out of the gravitational orbit of their heroes to become an individual. The process by which you can start to achieve this is straightforward, although it takes creative thinking and hard work!

Isolate a lick that particularly appeals to you, maybe one of the licks we've looked at in this book, or something gleaned from learning a solo. Once you're reasonably comfortable with playing the lick in its original form, try to transpose it to different keys. To do this you'll have to be able to visualise it in terms of the tonic note, or better still, a familiar chord shape.

The next thing you could try would be work out a version of the lick using a different scale. If, for example the lick used the Phrygian mode, you could adapt it to fit the Lydian or Aeolian modes. If the lick uses three note-per-string scale shapes this should be an easy process, otherwise you may need to work out how each pitch needs to be changed, using your ear as a guide.

Change the length of the phrase. If the lick moves through positions – keep going for twice as long, or perhaps practice shorter versions of the lick which can be inserted more easily into solos.

Analyse what makes up the lick and what it is that made you choose it. Is there an interesting sounding interval, sequential pattern, or perhaps the smooth flowing sound of legato and tapping piqued your interest? Whatever the DNA of the lick, set yourself the challenge of writing five licks that use that specific sound or technique. Don't worry if you feel like they are too similar, any reinterpretation of the material will enhance your creative thinking and musical understanding.

If you keep repeating this process, and record the results of your experimentation in a notepad, audio recording or tab/score editor on the computer, then you will soon develop a library of original ideas that have moved away from the style of whoever's lick you used as a launch pad.

This is only half the battle though, and the remaining task is to load this new vocabulary into your instinctive muscle memory so that it comes out in your natural playing. To stretch the well-worn language metaphor, you can usually tell when someone has consciously 'dressed up' their language with elaborate vocabulary to seem intelligent, as compared to when it is has been naturally acquired by osmosis.

The key to succeeding is reassuringly fun, after all the study and repetition. Look for a backing track with a feel that suits the licks you've been working on (there are plenty of 'jam tracks' for sale or on YouTube). Make sure that you can play your new licks in that key - then just play! You should pay attention to how you transition between phrases, and aim to link the new ideas into your existing playing. Given time, they will stop being new licks and become assimilated into your unique voice, especially if you use different variations interchangeably.

Taking Unusual Influences

One way to stand out is to take inspiration from different instruments and styles of music. Most guitarists listen to guitarists, copy their licks, and thus sound like guitarists! However, there are many who've managed to distinguish themselves by taking ideas from keyboard, violin, saxophone, banjo or instruments from other cultures like the koto and sitar.

The way notes are arranged on different instruments and the limitations of size or breath, mean that certain musical ideas are more accessible on some instruments than others.

While the guitar will always sound like a guitar, thinking about how we can copy the attributes of other instruments will lead us down new roads. Great examples include John 5 who's incorporated country licks derived from banjo and pedal steel into his metal vocabulary, Marty Friedman for his koto influenced bends, and guitarists like Paul Masvidal (Cynic) and Frederik Thordendal (Meshuggah) whose fusion influenced legato ideas come from saxophone players like John Coltrane and Michael Brecker, via jazz-rock legend Allan Holdsworth.

Building a Cohesive Style

While a good player can draw on the different textures and techniques to be expressive and maintain interest during a solo, a truly great player combines them seamlessly. This takes time and effort after first being comfortable with each technique individually. There are plenty of players who prove that speed and virtuosity are not prerequisites for great metal playing and little dashes of flashiness in an otherwise melodic and well thought-out solo can be much more effective than endless histrionics!

So, as a final thought, work on your technique, tone, theory and of course power stance!... but remember that the real goal is making powerful and emotionally engaging music. Regardless of the science behind the music, always ask yourself, 'does this move me?' and follow your ear!

Other Books from Fundamental Changes

The Complete Guide to Playing Blues Guitar Book One: Rhythm Guitar

The Complete Guide to Playing Blues Guitar Book Two: Melodic Phrasing

The Complete Guide to Playing Blues Guitar Book Three: Beyond Pentatonics

The Complete Guide to Playing Blues Guitar Compilation

The CAGED System and 100 Licks for Blues Guitar

Fundamental Changes in Jazz Guitar: The Major ii V I

Minor ii V Mastery for Jazz Guitar

Jazz Blues Soloing for Guitar

Guitar Scales in Context

Guitar Chords in Context

Jazz Guitar Chord Mastery (Guitar Chords in Context Part Two)

Complete Technique for Modern Guitar

Funk Guitar Mastery

The Complete Technique, Theory and Scales Compilation for Guitar

Sight Reading Mastery for Guitar

Rock Guitar Un-CAGED: The CAGED System and 100 Licks for Rock Guitar

The Practical Guide to Modern Music Theory for Guitarists

Beginner's Guitar Lessons: The Essential Guide

Chord Tone Soloing for Jazz Guitar

Heavy Metal Lead Guitar

Exotic Pentatonic Soloing for Guitar

Heavy Metal Rhythm Guitar

Voice Leading Jazz Guitar

The Complete Jazz Soloing Compilation

The Jazz Guitar Chords Compilation

Fingerstyle Blues Guitar

The Complete DADGAD Guitar Method

Printed in Great Britain
by Amazon